A Da Capo Press Reprint Series

**FRANKLIN D. ROOSEVELT
AND THE ERA OF THE NEW DEAL**
GENERAL EDITOR : FRANK FREIDEL
Harvard University

FARMERS ON RELIEF
AND REHABILITATION

Division of Research
Work Projects Administration

Research Monographs

Works Progress Administration
Division of Social Research
Research Monograph VIII

FARMERS ON RELIEF AND REHABILITATION

By Berta Asch and A. R. Mangus

DA CAPO PRESS • NEW YORK • 1971

126468

A Da Capo Press Reprint Edition

This Da Capo Press edition of *Farmers on Relief and Rehabilitation* is an unabridged republication of the first edition published in Washington, D.C., in 1937. It is reprinted by permission from a copy of the original edition owned by the Harvard College Library.

Library of Congress Catalog Card Number 78-165678
ISBN 0-306-70340-8

Published by Da Capo Press, Inc.
A Subsidiary of Plenum Publishing Corporation
227 West 17th Street, New York, N.Y. 10011
All Rights Reserved

Manufactured in the United States of America

FARMERS ON RELIEF
AND REHABILITATION

WORKS PROGRESS ADMINISTRATION
HARRY L. HOPKINS, Administrator
CORRINGTON GILL, Assistant Administrator

DIVISION OF SOCIAL RESEARCH
HOWARD B. MYERS, Director

FARMERS ON RELIEF AND REHABILITATION

By

BERTA ASCH

and

A. R. MANGUS

Research Monograph VIII

UNITED STATES
GOVERNMENT PRINTING OFFICE
WASHINGTON : 1937

LETTER OF TRANSMITTAL

Works Progress Administration,
Washington, D. C., June 15, 1937.

Sir: I have the honor to transmit an analysis of the social and economic characteristics of farm operators and farm laborers receiving assistance under the general relief and rural rehabilitation programs. The analysis contributes significant material on the incidence of relief in the various agricultural groups and thus provides necessary information for the determination of future policies for the relief of unemployment in rural areas. The report is based on data obtained through surveys of Current Changes in the Rural Relief Population, conducted by the Division of Research, Statistics, and Finance of the Federal Emergency Relief Administration.

The report emphasizes the fact that the depression in agriculture began long before 1929 and that the distress of the early 1930's merely accentuated farm problems of long standing. Chief among these problems are: the pressure of rural birth rates on farm opportunities; the attempt to farm lands which are submarginal in production or approaching submarginality; attempts to farm eroded lands and adoption of farming practices which are conducive to erosion; subdivision of farms into units too small to afford support for a family; concentration on commercial rather than subsistence farming; overcapitalization of farms and consequent heavy foreclosures; decline of certain extractive industries, especially lumbering and mining, with consequent loss of the supplementary income which many farmers depended on for an adequate budget; growth of the tenant system; and increase in low-paid wage workers in agriculture. The situation has become acute in recent years, due largely to the lack of parity of prices of farm products and to the cumulative influence of a succession of disastrous droughts. The extension of relief into rural areas has focused attention on the human needs of the low income farm families.

The study was made in the Division of Social Research, under the direction of Howard B. Myers, Director of the Division. The data were collected under the supervision of A. R. Mangus and T. C. McCormick, with the assistance of J. E. Hulett, Jr., and Wayne Daugherty. Acknowledgment is also made of the cooperation of the State Supervisors and Assistant State Supervisors of Rural Research who were in direct charge of the field work. The analysis of the data was made under the supervision of T. J. Woofter, Jr., Coordinator of Rural Research.

The report was prepared by Berta Asch, whose services were made available to the Works Progress Administration by the Resettlement Administration, and by A. R. Mangus; it was edited by Ellen Winston and Rebecca Farnham. Special acknowledgement is made of the contribution of T. J. Woofter, Jr., who wrote the Introduction and Chapters I, VI, and VIII. A. R. Mangus contributed Chapter VII and Appendix B—The Methodology of Rural Relief Studies.

Respectfully submitted.

CORRINGTON GILL,
Assistant Administrator.

Hon. HARRY L. HOPKINS,
Works Progress Administrator.

CONTENTS

ILLUSTRATIONS

FIGURES

Contents

FIGURE 9. Percent of all farm operators receiving relief grants or rehabilitation advances, by area, June 1935_____ 52

10. Usual occupation of heads of rural relief and rehabilitation households, June 1935_____ 58

11. Size of farms operated by farmers on relief in June 1935 and by all farmers reported in the 1935 Census of Agriculture__ 64

12. Grade attainment of heads of open country households on relief, October 1935_____ 70

13. Number of farm operators by usual occupation receiving Federal assistance in rural areas, October 1933–December 1935_ 74

14. Changes in estimated number of farm operators receiving general relief, March through June 1935_____ 84

15. Changes during month in estimated number of farm operators receiving general relief, July through December 1935_____ 84

PHOTOGRAPHS

Waste in the Cut-Over Area_____ Facing 8

Abandoned coal mine_____ Facing 10

Farmers at work on W. P. A. road project_____ Facing 22

On the move_____ Facing 42

A rehabilitation client_____ Facing 60

Rural school_____ Facing 70

Eroded cropland_____ Facing 90

Building a farm-to-market road_____ Facing 94

INTRODUCTION

THIS STUDY was undertaken to assemble information concerning the relief and rehabilitation needs of farmers and to clarify the problems of the farm families that became dependent on public assistance during the depression.

The specific objectives have been to describe the extent of the farm relief problem and the underlying causes of distress; the development of the administrative programs which were formulated to meet the situation; the types and amounts of assistance given farm households; the social characteristics of these households; the relation of farmers on relief to the land with respect to residence and tenure and their relation to the factors of production and experience; and the trend of farm relief through 1935.

The sections describing the social and economic characteristics of relief and rehabilitation clients are based mainly on an analysis of farm households receiving aid in June 1935. This month was selected because it was considered less subject to seasonal and administrative fluctuations than other months for which similar data are available.

Supplementary data, however, are drawn from relief studies that were made in February 1935 and October 1935 in the same sample areas as was the June study. Material is also drawn from previous Works Progress Administration studies, principally *Six Rural Problem Areas*, *Relief–Resources–Rehabilitation* and *Comparative Study of Rural Relief and Non-Relief Households*.[1] In chapter VII, "Relief Trends, 1933 Through 1935," use is made of reports of the Resettlement Administration and of the Works Progress Administration, and of the study made by the latter organization of cases opened and closed by relief offices between March and October 1935.

The data presented in this report were obtained by means of a sample enumeration.[2] The June relief study included 116,972 rural cases, in 300 counties representing 30 States, of which 37,854 were those of farm operators; 58,516 of the total rural cases were in 138

---

[1] Research Monographs I and II.
[2] For details of the sampling procedure, see appendix B.

counties representing 9 agricultural areas. Of these, 18,126 were farm operator households. The estimated United States and State totals were based on the larger sample.

The sample counties were systematically chosen as representative of varied types of agriculture in the States and areas surveyed. These counties contained 12.1 percent of all the farm operators in the States sampled [3] and 8.1 percent of farm operators in the areas sampled. The information on the schedules was obtained from case records in the county relief offices.

DEFINITIONS OF TERMS

This study is concerned with heads of families, either farm operators or farm laborers, 16 to 64 years of age. Those 65 years of age and over are arbitrarily excluded since they are considered as having passed their productive period. Farm operators include both farmers still remaining on their land and those forced to leave their farms [4] but whose usual occupation had been farming. In all areas, the study separates farm operators into two groups, *owners* and *tenants*, while in the Cotton Areas, a third group, *sharecroppers*, as distinguished from other tenants, is represented. *Farm owners* are farmers who own all or part of the land which they operate. *Farm tenants* are defined as operating hired land only, furnishing all or part of the working equipment and stock, whether they pay cash, or a share of the crop, or both, as rent. *Croppers* are tenants to whom the landlord furnishes all the work animals, who contribute only their labor, and who receive in return a share of the crop. *Farm laborers* are persons who work on a farm with or without wages under the supervision of the farm operator.[5] The major part of the discussion of laborers is confined to heads of families.

For purposes of this survey, a person was regarded as having had a *usual occupation* if at any time during the last 10 years he had worked at any job, other than work relief, for a period of at least 4 consecutive weeks. If the person had worked at two or more occupations, the one at which he had worked the greatest length of time was considered the usual occupation. If he had worked for an equal length of time at two or more occupations, the one at which he worked last was considered the usual occupation. A person on relief continuously from February to June was defined as *currently employed* in June if he had had nonrelief employment

---

[3] The State sample was based on 31 States, but Arizona was not included in the June survey.

[4] A farm is defined as having at least 3 acres, unless its agricultural products in 1929 were valued at $250 or more. *Fifteenth Census of the United States: 1930*, Population Vol. I, p. 2.

[5] See Appendix C—Glossary.

lasting 1 week or more during February, the month of the preceding survey.[6] For cases opened or reopened from March to June, a person was considered currently employed in June if he had had non-relief employment, including employment as farm operator or laborer, during the week in which the first order for relief was received. The type of current employment is referred to hereafter as *current occupation.*

AGRICULTURAL AREAS SURVEYED

Although relief and rehabilitation rates are given by States, this study is primarily based on data for nine major agricultural areas. They are: the Eastern Cotton Belt, which includes portions of North Carolina, South Carolina, Georgia, Alabama, Mississippi, Louisiana, and Arkansas; the Lake States Cut-Over Area in northern Minnesota, Wisconsin, and Michigan; the Western Cotton Area, including parts of Oklahoma and Texas; the Appalachian-Ozark

FIG. 1 - AREAS REPRESENTED AND COUNTIES SAMPLED

SURVEY OF THE RURAL RELIEF SITUATION
June 1935

AF-2161, W.P.A.

Area, including the mountainous sections of West Virginia, North Carolina, Tennessee, Kentucky, Missouri, and Arkansas; the Spring Wheat Area in the northern part of the Great Plains; the Winter Wheat Area in the southern part of the Great Plains; the Ranching Area scattered through the mountain States; the Hay and Dairy Area, which stretches from New York along the Great Lakes to

---

[6] This procedure for determining current employment was necessary as case records were not kept up-to-date with respect to employment status. It is justified by the fact that June is a peak month for agricultural employment and farm operators and laborers employed in February, a slack month, would normally continue their employment through the summer.

Wisconsin and Minnesota; and the Corn Belt in Ohio, Indiana, Illinois, South Dakota, Nebraska, Kansas, and Missouri. Figure 1 delineates these areas and indicates the counties sampled as representative of conditions in each area.

The first six regions constitute definite rural problem areas.[7] The Ranching Area may also be listed as a problem area, insofar as it has been affected by recent droughts. The Hay and Dairy Area and the Corn Belt are more nearly normal agricultural regions and as such are especially interesting for a study of the general farm relief problem. This is particularly true of the Corn Belt, which was especially benefited by the corn-hog program of the Agricultural Adjustment Administration.

---

[7] See Beck, P. G. and Forster, M. C., *Six Rural Problem Areas, Relief–Resources–Rehabilitation,* Research Monograph I, Division of Research, Statistics, and Finance, Federal Emergency Relief Administration, 1935, pp. 8 ff. This report also deals with the various aspects of the farm relief problem. However, the counties sampled differ from those covered by the present study, and the data refer to an earlier period.

SUMMARY

THE FARM FAMILIES that have received public assistance under the various Federal relief programs were only in part victims of the depression. In many cases, the need for outside aid was the result of long-standing agricultural maladjustments and adverse climatic conditions such as drought and flood.

A large majority of the farmers and farm laborers receiving public assistance, up to the summer of 1935, were clients of the general relief and rural rehabilitation programs of the Federal Emergency Relief Administration. During the last half of 1935, the Federal Works Program and the Resettlement Administration took over the bulk of the load.

LOCATION OF FARM RELIEF AND REHABILITATION CASES

Over a million farmer and farm laborer families in rural and urban areas were on relief and rehabilitation rolls in February 1935, and almost 600,000 farmers in rural areas received relief grants or rehabilitation advances under the Federal programs in June 1935.

The June farm relief load varied widely among the States. New Mexico, with more than one-third of its farmers receiving these types of Federal aid, was followed in order by the Dakotas, Oklahoma, and Colorado, with more than one-fifth of all farmers on relief or rehabilitation, and by Kentucky, Florida, Idaho, Montana, Minnesota, Pennsylvania, Arkansas, South Carolina, and Wyoming, each with 10 percent or more of their farm families receiving such aid. In the country as a whole, the proportion of all farm families receiving relief grants or rehabilitation advances in June averaged 9 percent.

The 14 States in which the relief load was concentrated contained only one-fourth of all farms in the United States in 1935; yet they contained over one-half of all farmers receiving relief grants or rehabilitation advances in June of that year. The concentration of relief in these States primarily reflects the effects of the 1934 drought and the long-standing ills of the Appalachian-Ozark Area with its poor soil and abandoned industries. At the same time, the heavy relief loads in these States, as compared with others suffering from similar unfavorable conditions, reflect differences in relief policies, more liberal in some sections than in others.

TYPES AND AMOUNTS OF RELIEF AND REHABILITATION

Types and amounts of relief grants and rehabilitation advances to farm families in June 1935 differed widely among various agricultural areas. Since the administration of both relief and rehabilitation was largely entrusted to the States, the available funds and the administrative policies of the various States, as well as differences in standard of living and employment status, caused variations in the aid granted.

Most of the employed as well as the unemployed heads of farm families on general relief rolls received work relief in June 1935. The presence on work relief rolls of farmers still operating their farms indicates either that other members of their families could attend to the farm duties or that their farming was of little consequence. Many were normally full-time farmers whose operations had been curtailed by the drought, and others were part-time farmers who had lost their usual supplementary employment.

Relatively fewer Negroes than whites had work relief in the two Cotton Areas, with the difference more marked in the Eastern Cotton Belt. In that area two-thirds of the white farmers on relief but less than one-half of the Negroes had work assignments.

Amounts of relief given in June 1935 in all areas combined averaged $13 for farm owners, $12 for farm laborers and tenants, and $9 for croppers. Negroes in all agricultural groups received lower relief grants than whites. Relief grants were smallest in the Appalachian-Ozark and Cotton Areas, reflecting the relatively low standard of living of those sections.

The proportion of all rehabilitation clients receiving subsistence goods (for meeting budgetary needs) and the proportion receiving capital goods (for productive purposes) were about the same (83 and 84 percent, respectively) for the total of all areas, but differences among areas were marked.

Rehabilitation advances ranged in amount from an average of $31 in the Spring Wheat Area to $416 for whites in the Western Cotton Area, reflecting to some extent the different stages of development of the program in the various areas. The average for all areas was $189.

Relatively fewer Negro than white clients in the Cotton Areas received capital goods, and Negroes received smaller advances than whites of both capital and subsistence goods.

SOCIAL CHARACTERISTICS OF RELIEF FAMILIES

Farmers on relief did not differ markedly in age from all farmers in the United States. Comparison of February and June data, however, indicates that the younger farmers and farm laborers (excluding the very young group, 16–24 years of age) left relief rolls in greater numbers than did the older clients during the spring planting season. As in the general population, owners on relief were about 9 years older on the average than tenants, while share-croppers and laborers were the youngest agricultural groups.

Relief families were found to be larger than those in the general population. In most areas, tenants had larger families than the other groups. Negro and white households were not consistently different in size.

Although the normal family (husband and wife, or husband, wife, and children) was the prevailing type on relief, the proportion of such families varied considerably by areas and by tenure groups. Broken families were found more frequently in the two Cotton Areas and in the self-sufficing areas (Lake States Cut-Over and Appalachian-Ozark) than in the regions where rural distress is of more recent origin. These four areas were the only ones where the mother-and-children type of family was found on rural relief in any considerable proportions. Nonfamily men were particularly important on the relief rolls in the Lake States Cut-Over Area, and nonfamily women on relief were of significance only in the Eastern Cotton Belt, where their presence on relief rolls reflects the influence of the considerable migration of males from the South.

Households with only one worker were found more frequently in the lower socio-economic groups. The number of workers increased with the size of the family, but it was not a proportionate increase.

Migration of farmers and farm laborers evidently increased during the drought and depression years. This trend would indicate that mobility, rather than being a cause of the need for relief, was, at least partially, the result of the need for relief. However, there was no clear-cut relationship between mobility and relief needs.

EMPLOYMENT STATUS AND RELATION TO THE LAND

More than one-tenth of the farmers on relief in rural areas lived in villages, while much larger proportions of farm laborers on relief lived in villages. Although in some agricultural regions farmers and farm laborers normally live in villages rather than in the open country, the residence distribution probably reflects to a large extent the influence of depression unemployment, which causes families to migrate from open country to village communities, with their greater promise of opportunities for employment or relief.

Nearly three-fourths of the heads of farm families on relief in June 1935 were farmers by usual occupation, and slightly more than one-fourth were farm laborers. Tenants other than sharecroppers made up over one-half of the farm operators on relief, farm owners accounted for about one-third, and sharecroppers for nearly one-eighth.

In all areas larger percentages of tenants than of owners were on relief, reflecting the less secure economic position of tenants as compared to owners. In both Cotton Areas sharecroppers were represented more heavily on relief than either owners or other tenants.

The overwhelming majority of farmers on relief were still operating farms at the time of the survey. In general, tenants (exclusive of croppers) on relief had not been able to remain on the land to the same degree as had farm owners. Sharecroppers on relief had a lower employment rate at their usual occupation than either other tenants or owners, and relief heads who were farm laborers by usual occupation had the lowest employment rate of all. Few agricultural workers had shifted into nonagricultural jobs. Heads of relief households with farm experience but not currently engaged in agriculture had left the farm, in most instances, during the depression.

While farmers and farm laborers were leaving the open country for the villages, there was a tendency among nonagricultural workers to move to the farm. This was especially true in the Lake States Cut-Over and Appalachian-Ozark Areas where loss of industrial jobs evidently caused workers to give major attention to farming in which they had formerly engaged part-time. The poor soil in these two areas made the land easy to obtain but hard to get a living from, so that the workers had to resort to relief.

The majority of the heads of farm households on relief who were unemployed or who had gone into some nonagricultural occupation had left the farm between July 1, 1934, and July 1, 1935. Few had left farming in the prosperous years 1925–1930.

The greater economic resources of owners and tenants, as compared with those of sharecroppers and laborers, are reflected in the periods which elapsed between the time they lost their usual tenure status or job and the time they appeared on relief rolls. The average farm laborer family head on relief, who was no longer employed as a farm laborer, was accepted for relief only 3 months after the loss of his usual type of job, and the average sharecropper, no longer employed as such, remained off relief rolls for only 5 months after losing his cropper status. Displaced tenants and owners, however, did not receive relief until 7 and 13 months, respectively, after they had lost jobs at their usual occupation.

FACTORS IN PRODUCTION

Farmers who were unable to support themselves and their families were found to be handicapped with respect to acreage operated, livestock owned, and education attained.

The average acreage of farms operated by owners and tenants on relief was much less than that of all owner and tenant farms reported by the 1935 Census of Agriculture. The average acreage reported in June for both groups was much less than that in February, indicating that farmers with larger acreages had been able to become self-supporting or to go on rehabilitation rolls more readily than those with smaller farms. This situation may be taken to indicate that as recovery in agriculture becomes more general the relief group will contain a larger proportion of chronic or marginal cases as measured by size of holdings.

Many farmers with adequate acreage were hampered in their efforts at self-support by lack of sufficient livestock. From a study made as of January 1, 1934, it is evident that fewer farm operators on relief owned livestock than farmers not on relief, and that the relief clients who did own livestock had fewer animals.

The farm families' need for Federal assistance was not caused by lack of agricultural experience. The great majority of the agricultural workers on relief and rehabilitation reported 10 years or more of farm experience.

One measurable index of personal ability of farm families on relief is their educational attainment. A study made as of 1933 showed that heads of rural relief families had consistently received less schooling than their nonrelief neighbors. In the present study, the majority of the heads of open country households on relief in October 1935 had not completed grade school. In no area was the average schooling higher than the eighth grade. However, the younger heads of open country households were better educated than the older heads, reflecting the trend toward increased educational opportunities in rural areas.

COMPARISON OF RELIEF AND REHABILITATION FAMILIES

When rehabilitation clients are considered separately from farm families receiving relief, some of the expected differences between the two groups do not appear. Neither the older nor the younger relief heads and neither the larger nor the smaller relief families appear to have been consistently selected for rehabilitation. Nor is there any evidence that the number of employable persons in the household influenced selection of families for rehabilitation. Relative stability of residence also was apparently not a determining factor.

On the other hand, in contrast with relief families, practically all rehabilitation clients lived in the open country. Also, the proportion of farm laborers was smaller among rehabilitation clients than among relief families. Size of farm was evidently a criterion

of selection, the farms of rehabilitation clients being larger than
those of relief families in most areas. Some tendency to select
normal families was evident. Unattached women especially were
almost unknown among rehabilitation clients, although unattached
men, mother-children, and father-children families were accepted in
considerable numbers in a few areas.

The rehabilitation program was primarily agricultural, but only
89 out of every 100 rehabilitation clients on the rolls in June 1935
were farmers or farm laborers by usual occupation. All but 2 out
of every 100, however, had had agricultural experience.

RELIEF TRENDS

The estimated number of farm operators in the United States
receiving Federal assistance, including emergency relief, advances
under the rehabilitation program, and Works Program earnings,
increased from 417,000 in October 1933 to 685,000 in February 1935
and then fell to 382,000 in October 1935. During the last months of
1935, the downward trend in the number of farm operators receiving
these types of Federal assistance was reversed as needs increased
during the winter season. By December, 396,000 farm operators were
receiving aid under the 3 programs.

In February 1935, when the relief load reached a peak in rural
areas, nearly 1,000,000 farm families in rural areas alone, including
those of farm operators and farm laborers, received general relief
grants or rehabilitation loans. The largest single factor accounting
for the peak relief load in February was drought, which resulted
in crop failures and loss of livestock.

Farm families left the general relief rolls rapidly after February
1935, with the expansion of the rural rehabilitation program and
with increasing agricultural prosperity. Of all agricultural cases
on relief in February, only 42 percent were carried forward through
the month of June, the remainder being closed or transferred to the
rural rehabilitation program.

Between July 1 and December 31, 1935, 551,000 farmers were
removed from the rolls of agencies expending F. E. R. A. funds.
About 186,000 of these found employment on the Works Program and
37,000 were transferred directly to the Resettlement Administration.
Of the 328,000 families completely removed from Federal aid, it is
estimated that about half became at least temporarily self-supporting, largely through sale of produce or through earnings at private
employment, and that the other half received aid from State or local
funds or were left without care from any agency.

The temporary nature of the self-support obtained by many of the
families in 1935 is indicated by the fact that out of 215,000 farm

operator families accepted for aid between July 1 and December 31 by agencies expending F. E. R. A. funds, four-fifths were former relief cases returning to the rolls. The reasons for opening relief cases in the July-October period are also significant, indicating that improvement in economic conditions had not been sufficient to offset the effects of the 1934 drought and other factors causing rural distress. Crop failure and loss of livestock were reported most frequently as reasons for applying for relief. Loss of earnings from employment was the second most important reason given—seasonal employment had come to an end or earnings had become so low that supplementary relief was required. Other families came on relief which had been existing on savings for some time and which listed exhaustion of these resources as their reason for applying. Increased needs with the approach of winter, loss of assistance from relatives and friends, failure of landlords to continue advances to croppers after the cotton harvest, appropriation of crop returns by creditors, and destruction of property by local floods were other reasons for opening of relief cases.

PROGRAMS OF RECONSTRUCTION

Any program for the reconstruction of American agriculture must take into account the conservation of human values as well as of soil and other natural resources. It must also be adaptable to the peculiar regional needs of different parts of the country.

Combined farming-industrial employment, proposed as a partial remedy for farm problems, is limited by the location and hours of industry. Retirement of submarginal lands from agriculture is an obvious necessity, but financial and legal difficulties stand in the way of measures which would be immediately effective. Restoring fertility to eroded or exhausted soil is a sound measure of economic reconstruction, and a program to control surplus production is necessary to secure economic stability for farmers. Crop control can be successful, however, only if planned in such a way that agricultural production is adjusted to rural population trends.

For some areas, the reform of the tenant system and the arrest of the increase of tenancy are of paramount importance, since tenancy has proved to be a stumbling block in the path of such constructive efforts as crop diversification, soil conservation, and cooperative marketing.

Equally important in agrarian reconstruction are programs for the conservation of human resources. The needs of destitute farm families in the past few years have been met on an emergency basis by direct relief, work relief, and rehabilitation loans and grants. Direct relief, whether in the form of E. R. A. benefits, State or local relief, or Resettlement grants, is often best suited to the needs of farmers for temporary assistance, even if it creates no lasting values. Work relief has the disadvantage of taking the farmer away from his land, unless it is limited to off-seasons or to nonfarming members of the family. Rural rehabilitation loans are desirable for many farmers since they provide the necessary credit at a reasonable rate of interest, farm plans worked out to fit the individual farm, and advice and supervision in the execution of these plans.

Guided migration is a basic need in rural reconstruction. Although the Government cannot arbitrarily move people out of blighted areas, it can offer advice to farmers who wish to leave an area in which they cannot support themselves.

Cooperation is recognized as one of the hopes of the smaller farmer in marketing and purchasing, in owning machinery and lands in common, and in meeting farm and home problems. Education to awaken the desire for a higher standard of living is another means of social reconstruction. The improvement of educational and other institutions in rural areas, however, calls for better financial support than is now available. Equalization funds are needed for health, education, and public welfare to reduce the financial inequalities between rural States and States which contain points of financial concentration—between rural counties and industrial cities.

The more fundamental measures for building a superior agrarian civilization in the United States are long-time measures, not planned for immediate results. Furthermore, they require national coordination and Federal financial support. Successful rehabilitation cannot be accomplished without a continuing course of action, uninterrupted by sudden shifts of policy such as have characterized relief and rehabilitation programs during the depression years.

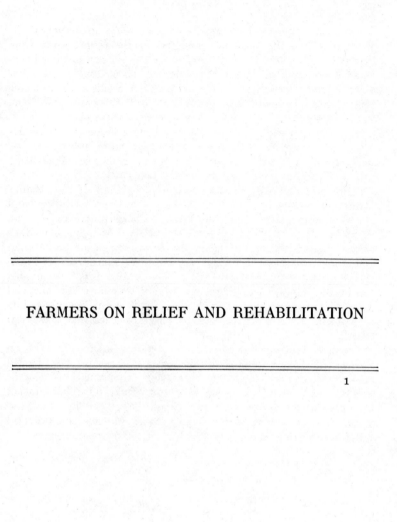

FARMERS ON RELIEF AND REHABILITATION

CHAPTER I

EXTENT AND CAUSES OF FARM DISTRESS

PUBLIC RELIEF of rural distress on a large scale has been a notable feature of the depression of the 1930's. In past periods of widespread destitution, the urban unemployed could usually step into a bread-line, find a place in a soup kitchen, or get direct financial aid from local public or private welfare agencies. Rural families, on the other hand, except in a few sections with long established systems of poor relief, usually had only their neighbors or the almshouse to turn to when their slender credit was exhausted. They could rarely expect assistance from welfare agencies of neighboring towns, whose resources were usually inadequate for their own needy townsfolk.

In the recent depression, as in earlier depressions, city governments recognized the necessity of providing assistance for the urban unemployed, but county governments discounted the needs of farmers within their jurisdiction, arguing that a farmer should be able to obtain the necessities of life from his own land, however bad market conditions might be. Under modern agricultural conditions, such an assumption is, of course, not supported by the facts. Even if he raises most of his foodstuffs, there will always be some necessary cash expenses that a farmer may not be able to meet. Moreover, under the one commercial crop system practiced in some agricultural regions, farmers either do not raise foodstuffs at all, or raise them in quantities insufficient for their own support. Again, farmers who normally raise their own foodstuffs may be prevented from doing so by drought or flood or other causes of crop damage, or by personal disability.

The depression of 1930–1935 was both prolonged and widespread in its effects. Moreover, it came at a crucial period in the development of American agriculture, when the country was due to reap the consequences of reckless and unplanned use of natural resources over a period of decades and when expanding commercial farming and increased mechanization were forcing radical readjustments in the relationship between land and labor. With the impact of the depression, bringing bank failures, a contracted market, and low prices, the weak spots in the agricultural structure gave way. Hundreds of thousands of farm families found themselves without savings or current income. Thousands were left without land or equipment. Other thousands faced a barren future on soil that had become useless for agriculture.

As more and more farm families lost their livelihood, it became clear that destitute farmers could no longer live on neighbors or credit. Their neighbors were frequently as badly off as they were. Many of their creditors were going bankrupt.

Consequently, when the Reconstruction Finance Corporation began to make relief loans in 1932 and when the Federal Emergency Relief Administration introduced direct grants in the spring of 1933, these benefits were made available to agricultural counties as well as to cities and towns. In June 1935, 31.5 percent of the 4,534,000 cases receiving Federal aid under the general relief program lived in rural areas.[1] Of the rural cases, 28 percent were farm operator families and 10 percent were farm laborer families (table 1). More than half of the 390,000 farm operators,[2] or 208,000, were tenants (exclusive of sharecroppers); about one-third, or 138,000, were farm owners; and the remaining 44,000 were sharecroppers. In addition, 203,612 families in rural areas received loans under the rural rehabilitation program during June 1935 [3] (table 2).

TABLE 1.—ESTIMATED NUMBER OF RURAL AND URBAN CASES RECEIVING RELIEF UNDER THE GENERAL RELIEF PROGRAM, AND USUAL OCCUPATION OF THE HEADS OF RURAL CASES, JUNE 1935

Residence and usual occupation	Cases under general relief program	
	Number	Percent
All cases	4,534,000	100.0
Rural [1]	1,427,000	31.5
Urban	3,107,000	68.5
Rural cases	1,427,000	100
Agricultural heads	537,000	38
Farm operators	[2] 390,000	28
Owners	138,000	10
Tenants [3]	208,000	15
Croppers	44,000	3
Farm laborers	147,000	10
All others	890,000	62

[1] Open country or centers of less than 2,500 population.
[2] Includes farm operators residing in towns of 2,500 to 5,000 population. The town cases constitute less than 2 percent of all cases.
[3] Exclusive of croppers in the 2 Cotton Areas.

Source: Smith, Mapheus and Mangus, A. R., *Cases Receiving General Relief in Urban and Rural Areas, July 1933–December 1935* (estimated), Research Bulletin, Series III, No. 1, Division of Social Research, Works Progress Administration, Aug. 22, 1936; and *Survey of Current Changes in the Rural Relief Population, June 1935.*

[1] That is, in the open country or in centers of less than 2,500 population.
[2] Exclusive of cases receiving both relief grants and rehabilitation advances. Such cases were considered rehabilitation clients.
[3] Throughout this report, the following points with regard to the rural rehabilitation load should be kept in mind: (1) The June sample of rehabilitation cases included approximately 9 percent that were also receiving general relief during June; (2) of the June rehabilitation sample, 80.4 percent of the household heads were farm operators by usual occupation; 8.1 percent were farm laborers; 8.4 percent were nonagricultural workers; while 3.1 percent reported no usual occupation; (3) a small but indeterminable number of rural rehabilitation clients had never been on relief rolls.

TABLE 2.—FARM OPERATORS IN RURAL AREAS RECEIVING RELIEF GRANTS AND REHABILITATION ADVANCES,[1] JUNE 1935, AND THEIR RATIO TO ALL FARM OPERATORS IN JANUARY 1935, BY STATE

State	Number of cases [2]			Ratio of combined case load to all farmers
	Total	Relief	Rehabilitation [3]	
United States, total	[4] 593,612	390,000	203,612	9
Oklahoma	58,310	50,100	8,210	27
Kentucky	54,045	53,500	545	19
Texas	40,939	18,000	22,939	8
Arkansas	28,098	9,100	18,998	11
South Dakota	27,733	9,800	17,933	33
Minnesota	23,842	13,200	10,642	12
Mississippi	23,260	10,900	12,360	8
North Dakota	22,633	22,600	33	27
Pennsylvania	22,573	22,200	373	12
Alabama	19,507	2,000	17,507	7
North Carolina	18,674	11,800	6,874	6
Georgia	17,894	5,500	12,394	7
South Carolina	17,579	11,500	6,079	11
Missouri	16,300	9,800	6,500	6
Tennessee	15,034	12,100	2,934	6
New Mexico	14,720	5,600	9,120	36
Illinois	14,633	13,800	833	6
Kansas	14,044	6,800	7,244	8
Colorado	13,917	7,000	6,917	22
Florida	13,107	7,400	5,707	18
Louisiana	12,910	2,200	10,710	8
Virginia	10,257	7,200	3,057	5
Michigan	10,179	8,000	2,179	5
Ohio	9,444	7,100	2,344	4
West Virginia	8,283	7,100	1,183	8
Wisconsin	8,281	6,800	1,481	4
Nebraska	8,077	5,700	2,377	6
Idaho	7,620	7,500	120	17
Montana	6,549	5,900	649	13
Iowa	6,228	5,000	1,228	3
Indiana	5,473	4,600	873	3
California	4,921	4,900	21	3
Washington	3,763	3,300	463	5
Utah	2,294	1,700	594	8
Wyoming	1,708	600	1,108	10
Maryland	1,700	1,700	----------	4
New York	1,697	1,600	97	1
Massachusetts	1,500	1,500	----------	4
Maine	1,254	900	354	3
Oregon	1,158	1,100	58	2
New Jersey	1,128	900	228	4
Arizona	957	800	157	5
Connecticut	454	400	54	1
Vermont	401	400	1	2
New Hampshire	213	100	113	1
Nevada	121	100	21	3
Delaware	100	100	----------	1
Rhode Island	100	100	----------	2

[1] Exclusive of cases under care that did not receive advances during June.
[2] These figures include farm operators residing in towns of 2,500 to 5,000 population. The town cases, however, constitute less than 2 percent of all cases.
[3] Including groups other than farm operators. See p. 4, footnote 3.
[4] Cases that received both relief grants and rehabilitation advances were considered rehabilitation cases.

Source: Relief data for States estimated on the basis of the Survey of Current Changes in the Rural Relief Population and the *United States Census of Agriculture: 1935;* rehabilitation data from the Rural Rehabilitation Division, Federal Emergency Relief Administration.

Some 2,000,000 farm families received relief at one time or another during the depression period. In a single month (February 1935)

well over 1,000,000 farmers and farm laborers [4] were receiving some type of public assistance.[5] Thus, at this time, families whose heads had usually been employed in agriculture constituted about one-fifth of the total relief load of the entire country.

LOCATION OF FARM RELIEF AND REHABILITATION CASES

The 593,612 farm operators receiving relief grants or rehabilitation advances [6] in June 1935 (table 2) constituted 9 percent of all farmers [7] in the United States as reported by the 1935 Census of Agriculture.[8] This proportion does not appear large when compared with the 18 percent of urban families on relief in June 1935.[9] In 21 States, in fact, the combined number of farm operators receiving relief grants or rehabilitation advances was less than 6 percent of all farmers, and in 13 States the ratio was from 6 to 8 percent. In 14 States, however, farmers receiving relief grants or rehabilitation advances in June 1935 accounted for from 10 to 36 percent of the total farmers.

New Mexico had the highest proportion of its farm operators on relief or rehabilitation, 36 percent. South Dakota followed with 33 percent, and North Dakota and Oklahoma each with 27 percent. About one-fifth of all farmers in Colorado and Kentucky were receiving such aid. Florida, Idaho, Montana, Minnesota, Pennsylvania, Arkansas, South Carolina, and Wyoming reported 10 to 18 percent of their farmers on either relief or rehabilitation rolls. These 14 States, which contained approximately one-fourth of all farms in the United States, included over one-half of all farmers in rural areas receiving public aid in June 1935.

All but two of these States are in drought or poor land regions (figure 2). Idaho, Montana, the Dakotas, and Minnesota form a belt

---

[4] These included 598,000 farm operators and 279,000 farm laborers who were heads of households on the general emergency relief program (a small percentage of the farmers lived in towns of 2,500–5,000 population, the rest in open country and villages) ; 135,000 cases under care of rural rehabilitation ; an undetermined number aided by sons in the Civilian Conservation Corps ; and about 166,000 displaced farmers or farm laborers living in cities and receiving urban or transient relief. These estimates of the Division of Research, Statistics, and Finance, Federal Emergency Relief Administration, exclude all farmers or farm laborers 65 years of age and over.

[5] Due to changes in economic status through improved crop conditions in some areas, to Agricultural Adjustment Administration benefit payments, and to seasonal employment or administrative orders, some farmers left the relief rolls while others, as their resources finally became entirely depleted, were forced to seek Federal assistance. Thus, the total number of families aided during the year was considerably larger than the number receiving emergency aid at any one time.

[6] Unduplicated total. Cases that received both relief grants and rehabilitation advances were considered rehabilitation cases.

[7] Because of lack of census data on farm laborer heads of households (unlike farm operators, farm laborers are not predominantly household heads), estimates of the percentage of farm laborer households on relief by States are not available.

[8] Ratios based on the Census of Agriculture tend to be slight overstatements as the farmers included in the present survey were not necessarily still on their farms. All farmers reported by the Census of Agriculture were actually operating farms at the date of enumeration.

[9] Table 1 and *Fifteenth Census of the United States: 1930*, Population Vol. VI.

across the northern part of the 1934 drought area. Wyoming forms a connecting link with Colorado, New Mexico, Oklahoma, and Arkansas, a chain of southwestern drought States cutting into the Dust Bowl and the cotton areas. Kentucky and Pennsylvania had large concentrations of farmers on relief in the Appalachian sections with their poor soil and abandoned mines.

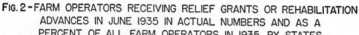

Fig. 2 – FARM OPERATORS RECEIVING RELIEF GRANTS OR REHABILITATION ADVANCES IN JUNE 1935 IN ACTUAL NUMBERS AND AS A PERCENT OF ALL FARM OPERATORS IN 1935, BY STATES

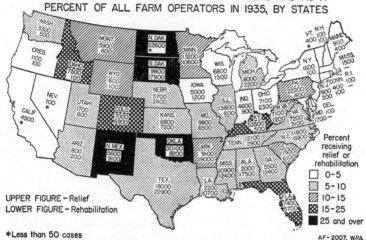

Heavy relief in Florida and South Carolina may be attributed to a number of local natural and economic conditions and to local administrative policies. These States were probably more liberal in accepting farm families for aid than were other southern States.

Rehabilitation clients in June were still concentrated to a large extent in the southern States, where the program was first developed. Of the 8 States with more than 10,000 clients receiving advances during the month, only 2 (South Dakota and Minnesota) were outside the South. The program had its smallest development on the west coast and in the northeastern States (figures 2 and 4).

BASIC FARM PROBLEMS

Part of the vast volume of rural need was due directly to depression factors. Farmers who had done fairly well in the past were victims of bank failures and vanishing markets. City workers and workers in rural industries lost their jobs and, without farm experience or capital, tried to make a living from the soil. Youth who would normally have gone to the cities and towns to work in industry stayed on the farm, crowding into an already overcrowded agriculture.

The depression was not directly responsible, however, for all the rural distress reflected in the heavy relief rolls. Federal relief brought to light a much more numerous group of farmers whose distress arose from long-run factors, who had led a precarious existence for some years prior to the depression because of these factors, or for whom the depression was the last straw in an accumulation of troubles outside their control.

Some of the accumulating hazards of American agrarian life [10] have been enumerated here. They show the variety and complexity of the forces which underlie rural distress and indicate the regional differences involved.

Farming on Poor Land,

In many parts of the country, farmers have been attempting for years to cultivate soil which was never suitable for farming or which has deteriorated beyond redemption.[11] Such soil has given them only the barest living and has made it impossible for them to better their condition. Had Federal relief not been made available, they might have continued more or less inarticulately to endure their extreme poverty unaided. The relief program served to bring their condition to light and to focus attention on the need for removing the impoverished land from cultivation.

The National Resources Board has estimated that about 450,000 farms in the United States, including 75 million acres, are of this submarginal type.[12] They are to be found for the most part in the hilly, dry, or forested parts of the country and in sections where the soil is light and sandy or seriously eroded.[13] Over one-half of the total acreage proposed for retirement from arable farming is in the Western Great Plains and the southeastern hilly cotton and tobacco regions, although scattered concentrations are found throughout the United States.

Excess Birth Rate in Poor Land Areas.

Poor land in itself is a sufficient hazard to farming, but when, as in the Appalachian-Ozark highlands and parts of the cotton areas, it is coupled with an excessive birth rate, the problem is greatly aggravated, and individual and family suffering multiplied. In

---

[10] Discussed in more detail by Beck, P. G. and Forster, M. C., *Six Rural Problem Areas, Relief–Resources–Rehabilitation,* Research Monograph I, Division of Research, Statistics, and Finance, Federal Emergency Relief Administration, 1935.

[11] *National Resources Board Report,* December 1, 1934, pp. 15–16.

[12] *Idem,* pp. 110, 127, 157 ff., 175 ff.

[13] *Idem,* p. 181.

Waste in the Cut-Over Area

the past, the high farm birth rate served to populate new areas and the cities. But desirable free homestead land was exhausted years ago and the covered wagon is no longer a means of escape from an overcrowded shack in the hills. The depression shut off the opportunity to make a living by migrating to cities and towns. There was nothing for the surplus rural population to do but remain, causing serious unbalance between population and land in many sections.

Soil Erosion.

Not only have some farmers been trying to grow crops on hopelessly poor soil, but others have been ruining good land by practices conducive to soil erosion or have failed to take necessary precautions to protect land subject to erosion. Warnings of soil erosion have been heard in many areas for years, but these have been ignored by farmers who were too eager for immediate results to care about the future. Other farmers could not afford the outlay necessary to prevent erosion or had such limited acreages that they had no choice but to use their land to the full, regardless of the danger of overcropping. In 1934, the National Resources Board reported that the usefulness for farming of 35 million acres had been completely destroyed, that the top soil was nearly or entirely removed from another 125 million acres, and that destruction had begun on another 100 million acres.[14]

Excessive cropping has been especially destructive on the dry land of the Western Great Plains, where quarter sections allotted to the settlers under the homesteading laws were too small for economic use of the land. The farmers were further led astray during the World War when they were encouraged to break more and more sod in order to meet the world demand for wheat. No provision was made against the effects of the inevitable dry years, and vast acreages of dry soil were left unprotected by grass or trees against the ravages of wind and sun.

The southern and western corn belts also contain much easily eroded soil which is being destroyed because the many small farmers in the area have been concentrating on clean-cultivated row crops. In the hilly southeastern section, cotton and tobacco are being grown for the market on land from which the top soil has been completely worn away. Cultivating the subsoil requires extensive use of fertilizer, which makes farming on such land an expensive and precarious business. The cost of fertilizer consumes a large part of the farmer's income and credit, and when the crop fails he is ready for the relief rolls.[15]

---

[14] *National Resources Board Report, op. cit.,* p. 17.

[15] Woofter, T. J., Jr., *Landlord and Tenant on the Cotton Plantation,* Research Monograph V, Division of Social Research, Works Progress Administration, 1936, chapter V.

Inadequate Size of Farms.

Small farms in areas which require large-scale methods often lead to practices conducive to soil erosion, as already pointed out. Even when soil erosion is not involved, the farms are often inadequate to make a stable income possible.[16] [Where productivity per acre is low, as in the western dry-farming regions and the hilly cotton areas, and where there is constant threat of drought, large acreages are required to compensate for low productivity and to build up reserves for years of crop loss. Farmers whose acreages are too small to provide such surpluses in good years are brought to dependency at the first year of crop failure.]

Extension of the One Cash Crop System.

The recent trend in American agriculture has been toward absolute dependence on a single cash crop—cotton, tobacco, corn, or wheat —to the exclusion of production of food and feed crops for home use. The small farmer who follows this practice is rarely able to accumulate reserves in good years for the year when his one crop fails or the market falls. When that time comes, he is left not only with no alternative source of income but also with no products for home consumption.

Overcapitalization of Farms.

During the World War and post-war years, farmers borrowed money and bought large acreages of land at inflated values in order to take advantage of high prices for foodstuffs. [They also invested heavily in machinery to be paid for at some future date. But before they could realize on their investment, the depression sent prices and land values tobogganing. Many were unable to meet real estate and chattel mortgage payments and were left in the hands of their creditors.]

[*Decline of Rural Industries*]

Natural resources, such as timber, coal, and other minerals, have been progressively and often wastefully depleted in certain parts of the country. [These formerly furnished small farmers with a means of earning the cash income necessary to supplement their limited agricultural production.] When these industries declined, the farmers became completely dependent on farms too small or too unproductive to support them. This situation is found in the Lake States Cut-Over and Appalachian-Ozark Areas in particular, and accounts in part for the heavy relief loads in those regions.

---

[16] *National Resources Board Report, op. cit.,* pp. 17 and 159.

Abandoned Coal Mine

The Tenant System.

An extremely low standard of living has been characteristic of tenant farmers in various parts of the country [17] since long before the depression. This has been particularly true of the South where the cotton tenant system, especially that phase of tenancy known as sharecropping, was developed to utilize the abundant supply of cheap and tractable labor.

Under the sharecropping system the tenant furnishes the labor of his entire family, as well as his own, for raising the cotton crop. The family receives in return the use of a piece of land, a house, work stock, equipment, subsistence goods, and the proceeds of half the crop, the other half being retained by the landlord. This system has become more and more widespread, until at the present time 50 percent of the tenants in some States are sharecroppers.[18]

While cotton was booming, the extreme poverty of the southern cotton tenant attracted little attention, but the depression and pre-depression years brought a crisis in the cotton market. Cotton acreage was extended after the war. Increases in production, however, coincided with a relatively decreasing demand both at home and abroad. The competition of artificial silk, increased production in foreign countries since the World War, and increased tariffs were some of the factors responsible. The results were decreasing prices since 1925 and a large carry-over from one season to another.

When the depression brought these conditions to a climax, acreage was sharply reduced, and tenants, especially sharecroppers, were displaced from the land. With no resources of any kind, and accustomed to depend on the landlord for every want,[19] large numbers of tenant farm families were left stranded, bewildered, and helpless.

The acreage reduction program of the Agricultural Adjustment Administration raised prices and helped the cotton growers by benefit payments. Most of the tenants' payments in the first years of the program, however, were applied by the landlords to old debts,[20] and tenants continued to be displaced from the farms, although at a much slower rate than before.

Assuming a permanently decreased demand for cotton, the tenant system of the South has produced a "stranded" population, a group of landless people with undeveloped capacities, who, unless some scheme for rehabilitation is devised, will be permanently in need of public assistance.

---

[17] For a detailed description of tenancy in the old Cotton Belt, see Woofter, T. J., Jr., *op. cit.*

[18] *United States Census of Agriculture: 1935.*

[19] Hoffsommer, Harold, *Landlord-Tenant Relations and Relief in Alabama,* Research Bulletin, Series II, No. 9, Division of Research, Statistics, and Finance, Federal Emergency Relief Administration, November 14, 1935.

[20] *Idem.*

Not so widely publicized, but more rapid of late, has been the increase in tenancy in the drought-stricken Great Plains Area, where discouraged owners are being replaced by tenants.

Farm Laborer Problem.

Insofar as farm laborers have formerly been employed by farmers now on relief, their need for relief is caused by the same factors that caused the need of their former employers. The depression also led to unemployment of farm laborers through restricting the demand for farm hands by farmers still able to carry on. It may be reasonably assumed, therefore, that the relief problem of farm laborers is to a greater extent a function of the depression than the result of long-run tendencies.[21]

In addition, the problem of migratory labor has grown markedly with the increase of large-scale one crop commercial farming. Since under this system laborers are needed for only a brief period while the one crop is being harvested, they must move on to other areas after a few weeks, and so on throughout the season. At best they can find employment for only a few months a year and their wages are not enough to carry them through the months of idleness. Because of their wandering existence, they are without roots in any community and cannot turn to neighbors or neighborhood grocers for help in off-seasons.[22]

---

[21] Inadequacies of available data make it impossible to ascertain the extent to which unemployment of farm laborers is due to displacement caused by increasing mechanization.

[22] For a detailed discussion of the migratory labor problem, see Webb, John N., *The Migratory-Casual Worker*, Research Monograph VII, Division of Social Research, Works Progress Administration, 1937.

CHAPTER II

RELIEF AND REHABILITATION PROGRAMS

ARLY IN 1933,[1] the Federal Government assumed responsibility for public assistance to the unemployed.[2] The Federal Emergency Relief Administration was established in May 1933 with a program of making cash grants to the States for direct or work relief under Federal supervision.[3] In the fall of that year, the Federal Surplus Relief Corporation was organized to assist the F. E. R. A. by purchasing and distributing commodities, such as foodstuffs and feed for livestock, to the States.[4]

Direct relief, whether in cash or in kind, was looked upon by the Administration as a "dole" which in the long run would tend to demoralize its recipients through prolonged idleness. Furthermore, direct relief created no equivalent for the money spent. Because of these objections, and because of the limited range of employment under the Public Works Administration, a program of work relief was early developed in a number of States.

In November 1933, the Civil Works Administration was set up to provide jobs quickly for the unemployed, both those on relief and those who had managed to stay off the rolls. Large numbers of rural cases were cared for under this program during the winter months, but as early as March employment under the Civil Works Program was discontinued in a number of States. On April 1, 1934, the C. W. A. work program gave way to the emergency work relief program of the F. E. R. A., designed for workers from relief rolls, with the few exceptions necessary to provide adequate supervision and administration. Although the emergency work relief program was intended to give employment to relief clients as a substitute for direct relief, such substitution was limited by available funds and by the

---

[1] Prior to this time, relief had been considered a local responsibility, although the Reconstruction Finance Corporation had been established to make loans to the States to assist them in caring for the unemployed.

[2] The agencies discussed in this chapter are limited to those which gave major assistance to farmers who either temporarily or permanently had lost their means of self-support.

[3] For a detailed history of the F. E. R. A., see Carothers, Doris, *Chronology of the Federal Emergency Relief Administration, May 12, 1933, to December 31, 1935*, Research Monograph VI, Division of Social Research, Works Progress Administration ; and Hopkins, Harry L., *Spending to Save*, New York : W. W. Norton & Company Inc., 1936.

[4] The F. S. R. C. was only in part a relief organization. In November 1935, its name was changed to Federal Surplus Commodities Corporation and its direction was brought under the Department of Agriculture.

fact that many households had no employable member. A large proportion of cases continued to receive direct relief, either alone or as
a supplement to work relief earnings.

Farmers and farm laborers, along with other workers on relief
rolls, shared in these early types of Federal relief and work programs
in varying degrees. Unemployed farm laborers and farmers who
had lost their farms presented in some respects the same problem
as other unemployed persons. They needed help to tide them over
until they could return to farming or find employment outside agriculture. It was discovered, however, as early as May 1933, that
thousands of farmers still on their farms also were without sufficient
means of subsistence. As soon as the F. E. R. A. began to function,
requests for help began to come into Washington headquarters from
the drought-stricken Southwest where farmers were losing their crops
and livestock. Direct relief was needed for the smaller farmers who
were unable to get loans for livestock feed from the Farm Credit
Administration or commercial agencies. The F. E. R. A. responded
with funds for direct relief and feed for such livestock as farm
families retained for their own use.

DROUGHT RELIEF [5]

By September 1933, the Northwest had been added to the drought
area and Federal relief activities had to be extended. A special
drought relief program was adopted in which various Federal agencies cooperated. The F. E. R. A. set aside a special fund for drought
relief for the purchase of grain, hay, and other feed. It also continued to give direct relief to farm families. The Bureau of Public
Roads established road building projects for drought farmers, whose
wages were paid first from relief funds and later by the C. W. A.,
while the P. W. A. assumed up to 30 percent of the cost of materials.
After April 1, 1934, the various State relief administrations continued
the road projects under their work programs.

The drought relief program was greatly expanded in 1934, when
more than half the land area of the United States suffered from
serious drought (figure 3). Under the Emergency Appropriation
Act of June 1934, the F. E. R. A. was allotted funds for relief and
land purchases. Relief took the form of food, clothing, household
supplies, and medical care; feed for subsistence livestock; seed for
forage crops; and employment on the work program, where wages
were paid in cash or credited against advances made for feed and
seed.

---

[5] *Monthly Reports of the Federal Emergency Relief Administration,* December 1933, pp.
8–9 ; February 1935, pp. 18–23 ; and November 1935, pp. 11–23.

Agencies cooperating with the F. E. R. A. in the drought relief program included State and local relief administrations; the Office of Emergency Conservation Work; the Extension Service of the Department of Agriculture, and its State and county agents; the Drought Relief Service of the Agricultural Adjustment Administration; the Farm Credit Administration; the Farm Debt Adjustment Service; and the Federal Surplus Relief Corporation which took the livestock purchased by the A. A. A. and had it processed for distribution among relief families.

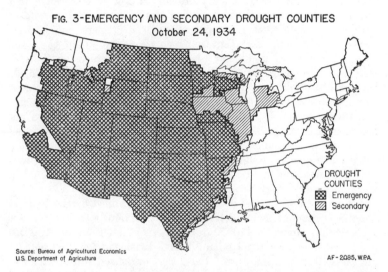

FIG. 3-EMERGENCY AND SECONDARY DROUGHT COUNTIES
October 24, 1934

DROUGHT
COUNTIES
Emergency
Secondary

Source: Bureau of Agricultural Economics
U.S. Department of Agriculture

AF-2085, W.P.A.

Orders to State administrators, effective March 1, 1935, and subsequently, provided that the Rural Rehabilitation Division of the F. E. R. A. should extend its activities to include drought relief cases. The special F. E. R. A. grants for drought relief rapidly decreased after that date, although large numbers of drought cases continued to be cared for throughout the summer and fall of 1935.

RURAL REHABILITATION

Farmers who could regain self-support, if provided with fertilizer, seed, tools, or work animals, presented another special problem to relief administrators when Federal aid was first extended. Early in the history of F. E. R. A., the relief administrations of southern States began to make advances of such capital goods to relief clients instead of giving them recurrent direct relief grants.

In April 1934, a special Rural Rehabilitation Division was established within the F. E. R. A. to develop this type of aid to farmers on a national scale. Its purpose was "to assist destitute farm families and other families residing in rural areas to become self-supporting and independent of emergency relief aid." [6]

This program recognized the variety of problems facing farmers who had been receiving drought or other emergency relief or whose resources were nearly exhausted. For those living on fertile land, it proposed to provide such resources as seed, livestock, equipment, buildings, building repairs, and more land if needed; to arrange debt adjustments if necessary; and to give training and advice in farm management and home economics. Displaced farmers would be relocated on the land. Farmers living on poor land would be moved to better land purchased under a land program in which the A. A. A. shared. Rural relief families living in towns having less than 5,000 inhabitants would be provided with subsistence gardens. Selected families would be transferred from the towns to subsistence farms. Families stranded by the decline of local industries would be encouraged to develop subsistence gardens and community farmsteads.[7]

All subsistence and capital goods provided under the rehabilitation program [8] would be assigned to cash value, charged against the families' accounts, and paid for by the farmers in cash, in kind, or in work on Federal work projects.[9]

Although these general objectives were determined by the Federal Emergency Relief Administration, the program was worked out under State control. The State emergency relief administrations organized their own rural rehabilitation divisions to outline policies and to conduct the programs. Later they organized Rural Rehabilitation Corporations which acted as the legal and financial agents of the rehabilitation divisions.

---

[6] "Rural Rehabilitation Program," *Monthly Report of the Federal Emergency Relief Administration*, May 1934, p. 6. For cooperating agencies, see p. 8 of that report.

[7] "The Rural Rehabilitation Program," *Monthly Report of the Federal Emergency Relief Administration*, August 1935, pp. 14–24.

[8] Capital goods refer to the goods classed as "rehabilitation goods" under the Federal Emergency Relief Administration rehabilitation program. These included the "purchase, rental, construction, or repairs of land, buildings, home equipment, livestock, work animals, feed, seed, fertilizer, equipment, farm tools, or machinery and any other capital outlays required to carry out the rural rehabilitation program for individual cases, groups and/or community projects." Subsistence goods under the Federal Emergency Relief Administration rehabilitation program included "cash and/or the types of services or commodities which are usually issued in the form of direct relief to general relief cases. Such commodities are: food, clothing, fuel, medical care, or any other necessities of life which the Rural Rehabilitation cases may need pending their complete rehabilitation."— From a letter to all State Emergency Relief Administrations, Attention Rural Rehabilitation Directors, Subject: "Rural Rehabilitation Program: Financial Policies and Procedures," December 26, 1934, Federal Emergency Relief Administration Form RD–22a.

[9] *First Annual Report, Resettlement Administration*, 1936, p. 9.

It is not surprising, therefore, that the programs in practice diverged somewhat from the original plan. Although administrative machinery was provided for organizing rehabilitation on a national scale, the program continued to be concentrated in the southern States. As the program was worked out in the States, rehabilitation "in place"[10] became the major type of aid provided, whereas the resettlement of farmers from submarginal to better lands was conducted on a much smaller scale.

The first F. E. R. A. grants specifically for rural rehabilitation, made in May 1934, went to seven southern States—Alabama, Georgia, Louisiana, North Carolina, Oklahoma, Texas, and Virginia; and six western States—Iowa, Kansas, Nebraska, Ohio, South Dakota, and Washington.[11] Due in part to the fact that it began late in the growing season, the program was slow in getting under way.

TABLE 3.—CASES RECEIVING REHABILITATION ADVANCES, BY MONTHS, APRIL 1934 THROUGH JUNE 1935 [1]

Year and month	Number of cases	Year and month	Number of cases
1934		**1935**	
April	325	January	72,222
May	18,071	February	87,350
June	27,423	March	172,886
July	30,776	April	209,951
August	34,372	May	205,433
September	40,092	June	203,612
October	46,011		
November	52,391		
December	68,610		

[1] Data revised as of Apr. 16, 1936.

Source: Division of Research, Statistics, and Records, Works Progress Administration.

In February 1935, fewer than 88,000 cases received advances under the rehabilitation program[12] (table 3) and more than half of these were in the 2 States of Alabama and Louisiana. Ninety-three percent of the total were in the 10 southern States of Alabama, Arkansas, Florida, Georgia, Louisiana, Mississippi, North Carolina, Oklahoma, South Carolina, and Texas. Outside of the South the only States with more than 100 cases were Illinois, Indiana, Michigan, Missouri, Ohio, and Washington (table 4).

---

[10] Rehabilitation "in place" included those cases in which the rehabilitation agency bought or leased land in the immediate vicinity and rented it to individual clients, or helped clients to obtain better leasing arrangements, as well as those in which the client was rehabilitated on the land which he already occupied.

[11] The State of Vermont also received a small grant.

[12] This figure excludes households which had received advances in previous months, but which had received none during February.

TABLE 4.—CASES RECEIVING ADVANCES UNDER THE RURAL REHABILITATION PROGRAM, FEBRUARY THROUGH JUNE 1935,[1] BY STATE

State	Number of cases receiving advances [2]				
	February	March	April	May	June
United States, total	87,350	172,886	209,951	205,433	203,612
Alabama	20,813	21,817	18,273	18,079	17,507
Arizona	17	48	89	163	157
Arkansas	9,942	17,372	19,014	19,115	18,998
California				2	21
Colorado		241	6,371	5,136	6,917
Connecticut	3	2	1	85	54
Delaware					
Florida	1,372	4,043	5,435	5,740	5,707
Georgia	6,978	9,908	12,161	12,457	12,394
Idaho	31	45	117	166	120
Illinois	584	2,350	1,276	750	833
Indiana	284	437	796	911	873
Iowa	16	73	266	864	1,228
Kansas		39	326	1,251	7,244
Kentucky			33	973	545
Louisiana	25,584	24,551	20,744	12,321	10,710
Maine	29	40	23	125	354
Maryland					
Massachusetts					
Michigan	1,414	1,540	1,898	2,014	2,179
Minnesota	26	17,509	21,725	16,439	10,642
Mississippi	5,331	8,978	10,711	12,439	12,360
Missouri	129	21,061	19,944	14,425	6,500
Montana		10	1,507	688	649
Nebraska	2	68	664	1,761	2,377
Nevada	15	25	22	22	21
New Hampshire			30	50	113
New Jersey			101	198	228
New Mexico			8,783	9,698	9,120
New York				65	97
North Carolina	1,052	4,485	6,122	6,781	6,874
North Dakota		2	2	16	33
Ohio	1,769	2,381	2,721	2,164	2,344
Oklahoma	401	2,437	4,852	6,948	8,210
Oregon				43	58
Pennsylvania			94	313	373
Rhode Island					
South Carolina	2,117	3,449	4,998	6,001	6,079
South Dakota	25	977	1,246	3,135	17,933
Tennessee		1,162	2,683	3,008	2,934
Texas	7,548	11,810	18,441	23,078	22,939
Utah	16	108	229	483	594
Vermont					1
Virginia	37	285	1,311	2,528	3,057
Washington	140	277	375	434	463
West Virginia	1,629	67	279	756	1,183
Wisconsin	46	15,289	16,114	11,632	1,481
Wyoming			174	2,176	1,108

[1] Data revised as of Apr. 16, 1936.
[2] The total number of clients under care, i. e., who still owed the Rehabilitation Corporation for advances, each month March to June inclusive, was as follows: March 250,531; April 294,537; May 315,746; June 366,945 (figures from unpublished reports; data for February 1935 not available).

Source: Division of Research, Statistics, and Records, Works Progress Administration.

Many of these cases, although nominally transferred from general relief to the rehabilitation division, had experienced no change in type of aid received. The large rehabilitation case loads in Alabama and Louisiana, for instance, do not mean that the rehabilitation programs were unusually comprehensive and far advanced in those

States. Wholesale transfers were followed by attempts to classify the clients and to work out differentiated programs. Even when this had been done, many cases continued to receive substantially the same types of aid as they had when on the general relief program, since general relief in some rural sections of the South had been on a loan basis for some time and in other sections rehabilitation advances of subsistence goods had the character of direct relief grants.

The predominance of the South in the early rehabilitation program may be explained by the prevailing tenant system, which had reduced many tenants, especially sharecroppers, to destitution. After the crop reduction program of the A. A. A. had been carried out, landlords, who no longer needed as many tenants and croppers as before or who were unwilling to furnish them with their subsistence for the coming season, were reluctant to reemploy these displaced tenants. The rural rehabilitation program, however, by "furnishing" the croppers and tenants,[13] made it possible for them to raise a crop in 1934.

Another reason for the predominance of the South in the early program may be that the region presented a relatively simpler problem than some other areas. Most of the farmers in need of relief were already on the land and could readily be rehabilitated "in place."

Between February and March 1935, the number of cases receiving rural rehabilitation advances doubled, as thousands of drought relief cases were transferred to the rolls. The numbers receiving aid also increased in April as the transfers of drought cases continued and as the beginning of the growing season caused a number of cases to be added to the rolls.

The transfer of drought cases, like the "furnishing" of sharecroppers, meant another modification of the rehabilitation program, because it made rehabilitation clients of many farmers who were in need not of any long-range rehabilitation but only of some emergency assistance, such as feed for livestock.

In June 1935, the 10 southern States which had 93 percent of all rural rehabilitation clients in February still contained about 60 percent of the cases. By that time, however, the rehabilitation program had been so extended that only 11 of the 48 States had less than 100 rehabilitation clients or none at all (table 4 and figure 4).

During this period of expansion a certain amount of shifting was occurring in the rehabilitation rolls. The total number of clients under care at any time from April 1934 through June 1935 was

---

[13] The practice of making subsistence advances is known locally as "furnishing." For a discussion of this practice, see Woofter, T. J., Jr., *Landlord and Tenant on the Cotton Plantation*, Research Monograph V, Division of Social Research, Works Progress Administration, 1936, pp. 59 and 63.

398,000.[14] Since the total number of cases on the records in June was only 367,000, it appears that about 30,000 cases had been closed in the 15-month period. Some of these were clients who had repaid advances; others had been considered unsatisfactory clients for rehabilitation and had been dropped from the program.

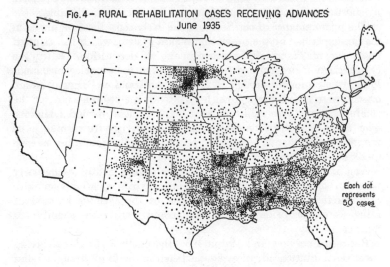

FIG. 4 – RURAL REHABILITATION CASES RECEIVING ADVANCES
June 1935

Each dot
represents
50 cases

NUMBER OF CASES

ALABAMA	17,507	IOWA	1,228	NEBRASKA	2,377	RHODE ISLAND	—
ARIZONA	157	KANSAS	7,244	NEVADA	21	SOUTH CAROLINA	6,079
ARKANSAS	18,998	KENTUCKY	545	NEW HAMPSHIRE	113	SOUTH DAKOTA	17,933
CALIFORNIA	21	LOUISIANA	10,710	NEW JERSEY	228	TENNESSEE	2,934
COLORADO	6,917	MAINE	354	NEW MEXICO	9,120	TEXAS	22,939
CONNECTICUT	54	MARYLAND	—	NEW YORK	97	UTAH	594
DELAWARE	—	MASSACHUSETTS	—	NORTH CAROLINA	6,874	VERMONT	1
FLORIDA	5,707	MICHIGAN	2,179	NORTH DAKOTA	33	VIRGINIA	3,057
GEORGIA	12,394	MINNESOTA	10,642	OHIO	2,344	WASHINGTON	463
IDAHO	120	MISSISSIPPI	12,360	OKLAHOMA	8,210	WEST VIRGINIA	1,183
ILLINOIS	833	MISSOURI	6,500	OREGON	58	WISCONSIN	1,481
INDIANA	873	MONTANA	649	PENNSYLVANIA	373	WYOMING	1,108

UNITED STATES TOTAL   203,612

AF – 2087, W. P. A.

The type of capital or rehabilitation goods advanced to clients varied from area to area according to the type of farming. In the cotton areas, mules or oxen, and fertilizer were usually advanced to rehabilitation clients. In Tennessee,[15] the rehabilitation advances included fertilizer, seed, and livestock. In a Wisconsin county, cows, horses, pigs, and hens were supplied, as were seed and implements.

[14] Division of Research, Statistics, and Records, Works Progress Administration. Data revised as of December 15, 1936.

[15] The following information is based on various county reports obtained in connection with the Survey of Current Changes in the Rural Relief Population.

Advances for equipment sometimes took the form of refinancing loans for machinery (for example, in Olmsted County, Minnesota). In some cases advances were also made for building materials, and at least in Hawkins County, Tennessee, mortgages were secured with the help of rehabilitation advances.

Only in a few cases were the rehabilitation clients advanced money with which to buy livestock or farm equipment and in those cases the clients were required to make account of their expenditures. Usually, the rehabilitation agency assisted the farmer in selecting the required goods and made payment for him in the name of the Rehabilitation Corporation. For durable goods and livestock, which were bought in this way and sold to the client under a conditional sales contract, the Corporation retained the title.

The terms for repayment of rehabilitation loans showed variations by States and even by counties. Usually, advances for capital goods were repayable over a fairly long period, while advances for subsistence goods, since they were goods of a perishable character, were to be repaid within 1 year. Crop mortgages and notes were given as security. Interest on these advances was fixed in accordance with local rates; in some States no interest was charged until the notes reached maturity; in others the advances were free of interest for the first year. In order to facilitate repayment, some rehabilitation agencies accepted payment in marketable produce. In a number of instances, especially in regions where there were no money crops, due particularly to drought, the rehabilitation clients were given employment on work projects and thus were enabled to pay back part of their advances.

A number of States made relief grants to rehabilitation cases. As late as June 1935, about 9 percent of the rehabilitation clients also received relief grants, according to data from the nine sample areas.[16]

After the responsibility for the rural rehabilitation program was transferred from the Federal Emergency Relief Administration to the Resettlement Administration on June 30, 1935, it was taken out of the hands of the States and became centralized under Federal authority. Thus, more uniform policies were made possible.

Rehabilitation loans to farmers continued under the new regime, the Resettlement Administration providing farm management plans and supervision to its standard loan clients, charging interest of 5 percent and limiting the period of a loan to 5 years.[17] In addition, the Resettlement Administration made loans to emergency cases, for whom no farm plan was drawn up. Beginning in November 1935

---

[16] See chapter I, footnote 3.

[17] Taeuber, Conrad, *The Work of the Resettlement Administration in the Works Program*, Division of Research, Statistics, and Records, Works Progress Administration, December 1, 1935, Appendix C-1.

when the Federal Emergency Relief Administration was about to terminate direct relief grants, the Resettlement Administration introduced direct grants for certain needy farmers. The Resettlement Administration also encouraged cooperative purchase of farm equipment through loans.

During the transition period from State-controlled rehabilitation corporations under F. E. R. A. to a Federal-controlled rehabilitation program under the Resettlement Administration, the number of farmers aided by the rural rehabilitation program declined. From 367,000 clients on the records in June 1935 under the F. E. R. A., the number had fallen to 351,000 by July 31 and to 314,000 by November 15,[18] including those in debt to the Administration for past loans as well as those receiving advances during the month. Including only those receiving advances during the month, the number fell from 204,000 clients in June to 58,000 in October, and then rose to 156,000 in December, comprising 26,000 loan cases and 130,000 grant cases.[19]

WORKS PROGRAM

In July 1935, the F. E. R. A. work program began to be supplanted by the new Federal Works Program, coordinated by the Works Progress Administration, which was the major employing agency.[20] One important respect in which the new Works Program differed from the F. E. R. A. work program was that the workers were paid a monthly security wage rather than a relief grant based on their budget deficiency. With the inauguration of the Works Program, the Federal Government announced its intention of terminating direct relief, and of turning over to the States and localities the responsibility for all persons in need, over and above the 3,500,000 workers who were to receive jobs on the new program.

The shift from Federal work and direct relief to Federal jobs and local relief began slowly during the summer and fall and was finally accomplished in November and December of 1935, when the quota on Works Program employment was approximated and all Federal direct relief, with minor exceptions, ended. Farmers in need of aid who were not employed on Works Program projects, or cared for by Resettlement Administration grants or loans, became the responsibility of State and local relief agencies.

---

[18] *First Annual Report, Resettlement Administration*, 1936, pp. 9–10.
[19] See chapter VII, table 30.
[20] *Report on the Works Program,* Works Progress Administration, March 16, 1936, pp. 1–10.

Farmers at Work on W. P. A. Road Project

CHAPTER III

RELIEF GRANTS AND REHABILITATION ADVANCES

TYPES AND AMOUNTS of relief grants and rehabilitation advances varied widely by agricultural groups and by areas. As the administration of both relief and rehabilitation was largely entrusted to the States, there were no uniform rulings to determine whether direct or work relief should be extended, or whether rehabilitation advances should take the form of subsistence or capital goods. Neither were there any uniform standards for the amount of relief grants per family or the value of rehabilitation advances, although the recommended procedure for determining relief grants was on a budget deficiency basis established by social workers, while rehabilitation advances were to be determined on the basis of individual farm plans developed by the county rural rehabilitation supervisors. Differences in the availability of funds were also a factor in determining amounts granted.

In general, the various groups within agriculture might be expected to receive different types and amounts of aid according to differences in standard of living and need for assistance. Where farmers were still on the land, for instance, except in areas of extreme drought, it might not be feasible for them to leave their crops at certain times of the year to work on relief projects. Furthermore, they might be able to furnish part of their living from their own land and thus require only supplementary direct relief. On the other hand, an unemployed farm laborer living in a village might best be served by work relief. Similarly, a farm owner on rehabilitation might require advances of only feed and seed, while a laborer who was being established as a rehabilitation farmer would necessarily require both working capital and subsistence goods.

TYPES OF RELIEF

Both direct relief and work relief [1] were given to destitute farm families. In some cases they received only one type of relief; in others they received both types concurrently. Moreover, largely due to the fact that farm operators who were still on their farms were considered to be employed, work relief was given to employed workers as well as to the unemployed.

---

[1] For a discussion of types of relief programs, see chapter II.

23

The fact that work relief was given to employed workers reflects the inadequacy of much of this employment. It is true that the definition of current employment used in this survey—1 week or more of employment during the month—permits a situation in which a laborer might work during the first part of the month and go on relief during the last part; he would be recorded as receiving relief and working at the same time, merely because the two conditions occurred during the same month. However, it may be assumed that in the great majority of these cases relief and employment actually did coincide, and that relief was given to supplement insufficient earnings from private employment.

In regard to farmers who received work relief while operating farms, it might be assumed that employment on relief projects in the month of June would interfere with their work on the farm and retard the process of rehabilitation. However, many farmers on relief were, in normal times, only part-time farmers; others could leave the farming activities to some other member of the household; and still others had been prevented by drought or flood from putting in full-time work on their farms.

In February, 75 percent of all the farm operators on relief who were currently operating farms were receiving work relief or drought relief,[2] while 60 percent of the currently employed farm laborers received these types of relief. In June, the proportions of currently employed farm families receiving work relief were still high—74 percent for farm operators and 60 percent for farm laborers[3] (appendix tables 1 and 2).

Active farmers and employed farm laborers participated in work relief to a greater extent than did rural workers employed in nonagricultural industries. This may have been partly due to administrative policies. It was probably also due, in part, to the fact that in this study farmers were considered employed if they were operating their land, whether or not this activity brought in any net income or took any considerable part of their time; whereas nonagricultural workers were considered employed only if they put in some hours of work and received some income.[4]

---

[2] Work relief, in this context, comprises work relief only and work relief combined with direct relief. Drought relief consisted primarily of cash payments for work on approved projects although in an undetermined proportion of cases drought relief consisted of direct relief only.

[3] The 2 months of February and June are not directly comparable since statistical and administrative procedures included drought relief cases in February, but eliminated them in June after they had been transferred to the Rural Rehabilitation Division of the Federal Emergency Relief Administration. The June data undoubtedly furnish more accurate information than the February data as to the role of work relief among the farm relief clients.

[4] Exceptions to this latter group include a small number of workers employed on "own account," such as proprietors of small businesses and commission salesmen.

A greater proportion of employed farm laborers than of employed nonagricultural workers received work relief in all areas in February, but this was true of only three areas in June. This difference would indicate that the February employment of nonagricultural workers was more remunerative than the employment of farm laborers in that month. The latter were probably employed to a greater extent at odd jobs which left them more time to fill work relief assignments. As the agricultural season advanced, either the employment of farm laborers became more substantial, or administrative policy was opposed to extending them supplementary work relief.

Tenants (exclusive of sharecroppers) shared in the work relief program more than any other farm group in June in most areas (appendix table 2). They shared in the work relief program to a higher degree than farm owners [5] in all areas except the Eastern Cotton Belt (figure 5). In six of the nine areas, a higher percentage of tenants than owners received direct relief combined with work relief, the combination carrying higher benefits than either work or direct relief separately (appendix tables 3 and 4).

Employed farm laborers generally were given less work relief than farm owners, although more employed farm laborers than farm owners received direct and work relief combined. Employed laborers usually received much less work relief than tenants.

The great majority of the employed sharecroppers in both Cotton Areas received work relief, either alone or in combination with direct relief.

Negroes in all agricultural groups received less work relief than the whites in both Cotton Areas, but the differences tended to be more marked in the Eastern Cotton Belt. While about two-thirds of each of the white farm tenure groups in that area received work relief, only a little over one-half of the Negro owners and croppers and one-third of the Negro tenants received work relief. Only one-fourth of the employed Negro farm laborers compared with three-fourths of the employed white farm laborers were given work relief.

In all but one area, drought relief was extended to workers currently employed in nonagricultural industry in February 1935 (appendix table 1). In the Winter Wheat Area, 40 percent of the cases on relief with heads currently employed in nonagricultural industries received this type of relief. The role which drought relief played in the various areas depended, of course, on administrative policies as well as on the actual drought situation.

---

[5] The small number of farm managers are combined with farm owners in all tables.

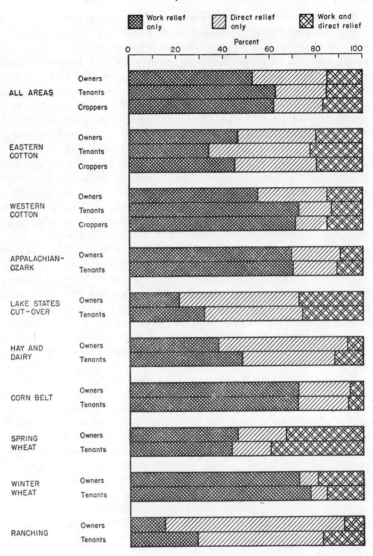

FIG. 5 – TYPE OF RELIEF RECEIVED BY RURAL HOUSEHOLDS
WITH HEADS CURRENTLY ENGAGED AS
FARM OPERATORS, BY AREA

June 1935

AF-2073, W.P.A.

AMOUNTS OF RELIEF

Average relief grants were uniformly low, but they varied considerably among the different areas. The two Cotton Areas and the Appalachian-Ozark Area stand out with the lowest median relief grants per family for all agricultural groups (table 5 and figure 6). In these three areas, median grants for all agricultural groups were $10 or less in June 1935, and 90 percent or more of all grants were less than $20 (appendix table 5). The influence of administrative policies cannot be entirely discounted, but it is safe to assume that the low standard of living prevailing in these three areas was a determining factor in fixing the relief grants at this low level. The Lake States Cut-Over Area also is not a prosperous area, but it ranks second highest with regard to median relief amounts when all agricultural groups are taken together. Only one-half of the cases received less than $20, and 36 percent received from $20 to $39 in relief grants. The highest grants were in the Hay and Dairy Area with an average grant of $22 in June 1935. The average amounts of relief are per family and not per capita, and therefore do not take into consideration the size of the relief households,[6] but when the two sets of data are compared, little or no relationship is apparent (tables 5 and 13 and appendix table 7).

The average amounts of relief also varied somewhat by tenure groups. In seven of the nine areas, tenants by usual occupation received higher average grants than owners in June 1935 (table 5 and figure 6).

TABLE 5.—AVERAGE [1] AMOUNT OF RELIEF RECEIVED BY RURAL HOUSEHOLDS, BY USUAL OCCUPATION OF THE HEAD AND BY AREA, JUNE 1935 [2]

[138 counties representing 9 agricultural areas]

Area	Agriculture					Nonagriculture
	Total	Owners	Tenants [3]	Croppers	Laborers	
All areas	$12	$13	$12	$9	$12	$15
Eastern Cotton:						
Total	9	9	10	10	8	12
White	10	10	12	10	9	14
Negro	7	9	6	9	7	10
Western Cotton:						
Total	9	9	10	9	8	9
White	9	9	10	9	8	10
Negro	8	8	9	8	7	7
Appalachian-Ozark	10	10	9	_____	11	12
Lake States Cut-Over	20	19	25	_____	18	21
Hay and Dairy	22	20	21	_____	23	23
Corn Belt	16	13	16	_____	17	18
Spring Wheat	18	17	18	_____	17	23
Winter Wheat	12	14	12	_____	11	15
Ranching	18	18	20	_____	17	16

[1] Median.
[2] Exclusive of cases opened, reopened, or closed during the month.
[3] Exclusive of croppers in the 2 Cotton Areas.

[6] Variations in the method of enumeration of cases by the different relief agencies may influence the size of cases.

The Negro farm families consistently received smaller amounts of relief than white families. The difference was most marked for the Negro tenants of the Eastern Cotton Belt who received $6 a month as compared with $12 for the white tenants. As was shown in a previous study,[7] these differences cannot fully be explained by the size of white and Negro relief households. It may be assumed, therefore, that the lower standard of living usually prevailing among the Negroes was made the basis of differentiation.

The nonagricultural workers by usual occupation received somewhat higher relief benefits in June 1935 than all groups of farm operators and farm laborers in most areas (table 5). This difference

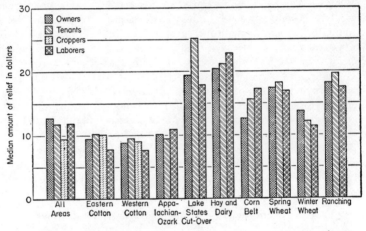

FIG. 6 - MEDIAN AMOUNT OF RELIEF RECEIVED BY RURAL HOUSEHOLDS WITH AGRICULTURE AS THE USUAL OCCUPATION OF THE HEAD, BY AREA *

June 1935

*Exclusive of cases opened, reopened, or closed during the month

AF-2133, W.P.A.

is probably related to the fact that nonagricultural workers have less opportunity than agricultural workers to provide themselves with foodstuffs from their own land.

TYPES OF REHABILITATION ADVANCES

Subsistence goods [8] were advanced to 83 percent of the rehabilitation clients, while capital goods were advanced to 84 percent of the clients (table 6). There were great variations among the different

---

[7] Mangus, A. R., *The Rural Negro on Relief, February 1935,* Research Bulletin H–3, Division of Research, Statistics, and Finance, Federal Emergency Relief Administration, October 17, 1935, pp. 6–7.

[8] For definitions of subsistence and capital goods, see chapter II.

areas.[9]   In the Hay and Dairy and Lake States Cut-Over Areas, only 32 and 38 percent, respectively, of the cases received advances for subsistence goods.   On the other hand, both Cotton Areas listed more than 97 percent of their cases as receiving advances for subsistence goods.

Fewer clients received advances for capital goods than for subsistence goods in the Cotton, Wheat, and Ranching Areas, an indication that a fairly high proportion of the clients received nothing but subsistence goods.   In some of the southern States a distinction was made between rehabilitation clients who were capable of managing advances of capital goods and those who were considered incapable, and this may furnish an explanation for the lower percentages of cases with capital goods advances in the Cotton Areas.   In both Cotton Areas, the percentage of Negro cases with advances for capital goods was somewhat smaller than the corresponding figure for the white rehabilitation clients.   In some States, it appears that a relatively large number of Negro clients were not considered capable of handling advances for capital goods.

TABLE 6.—TYPE AND AMOUNT OF TOTAL ADVANCES TO RURAL REHABILITA-
TION CLIENTS,[1] BY COLOR AND BY AREA, JUNE 1935

[138 counties representing 9 agricultural areas]

Area	Number of cases [1]	Average amount of advances	Advances for capital goods		Advances for subsistence goods	
			Percent receiving advances	Average amount	Percent receiving advances	Average amount
All areas	14,428	$189	84.0	$168	83.1	$58
Eastern Cotton:						
Total	6,288	175	90.3	119	97.9	69
White	4,028	205	91.2	145	98.8	74
Negro	2,260	122	88.8	73	96.3	60
Western Cotton:						
Total	2,332	388	91.1	362	97.3	60
White	1,872	416	91.8	387	97.3	62
Negro	460	276	88.3	257	97.4	51
Appalachian-Ozark	904	153	92.3	133	76.5	40
Lake States Cut-Over	770	104	98.7	67	38.2	100
Hay and Dairy	1,386	168	89.6	176	32.0	31
Corn Belt	1,284	116	68.2	144	62.5	28
Spring Wheat	948	31	20.5	44	94.3	24
Winter Wheat	310	187	86.5	178	87.7	39
Ranching	206	182	69.9	201	77.7	53

[1] Only cases receiving advances during the month are included.   The amounts include grants during previous months as well as during June.

Advances for capital goods were predominant in the Hay and Dairy, Corn Belt, Lake States Cut-Over, and Appalachian-Ozark Areas, regions of general and self-sufficing farms.   In such areas, farmers usually raise their own foodstuffs and hence are less in need of subsistence than farmers following the one crop system.

---

[9] It may be pointed out that the sample was selected as representative of the ‚relief situation and cannot, therefore, be considered as wholly representative of rural rehabilitation clients.

AMOUNTS OF REHABILITATION ADVANCES

The money value of the advances given to clients varied from $31, the average advance in the Spring Wheat Area, to $416 for whites in the Western Cotton Area (table 6). Next to the Western Cotton Area, the Winter Wheat and Ranching Areas paid the highest average advances. In terms of advances for capital goods alone, the Western Cotton Area again held first rank. When subsistence advances alone were considered, the Lake States Cut-Over Area was found to have given the highest amounts, averaging $100, followed by the Eastern Cotton Belt with $69. Moreover, the Lake States Cut-Over was the only area in which the average value of advances for subsistence goods exceeded the average value of advances for capital goods.

The Negroes of the two Cotton Areas received considerably smaller advances than the whites in both capital and subsistence goods.

Differing administrative policies probably were the primary reason for the wide range in amount of advances. The various States based their rehabilitation programs on different principles, and these programs, moreover, were in various stages of development at the time of the survey. Differences in type of farming and standard of living may also have led to differing financial requirements for rehabilitation.

CHAPTER IV

SOCIAL CHARACTERISTICS OF RELIEF AND REHABILITATION HOUSEHOLDS

THE TYPICAL FARMER on relief or rehabilitation in June 1935 was about 40 years old. He was married and had three or four children, for whom he was the sole breadwinner. He had lived in his present county of residence for at least 10 years.

The typical farm laborer head of a relief or rehabilitation household was 32 to 36 years old, was married, and had two or three children. Like the typical farmer, he was the only worker in his family and had been a resident of the county for at least a decade.

These composite pictures of the average farm families [1] receiving aid in June 1935 indicate that the majority of such families were similar to farm families in the general population with respect to age and composition, although somewhat larger than average in size. Certain variations come to light when relief and rehabilitation clients are studied separately in the nine areas.

AGE OF HEADS OF RELIEF HOUSEHOLDS

Farmers on relief [2] did not differ markedly in age from all farmers in the United States in 1930 (table 7). Farm owners on relief proved

TABLE 7.—AGE OF ALL FARMERS IN THE UNITED STATES, 1930, AND OF FARMERS [1] ON RELIEF, JUNE 1935

Tenure status	Median age in years	
	All farmers, 1930 [2]	Relief farmers, [3] June 1935
Farm operators	43.3	40.8
Owners	47.5	46.6
Tenants, including croppers	37.6	37.9

[1] By usual occupation.
[2] *Fifteenth Census of the United States: 1930*, Agriculture Vol. IV.
[3] Based on data for 138 counties representative of 9 agricultural areas.

---

[1] The terms "families" and "households" are used interchangeably in this chapter.
[2] Since only 1.4 percent of all farm operators in the sample were not heads of households, the small number of nonheads is disregarded in the discussion.

31

to be only about 11 months younger and tenants, including croppers, about the same age as the same tenure groups in the general farm population.[3]

The slightly lower average age of farm owners on relief, as compared with farm owners in the general farm population, suggests that, on the whole, the older farm owners were somewhat less likely to apply for relief than the younger ones because their economic resources were greater. The similarity of the average ages for tenants in both categories may indicate that tenancy contains elements of insecurity which are likely to affect all age groups [4] and make them equally susceptible to the need for public support.

There is some indication that the younger farmers and farm laborers found it easier to leave the relief rolls during the spring planting season. Comparison was made of the age distribution of all heads of farm families on relief in February and June 1935 (tables 8 and 9). In the nine areas, taken as a whole, the age group 55–64 years was larger for all agricultural groups in June than in February. The very young farmers, those 16–24 years of age, however, tended to remain on relief throughout the spring and early summer. Not only farmers, but also farm laborers, 16–24 years of age, made up a larger part of the June than of the February rural relief load in most areas.

Owners on relief were about 9 years older, on the average, than tenants (including croppers) ; this difference is similar to that found in the general population (table 7). Tenancy precedes ownership in the life of many farmers, and this fact probably accounts for the considerable difference in age.

The sharecroppers in the two Cotton Areas were younger than the other tenants in those areas. This would be expected since the sharecropping contract does not call for any capital on the part of the cropper, and young people can easily become croppers. In both Cotton Areas the croppers were about the same age as the farm laborers.

---

[3] Comparisons could not be made by areas or for farm laborers since census data on the age grouping of farmers are not available by counties, and since no census data on this point for farm laborers are available. Both groups of figures pertain only to the age group 16–64 years, because, owing to the definition used in this survey, only persons within these age limits are classified as having a usual occupation.

[4] When age distributions of owner and tenant heads in rural farm areas of the United States, exclusive of women heads, were compared with those of the relief population, fewer owners and more tenants were found in the 45–64 year group on relief than in the general population. Sources : Table 8 and *Fifteenth Census of the United States: 1930*, Population Vol. VI.

In all areas, farm laborers were younger than owners or tenants (exclusive of croppers), reflecting the situation in the total farm population. However, it is possible that the farm laborers on relief, in contrast to farm operators, were older than the laborers in the general population. In general, wages for married and unmarried farm laborers are the same with no differential, except possibly in perquisites. Thus, the married laborers, who were also the older ones, were more likely to go on relief when their wages suffered severe cuts during the depression and were no longer adequate to support a family.

TABLE 8.—AGE OF HEADS OF FARM HOUSEHOLDS [1] ON RELIEF, BY AREA, FEBRUARY 1935

[138 counties representing 9 agricultural areas]

Area and usual occupation	Total		Age in years				
	Number	Percent	16–24	25–34	35–44	45–54	55–64
All areas:							
Owners	10,978	100.0	2.4	13.9	26.6	33.7	23.4
Tenants [2]	17,411	100.0	6.7	32.9	28.1	21.2	11.1
Croppers	5,486	100.0	11.3	33.0	25.6	19.5	10.6
Farm laborers	10,735	100.0	14.4	34.7	22.2	16.5	12.2
Eastern Cotton:							
Owners	835	100.0	2.0	15.7	20.5	37.0	24.8
Tenants	1,327	100.0	5.4	23.0	28.4	23.8	19.4
Croppers	2,401	100.0	9.6	28.6	29.1	20.7	12.6
Farm laborers	2,659	100.0	15.1	31.1	22.5	18.0	13.3
Western Cotton:							
Owners	1,739	100.0	2.2	15.2	24.9	31.4	26.3
Tenants	3,957	100.0	6.3	36.0	26.9	20.3	10.5
Croppers	3,085	100.0	13.1	36.3	22.9	18.6	9.1
Farm laborers	2,721	100.0	16.5	34.7	20.3	16.1	12.4
Appalachian-Ozark:							
Owners	2,535	100.0	3.9	16.2	27.2	28.8	23.9
Tenants	4,015	100.0	10.7	34.7	23.8	19.1	11.7
Farm laborers	555	100.0	14.8	41.9	23.1	11.9	8.3
Lake States Cut-Over:							
Owners	1,339	100.0	1.3	11.4	26.9	42.0	18.4
Tenants	393	100.0	2.6	33.3	29.0	21.9	13.2
Farm laborers	133	100.0	14.3	56.4	13.5	4.5	11.3
Hay and Dairy:							
Owners	1,618	100.0	2.3	11.0	30.5	36.3	19.9
Tenants	1,648	100.0	4.1	29.0	33.6	23.7	9.6
Farm laborers	1,506	100.0	12.2	34.2	22.7	20.7	10.2
Corn Belt:							
Owners	890	100.0	.9	12.1	24.5	35.6	26.9
Tenants	3,024	100.0	5.5	28.9	31.4	24.9	9.3
Farm laborers	2,050	100.0	10.4	34.0	25.1	16.2	14.3
Spring Wheat:							
Owners	1,234	100.0	1.8	13.5	31.3	29.8	23.6
Tenants	2,023	100.0	5.4	39.9	27.6	18.0	9.1
Farm laborers	369	100.0	19.5	52.0	9.8	9.5	9.2
Winter Wheat:							
Owners	339	100.0	6.2	16.5	14.5	37.1	25.7
Tenants	735	100.0	5.3	34.4	30.9	18.4	11.0
Farm laborers	247	100.0	18.6	34.0	25.5	13.4	8.5
Ranching:							
Owners	449	100.0	.9	12.2	26.5	34.6	25.8
Tenants	289	100.0	4.8	29.1	33.9	21.5	10.7
Farm laborers	495	100.0	14.7	32.8	27.5	13.3	11.7

[1] With agriculture as the usual occupation.
[2] Exclusive of croppers in the 2 Cotton Areas.

TABLE 9.—AGE OF HEADS OF FARM HOUSEHOLDS [1] ON RELIEF, BY AREA, JUNE 1935

[138 counties representing 9 agricultural areas]

Area and usual occupation	Total		Age in years				
	Number	Percent	16–24	25–34	35–44	45–54	55–64
All areas:							
Owners	6,416	100.0	4.1	14.3	25.3	30.6	25.7
Tenants [2]	9,684	100.0	8.8	32.2	26.1	21.4	11.5
Croppers	2,024	100.0	9.8	32.0	24.0	19.7	14.5
Farm laborers	6,850	100.0	14.3	32.0	22.6	17.9	13.2
Eastern Cotton:							
Owners	458	100.0	3.1	10.9	17.9	33.6	34.5
Tenants	646	100.0	5.0	22.0	23.5	28.1	21.4
Croppers	1,066	100.0	8.3	27.9	27.7	20.5	15.6
Farm laborers	1,502	100.0	12.1	26.7	25.0	20.5	15.7
Western Cotton:							
Owners	300	100.0	3.3	14.0	22.7	33.3	26.7
Tenants	1,238	100.0	9.4	28.7	25.2	24.6	12.1
Croppers	958	100.0	11.5	36.5	19.8	18.8	13.4
Farm laborers	1,448	100.0	15.1	30.5	24.3	17.9	12.2
Appalachian-Ozark:							
Owners	2,610	100.0	5.9	15.9	26.5	28.4	23.3
Tenants	3,904	100.0	12.5	33.8	23.4	18.7	11.6
Farm laborers	516	100.0	25.2	35.7	17.4	10.5	11.2
Lake States Cut-Over:							
Owners	660	100.0	2.1	16.4	26.1	31.2	24.2
Tenants	184	100.0	4.3	26.1	40.2	20.7	8.7
Farm laborers	144	100.0	26.4	41.6	12.5	5.6	13.9
Hay and Dairy:							
Owners	726	100.0	4.4	8.5	26.2	38.6	22.3
Tenants	762	100.0	3.7	27.3	32.3	27.0	9.7
Farm laborers	1,004	100.0	10.4	35.8	23.1	19.9	10.8
Corn Belt:							
Owners	394	100.0	2.0	10.7	20.3	31.0	36.0
Tenants	1,170	100.0	4.8	27.5	28.7	27.2	11.8
Farm laborers	1,454	100.0	10.9	30.7	22.6	20.1	15.7
Spring Wheat:							
Owners	864	100.0	2.1	15.0	27.5	29.7	25.7
Tenants	1,212	100.0	6.9	44.4	26.9	15.2	6.6
Farm laborers	244	100.0	21.3	48.4	10.7	9.8	9.8
Winter Wheat:							
Owners	110	100.0	9.1	21.8	14.5	32.8	21.8
Tenants	386	100.0	8.3	32.6	30.6	19.7	8.8
Farm laborers	204	100.0	22.6	41.2	17.6	10.8	7.8
Ranching:							
Owners	294	100.0	1.4	15.0	29.9	22.4	31.3
Tenants	182	100.0	5.5	32.9	28.6	16.5	16.5
Farm laborers	334	100.0	15.6	28.1	26.3	18.0	12.0

[1] With agriculture as the usual occupation.
[2] Exclusive of croppers in the 2 Cotton Areas.

Farm labor is now, to a larger extent than formerly, a permanent occupation and is no longer only the first rung of the agricultural ladder. This is indicated by the fact that about one-third of the farm laborers who were heads of households were between 45 and 64 years of age (table 11). The predominant age group, however, was 25–34 years.

The majority of the farm laborers on relief in five out of nine areas were not heads of households, the proportion ranging as high as 89 percent (table 11). These were overwhelmingly in the age group 16–24 years. They were for the most part sons and daughters of farmers, working on the home farm.

The average ages of the different agricultural groups varied little by area (table 10 and figure 7). Such variations as appear cannot be adequately interpreted since no corresponding data for the general population are available.

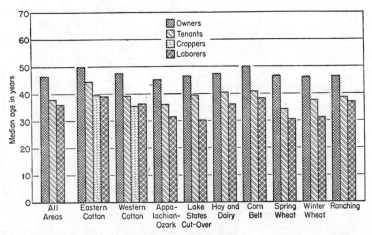

FIG. 7 – MEDIAN AGE OF HEADS OF RURAL RELIEF HOUSEHOLDS WITH AGRICULTURE AS THE USUAL OCCUPATION, BY AREA

June 1935

AF-1069, W.P.A.

TABLE 10.—AGE OF HEADS OF FARM HOUSEHOLDS [1] ON RELIEF, BY COLOR, BY RESIDENCE, AND BY AREA, JUNE 1935

[138 counties representing 9 agricultural areas]

	Median age in years											
	Farm operators									Farm laborers		
Area	Owners			Tenants [2]			Croppers					
	Total	Open country	Village	Total	Open country	Village	Total	Open country	Village	Total	Open country	Village
All areas	46.5	46.3	48.3	37.9	37.5	41.3	------	------	------	36.1	35.7	36.9
Eastern Cotton:												
Total	49.9	49.9	49.9	44.3	43.8	46.6	39.5	39.4	39.7	39.0	38.8	39.6
White	49.8	49.8	49.9	43.6	42.9	47.5	38.8	38.8	38.7	37.6	37.9	35.5
Negro	50.2	50.3	49.5	45.3	45.4	44.5	41.4	41.9	40.6	40.4	40.1	41.2
Western Cotton:												
Total	47.5	47.0	50.1	39.2	38.9	41.6	35.5	34.8	39.9	36.3	35.7	37.7
White	47.6	47.0	50.2	38.9	38.5	41.0	34.3	34.0	37.8	35.9	35.2	37.7
Negro	47.2	47.0	49.5	40.7	40.2	45.8	39.5	38.5	44.5	37.9	37.8	38.0
Appalachian-Ozark	45.1	45.0	46.6	36.1	36.0	38.3	------	------	------	31.5	31.9	30.1
Lake States Cut-Over	46.3	46.2	55.2	39.4	38.9	47.0	------	------	------	30.2	29.9	31.2
Hay and Dairy	47.3	47.2	48.0	40.4	40.3	41.2	------	------	------	36.1	35.9	36.7
Corn Belt	50.0	50.2	49.5	40.7	39.5	43.6	------	------	------	38.2	37.9	38.5
Spring Wheat	46.3	46.0	56.2	34.2	34.3	33.3	------	------	------	30.4	29.8	31.8
Winter Wheat	45.9	45.4	54.5	37.5	36.4	42.2	------	------	------	31.2	31.4	28.8
Ranching	46.2	47.8	42.2	38.5	37.7	39.5	------	------	------	36.9	35.3	37.6

[1] With agriculture as the usual occupation.   [2] Exclusive of croppers in the 2 Cotton Areas.

TABLE 11.—AGE OF FARM LABORERS [1] ON RELIEF, BY FAMILY STATUS AND
BY AREA, JUNE 1935

[138 counties representing 9 agricultural areas]

Family status and area	Total		Age in years				
	Number	Percent	16–24	25–34	35–44	45–54	55–64
All areas:							
Heads	6,850	100.0	14.3	32.0	22.6	17.9	13.2
Members	11,804	100.0	76.9	14.6	4.5	2.6	1.4
Eastern Cotton:							
Heads	1,502	100.0	12.1	26.7	25.0	20.5	15.7
Members	2,234	100.0	67.0	16.4	9.5	5.2	1.9
Western Cotton:							
Heads	1,448	100.0	15.1	30.5	24.3	18.0	12.1
Members	1,778	100.0	79.5	11.9	3.9	2.8	1.9
Appalachian-Ozark:							
Heads	516	100.0	25.2	35.7	17.4	10.5	11.2
Members	4,276	100.0	77.9	14.5	4.3	2.1	1.2
Lake States Cut-Over:							
Heads	144	100.0	26.4	41.7	12.5	5.5	13.9
Members	444	100.0	73.9	20.3	2.7	2.2	.9
Hay and Dairy:							
Heads	1,004	100.0	10.4	35.9	23.1	19.9	10.7
Members	868	100.0	82.0	10.8	3.7	1.4	2.1
Corn Belt:							
Heads	1,454	100.0	10.9	30.8	22.5	20.1	15.7
Members	760	100.0	75.5	19.2	2.9	1.3	1.1
Spring Wheat:							
Heads	244	100.0	21.3	48.4	10.7	9.8	9.8
Members	1,166	100.0	85.9	12.4	.5	1.0	.2
Winter Wheat:							
Heads	204	100.0	22.6	41.2	17.6	10.8	7.8
Members	118	100.0	72.9	23.7	1.7	----------	1.7
Ranching:							
Heads	334	100.0	15.6	28.1	26.3	18.0	12.0
Members	160	100.0	83.8	13.7	----------	2.5	----------

[1] By usual occupation.

The average age of farm owners on relief was greater in the
village than in the open country in most areas (table 10),[5] possibly
due in part to the fact that older farm owners often retire to
villages. This explanation is not completely satisfactory, however,
because two-thirds of the village farm owners were still engaged
in their usual occupation (appendix table 11).

In practically all areas, the average age of tenants also was higher
in the village than in the open country (table 10), but unlike the
owners, the majority of the tenants in the villages were unemployed
(appendix table 11). Only in the Appalachian-Ozark Area were a
majority of the tenants in villages employed at their usual occupation.

AGE DIFFERENCES BETWEEN RELIEF AND REHABILITATION CLIENTS

Age did not appear to be a determining factor in the selection of
rehabilitation clients. It might be expected either that older farmers

[5] The Works Progress Administration Labor Inventory shows that the median age of
both farm operators and farm laborers in cities was 4 years higher than the median age
of those in rural districts in March 1935. The median age of farm laborers was 31.3
years in cities and 27.2 years in rural areas, according to Labor Inventory data, and the
median age for farmers was 44.2 years in the urban areas compared with 40.0 years in
rural areas. Source: Division of Social Research, Works Progress Administration.

would have been preferred as rehabilitation clients because of their
longer experience, or that younger farmers would have been preferred because of their greater physical strength. Median ages
indicate, however, that there was no consistent selection of clients
on the basis of age by area (tables 10 and 12). In six out of nine
areas the younger owners appeared to be favored as rehabilitation
clients, and in five of the areas the older tenants were chosen.
In six areas the younger farm laborers and in two areas the older
ones were selected for rehabilitation. Croppers accepted for rehabilitation were younger than relief clients in the Eastern Cotton
Belt and older in the Western Cotton Area. In most areas, however, there were fewer owners and tenants in the oldest group,
55–64 years of age, among rehabilitation clients than among relief
clients (table 9 and appendix table 6).

TABLE 12.—AGE OF HEADS OF RURAL REHABILITATION HOUSEHOLDS,[1] BY
COLOR AND BY AREA, JUNE 1935

[138 counties representing 9 agricultural areas]

	Median age in years			
Area	Farm operators			Farm laborers
	Owners	Tenants [2]	Croppers	
All areas	45. 6	39. 0		32. 0
Eastern Cotton:				
Total	45. 5	39. 7	36. 7	31. 5
White	44. 0	38. 3	37. 7	31. 3
Negro	47. 9	42. 4	34. 6	32. 2
Western Cotton:				
Total	47. 2	38. 3	37. 6	33. 4
White	45. 3	38. 1	37. 3	33. 2
Negro	50. 1	39. 8	39. 1	35. 5
Appalachian-Ozark	43. 4	38. 0		32. 8
Lake States Cut-Over	47. 3	40. 5		32. 0
Hay and Dairy	45. 4	40. 0		36. 0
Corn Belt	45. 0	38. 8		31. 4
Spring Wheat	45. 1	36. 9		29. 1
Winter Wheat	45. 9	38. 1		27. 0
Ranching	42. 4	44. 1		33. 3

[1] With agriculture as the usual occupation.
[2] Exclusive of croppers in the 2 Cotton Areas.

SIZE OF HOUSEHOLDS

The average farm relief and rehabilitation family proved to be
larger than the average farm family in the general population.[6]
The average size of the farm relief household was larger in each area

[6] Also, see Beck, P. G. and Forster, M. C., *Six Rural Problem Areas, Relief–Resources–
Rehabilitation*, Research Monograph I, Division of Research, Statistics, and Finance, Federal
Emergency Relief Administration, 1935, pp. 43–44. and McCormick, T. C., *Comparative Study
of Relief and Non-Relief Households,* Research Monograph II, Division of Social Research,
Works Progress Administration, 1935, pp. 22–25.

than the highest State average size of rural farm family in the general population [7] of the area.

Tenants, exclusive of croppers, had families as large as or larger than those of other groups on relief and rehabilitation in all but two areas (table 13). The farm laborers had the smallest families of any agricultural group, as might be expected from the fact that they were the youngest group (with the exception of sharecroppers) among the heads of farm families.

TABLE 13.—SIZE OF RURAL RELIEF AND REHABILITATION HOUSEHOLDS, BY USUAL OCCUPATION OF THE HEAD AND BY AREA, JUNE 1935

]138 counties representing 9 agricultural areas]

Area	Median number of persons per household									
	Agriculture								Nonagriculture	
	Farm operators						Farm laborers			
	Owners		Tenants [1]		Croppers					
	Relief	Rehabilitation	Relief	Rehabilitation	Relief	Rehabilitation	Relief	Rehabilitation	Relief	Rehabilitation
All areas	5.5	5.4	5.4	5.5	4.9	5.6	4.5	4.6	4.5	5.2
Eastern Cotton:										
Total	4.9	5.7	5.6	5.8	4.9	5.7	4.6	4.7	4.1	5.1
White	4.9	5.7	5.4	5.8	5.0	5.8	4.9	4.7	4.5	5.4
Negro	5.5	5.8	6.1	5.9	4.4	5.5	4.2	4.8	4.0	4.4
Western Cotton:										
Total	5.0	5.5	5.4	5.4	4.8	5.2	4.8	4.9	4.3	5.0
White	4.9	5.4	5.3	5.4	4.7	5.2	4.9	4.8	4.4	5.1
Negro	5.3	5.6	5.9	5.2	5.3	5.4	4.6	5.4	4.2	4.7
Appalachian-Ozark	5.9	6.7	5.4	5.7			4.5	5.3	4.8	6.2
Lake States Cut-Over	5.0	4.8	6.3	5.2			3.3	4.5	4.2	5.1
Hay and Dairy	5.6	4.8	6.0	4.7			4.5	4.6	4.6	5.3
Corn Belt	4.9	5.0	5.0	5.1			4.6	3.8	4.4	4.9
Spring Wheat	6.1	5.6	5.3	5.2			3.6	3.4	4.8	5.0
Winter Wheat	5.0	4.4	5.1	5.2			4.0	3.8	4.3	3.5
Ranching	4.9	5.4	5.0	5.9			4.4	4.2	4.3	5.3

[1] Exclusive of croppers in the 2 Cotton Areas.

No consistent differences in size of Negro and white households in the two Cotton Areas were shown (table 13). Families of Negro owners and tenants on relief were slightly larger than those of whites in both areas, and the same was true of rehabilitation cases except among tenants in the Western Cotton Area. On the other hand, Negro cropper families on relief in the Eastern Cotton Belt were smaller, on the average, than white cropper families. This may be explained by the preference of many landlords not only for

---

[7] Data on the size of family in the general population are available only on a State basis so that a direct comparison with the area data of this study was not possible. The area data for farm operators were compared with the corresponding figures for the States represented in each of the nine sample areas. Source: *Fifteenth Census of the United States: 1930*, Population Vol. VI, table 6.

large families but for large Negro families so that such families would be less likely to be on relief during the growing season. Moreover, it was a common practice of the landlords to "split" their Negro cropper families and let the aged members of the family go on relief.[8] Thus many relief cases were classified as one-person families, reducing the average size of family.

The small size of Negro farm laborer families, as compared with white farm laborer families, is probably caused by differences in the family composition of white and Negro cases on relief, the Negro laborers having more broken families and one-person households than the white laborers (appendix table 7).

When relief and rehabilitation figures are compared by areas, size of family does not appear to have been a primary criterion for the selection of rehabilitation clients.[9] In some areas, rehabilitation families were larger; in others, they were smaller than the corresponding relief groups (table 13).

FAMILY COMPOSITION

An effort was made to determine which types of family were most likely to come on relief, the normal families—husband-wife, husband-wife-children—or the broken families and the one-person households. In the absence of comparable data for the general population, only the existing relief data (appendix tables 7 and 8) and general information on the social structure of farm families could be utilized.

In all areas the normal family was the prevailing type on relief but it varied in importance among areas and agricultural groups. The Corn Belt, the Spring and Winter Wheat, and the Hay and Dairy Areas had the highest proportions of normal families, while the Eastern Cotton Belt and the Lake States Cut-Over Area had the lowest proportions. In one relief group in the Eastern Cotton Belt—Negro laborers—normal families accounted for only 41 percent of the total. Farm owners had the smallest proportions of normal families in six of the nine areas, while tenants had the largest proportions in all areas.

Next to the normal family, the nonfamily man was the type of household which appeared most frequently on farm relief rolls, accounting for 7 percent of farm operator and 10 percent of farm laborer households on relief. The proportions were especially high in the Lake States Cut-Over Area, particularly among farm laborer households, more than one-third of which consisted of unattached

---

[8] Mangus, A. R., *The Rural Negro on Relief, February 1935*, Research Bulletin H–3, Division of Research, Statistics, and Finance, Federal Emergency Relief Administration, October 17, 1935, p. 6.

[9] See appendix tables 9 and 10 for distributions of relief and rehabilitation households by size.

men. This high percentage reflects the comparative youth of the farm laborers in that area (median age, 30 years), and possibly also the influx of single men into the mines and lumber camps of the area before the depression. After mines and lumber camps were abandoned, many of these recent migrants doubtless became farm laborers.

The Cotton Areas showed relatively high proportions of broken families of all types, especially among Negroes. Eleven percent of both white and Negro farm operator households on relief in the Eastern Cotton Area were of the mother-children type of family, and among farm laborer families on relief more than one-third of the Negro and more than one-sixth of the white cases were of this broken type. Nonfamily women also had a larger representation in the Eastern Cotton Area than elsewhere, accounting for 13 percent of Negro farm laborer cases and 8 percent of both Negro and white owners. Likewise, the father-children type of family was more frequent in the Cotton Areas than in other regions. This type was most important among Negro farm owners in the Western Cotton Area (7 percent) and white tenants and croppers in the Eastern Cotton Belt (5 percent).

The large proportions of mother-children families and unattached women in the Cotton Areas probably reflect the migration of males from the South, a phenomenon which has been more notable in the Eastern Cotton Belt, for whites as well as for Negroes, than in any other agricultural area during the past decade. The migration of males from the Western Cotton Area, also reflected in the data, probably represents more of a depression phenomenon, as the area was more recently settled.

The greater proportions of mother-children households among Negro tenants, croppers, and laborers, and of nonfamily men among Negro croppers and other tenants, in both Cotton Areas, as compared to the proportions of such families among whites, probably results from the attitude toward the Negro in these areas. The types of families which would naturally be in the most desperate straits, such as widows with children, or aged men, tended to be over-represented among Negro relief clients, while normal families with able-bodied male members tended to be underrepresented. The practice of splitting Negro families, referred to above, also helps to account for the large proportion of broken families.

Normal families were preferred as rehabilitation clients, as indicated by a comparison of relief and rehabilitation data (appendix tables 7 and 8). The proportion of normal families was higher on rehabilitation than on relief among owners and croppers in all areas and among other tenants in all but two areas. The relatively small number of laborers accepted for rehabilitation in the Cotton Areas reflects the same trend toward the selection of normal families.

It might appear that broken families were considered good risks for rehabilitation, as shown by the rather high ratio of mother-children families on rehabilitation in the Negro farm laborer group of the Eastern Cotton Belt and the comparatively high percentage of father-children families among owners in the Winter Wheat Area, Negro owners in the Western Cotton Area, and Negro tenants in the Eastern Cotton Belt. In the Lake States Cut-Over, Hay and Dairy, and Spring Wheat Areas, nonfamily men were well represented among farm owners on rehabilitation, and in practically all areas and agricultural groups they had some representation. On the other hand, the presence of such households on rehabilitation rolls may be interpreted as evidence that in certain States the rehabilitation program was largely a relief program, especially in its early stages. Few nonfamily women, however, were found among rehabilitation clients in any area or agricultural group.

EMPLOYABILITY

The number of workers [10] per relief or rehabilitation household is important in any consideration of the possibility of the family again becoming entirely independent. The more workers in a family, the greater the chance for this family to become self-supporting again, unless the number of dependent members of the household increases proportionately.

The percentage of relief and rehabilitation households with only one worker tended to increase as the occupational status of the family declined, assuming that the highest agricultural group is that of owner, followed in order by tenant, cropper, and laborer (appendix tables 9 and 10). These differences largely reflected the existing age differences among the various agricultural groups.[11] In general this held true not only for the total, but also for households of different sizes.[12] In other words, the older the head of a family, the higher the occupational status of the family, the more workers it had on the average, and the greater the likelihood that the children were already old enough themselves to be workers.

Although the number of workers increased with the size of the family, it was not a proportionate increase. The number of family

---

[10] Persons 16–64 years of age working or seeking work.

[11] There is, of course, the possibility that the second worker in the family is the wife, but the division of labor practiced in the American farm family practically limits such cases to the cotton-growing South.

[12] Data available in the files of the Division of Social Research, Works Progress Administration, show that this occupational difference appeared also in each of the nine sample areas.

members to be supported also tended to increase. Therefore, it was not surprising that large families came on relief, although a fairly high percentage of them had two or three and even more workers.

There is no evidence that families with more than one worker were given preference for rural rehabilitation. Rehabilitation households included larger proportions of one-worker families among farm owners and larger proportions with two or more workers among sharecroppers than did relief households. There were no marked differences for tenants or laborers.

CHANGES IN RESIDENCE

Migrations of agricultural workers evidently increased during the drought and depression years. This is indicated by data in chapter V on the residence distribution of farm families, and the more detailed information presented here on intercounty movements both during the depression period and during the entire life of the farmers and farm laborers.[13]

In a study made in October 1933 [14] it was found that farmers on relief had changed residence across county or State lines more often than those who had not up to that time received aid. It was suggested that this fact might reflect greater instability on the part of farmers in need of public assistance.

It is readily understandable, however, that the depression would have caused an increased mobility among farmers.[15] Mobility data for the relief population would reflect such movements because the prosperous farmer, who was not adversely affected by the depression, would have no reason to move during a time of general economic instability. Thus, the relief group would naturally appear more mobile than the nonrelief group. Mobility, rather than being a cause of the need for relief, seems to have been at least partially the result of the need for relief.

The degree of mobility cannot be made the basis for judgment, however. A higher rate of mobility does not necessarily reflect unfavorably on the character of the relief population. Nor is a high relief rate necessarily accompanied by high mobility. Generalizations of this type are not justified in the light of the specific situation prevailing in the United States. The stability of the European peasant has never been an ideal after which the American farmer strove; on the contrary, the pioneer tradition not only created instability but even regarded it as a virtue. The commercialization of farming tended to

---

[13] The mobility data are limited by the fact that no information was secured on intracounty movements and that there was no way of checking on farm families that had moved out of the county.

[14] McCormick, T. C., *op. cit.,* pp. 17–20.

[15] The back-to-the-land movement would affect the picture only as far as those returning became farmers.

Reséttlement Administration (Mydans)

On the Move

foster mobility, and the expansion of tenancy increased these tendencies. Furthermore, any judgment on stability or instability of farm laborers would have to be based on a study of individual cases because the influence of the labor market has to be taken into account.

In the Appalachian-Ozark Area, a definite "problem area," there had been very little movement from one county to another. Seventy-five percent of the farm operators and seventy-one percent of the farm laborers on relief had lived in the same county since birth (table 14). This undoubtedly reflects the high degree of stability prevailing in the general population of the area. The noncommercial, self-sufficing character of most of the farms and the remoteness of many of the mountain valleys have created an economic and social structure almost completely lacking in dynamic factors.[16] Correspondingly, only a small percentage (7 percent) of the farm operators on relief had moved into the county of residence since 1929, and the number of immigrating farmers from other States was a mere 1 percent.

TABLE 14.—CHANGES IN RESIDENCE OF HEADS OF RELIEF AND REHABILITATION FARM HOUSEHOLDS,[1] BY AREA, JUNE 1935

[138 counties representing 9 agricultural areas]

Change in residence	All areas	Eastern Cotton	Western Cotton	Appalachian-Ozark	Lake States Cut-Over	Hay and Dairy	Corn Belt	Spring Wheat	Winter Wheat	Ranching
FARM OPERATORS ON RELIEF										
Number	17,894	2,152	2,430	6,506	832	1,480	1,552	1,994	476	472
Percent	100.0	100.0	100.0	100.0	100.0	100.0	100.0	100.0	100.0	100.0
Lived in county since birth	50.0	53.9	33.0	75.2	10.6	39.3	41.2	28.4	19.3	25.0
Moved to county in 1929 or earlier	38.4	30.1	51.5	18.0	75.2	46.4	39.3	66.6	55.1	62.7
Moved to county since 1929	11.6	16.0	15.5	6.8	14.2	14.3	19.5	5.0	25.6	12.3
From within State	9.2	13.8	12.0	5.7	9.1	10.7	16.0	3.4	19.3	8.9
From another State	2.4	2.2	3.5	1.1	5.1	3.6	3.5	1.6	6.3	3.4
FARM LABORERS ON RELIEF [2]										
Number	6,738	1,494	1,388	514	142	1,004	1,444	224	200	328
Percent	100.0	100.0	100.0	100.0	100.0	100.0	100.0	100.0	100.0	100.0
Lived in county since birth	41.6	52.7	25.8	70.8	29.6	44.4	40.0	38.4	16.0	33.5
Moved to county in 1929 or earlier	38.7	28.0	50.6	17.1	47.9	38.8	41.4	42.0	48.0	47.0
Moved to county since 1929	19.7	19.3	23.6	12.1	22.5	16.8	18.6	19.6	36.0	19.5
From within State	14.1	11.7	18.3	9.8	11.3	12.2	14.3	13.4	30.0	10.4
From another State	5.6	7.6	5.3	2.3	11.2	4.6	4.3	6.2	6.0	9.1
FARM OPERATORS ON REHABILITATION										
Number	10,734	5,028	1,696	708	470	496	1,060	850	278	148
Percent	100.0	100.0	100.0	100.0	100.0	100.0	100.0	100.0	100.0	100.0
Lived in county since birth	46.8	60.0	40.0	65.8	5.1	33.9	43.6	14.1	13.7	13.5
Moved to county in 1929 or earlier	39.3	29.0	42.0	21.5	80.4	49.2	38.9	70.8	64.0	56.8
Moved to county since 1929	13.9	10.4	18.0	12.7	14.5	16.9	17.5	15.1	22.3	29.7
From within State	10.5	8.2	15.8	7.9	7.7	12.5	12.8	11.6	13.7	14.9
From another State	3.4	2.2	2.2	4.8	6.8	4.4	4.7	3.5	8.6	14.8

[1] With agriculture as the usual occupation.
[2] Because of the relatively small number of cases in the sample, comparable data for farm laborer heads of rural rehabilitation households were omitted.

[16] The fact that there was a considerable migration from this area to the industrial cities of the North and East is no contradiction of the above statement which refers only to the population which stayed in the area.

At the other end of the scale was the Lake States Cut-Over Area, another self-sufficing, noncommercial, poor land region, where only 11 percent of the farm operators on relief had lived in the same county since their birth. Part-time farmers who work in the mines and the lumber camps make up a large part of the general population of that region. As they came into the area with the development of these industries, a considerable mobility was to be expected. This is corroborated by the fact that 75 percent of the farm operators on relief moved into the county in 1929 or earlier, a migration that was evidently not prompted by the depression and thus was not a characteristic of the relief population as such. Moreover, 74 percent of the farmers on relief had lived in the county of residence for 10 years or more (table 15). About 14 percent of the farmers on relief had moved into the county since 1929. Since more than one-third of these came from other States, many of them may have been urban unemployed returning to the land. Others may have been displaced farmers from the drought areas.

There had been much more recent migration among the farmers of the Winter Wheat Area than among those of any other region (tables 14 and 15). Only 19 percent had lived in the same county since birth, 55 percent had moved to the county of residence in 1929 or earlier, and 26 percent had moved in since 1929. These data may merely reflect the comparatively recent settlement of the area and do not necessarily point to a high mobility of the relief population. Over 40 percent of the farmers on relief had lived continuously in the county of residence for less than 10 years, a fact which might indicate that depression and drought led to an increased mobility,[17] and that such increased mobility was characteristic of the relief population only. However, three-fourths of the recent movements recorded had been within the State.

The Spring Wheat Area, in sharp contrast with the Winter Wheat Area, showed little mobility on the part of farmers on relief. In spite of the drought, only 5 percent of all farmers on relief in the Spring Wheat Area had moved into the county since 1929. Less recent settlement in the Spring Wheat Area than in the Winter Wheat Area is reflected in the higher percentage of farm operators who had always lived in the county (28 percent) or moved to the county in 1929 or earlier (67 percent), with 87 percent reporting continuous residence of 10 years or more.

---

[17] The respective magnitude of these factors cannot be gauged due to lack of data on the exact time of these movements.

TABLE 15.—LENGTH OF LAST CONTINUOUS RESIDENCE IN COUNTY OF HEADS OF FARM HOUSEHOLDS [1] ON RELIEF, BY AREA, JUNE 1935

[138 counties representing 9 agricultural areas]

Length of last continuous residence	All areas	Eastern Cotton	Western Cotton	Appalachian-Ozark	Lake States Cut-Over	Hay and Dairy	Corn Belt	Spring Wheat	Winter Wheat	Ranching
FARM OPERATORS										
Number	17,984	2,152	2,462	6,510	844	1,482	1,556	2,014	490	474
Percent	100.0	100.0	100.0	100.0	100.0	100.0	100.0	100.0	100.0	100.0
Less than 5 years	9.9	13.0	13.5	5.7	12.3	10.9	17.1	5.0	23.7	11.8
5–9 years	9.9	11.1	15.6	5.2	14.2	14.4	12.5	7.8	17.5	8.4
10 years and over	80.2	75.9	70.9	89.1	73.5	74.7	70.4	87.2	58.8	79.8
OWNERS										
Number	6,374	454	300	2,608	660	722	392	836	110	292
Percent	100.0	100.0	100.0	100.0	100.0	100.0	100.0	100.0	100.0	100.0
Less than 5 years	5.3	4.9	6.7	2.6	10.0	8.6	11.2	1.7	10.9	9.6
5–9 years	7.2	5.7	12.0	4.6	11.8	11.9	7.7	6.0	14.5	6.8
10 years and over	87.5	89.4	81.3	92.8	78.2	79.5	81.1	92.3	74.6	83.6
TENANTS [2]										
Number	9,612	642	1,220	3,902	184	760	1,164	1,178	380	182
Percent	100.0	100.0	100.0	100.0	100.0	100.0	100.0	100.0	100.0	100.0
Less than 5 years	11.7	11.2	14.4	7.7	20.7	13.2	19.1	7.3	27.4	15.4
5–9 years	10.5	9.3	16.2	5.6	22.8	16.8	14.1	9.2	18.4	11.0
10 years and over	77.8	79.5	69.4	86.7	56.5	70.0	66.8	83.5	54.2	73.6
CROPPERS										
Number	1,998	1,056	942	--------	--------	--------	--------	--------	--------	--------
Percent	100.0	100.0	100.0	--------	--------	--------	--------	--------	--------	--------
Less than 5 years	16.1	17.6	14.4	--------	--------	--------	--------	--------	--------	--------
5–9 years	15.1	14.4	15.9	--------	--------	--------	--------	--------	--------	--------
10 years and over	68.8	68.0	69.7	--------	--------	--------	--------	--------	--------	--------
FARM LABORERS										
Number	6,768	1,496	1,402	514	144	1,004	1,446	228	204	330
Percent	100.0	100.0	100.0	100.0	100.0	100.0	100.0	100.0	100.0	100.0
Less than 5 years	16.5	15.4	20.5	10.9	18.1	13.9	15.8	18.4	28.4	14.5
5–9 years	16.5	12.6	20.7	5.8	12.5	15.9	19.8	11.4	27.5	18.2
10 years and over	67.0	72.0	58.8	83.3	69.4	70.2	64.4	70.2	44.1	67.3

[1] With agriculture as the usual occupation.
[2] Exclusive of croppers in the 2 Cotton Areas.

The Eastern Cotton Belt showed greater stability than any other area except the Appalachian-Ozark. More than one-half of all farm operators on relief in that area had lived in the county since their birth, and three-fourths of them reported 10 years or more of continuous residence. However, 16 percent had established residence since 1929. It is possible that among these 16 percent, of which the great majority came from within the same State, there were cases of back-to-the-farm migration. The data probably overemphasize stability, however, due to the tendency of tenants to move frequently within the county.

In the Western Cotton Area, only one-third of the farmers on relief had lived in the same county since birth, probably reflecting the much more recent settlement of this area as compared with the Eastern Cotton. The proportion of farmers who moved into the county of residence in 1929 or earlier (52 percent) is considerably higher than the corresponding percentage for the Eastern Cotton Belt (30 percent).

In the Corn Belt, about one-fifth of the farmers on relief had moved to their present county of residence during the depression, and four-fifths of this migration took place within the State. Foreclosures may have been partially responsible for these recent movements.

The farm laborers on relief did not differ greatly from the farm operators with regard to mobility. The percentage of those who had lived in the same county since their birth was usually either equal to or, in some areas (Spring Wheat, Lake States Cut-Over, Hay and Dairy, and Ranching), considerably higher than that of the farmers. However, migration into the county of residence since 1929 had been more marked in the farm laborer group than in the farm operator group in all areas but the Corn Belt. The difference was especially striking in the Spring Wheat Area.

The extent to which the location and policies of relief offices and the existence of C. W. A. and other work projects were responsible for movements of relief clients cannot be determined on the strength of the available statistical material. The data on continuous residence in the county indicate a slightly higher mobility of farm laborers than of farm operators but, on the whole, the stability of the group within county limits is marked. This is probably explained in part by the fact that the data exclude migratory workers as well as those farm laborers who, under the impact of unemployment, became transients.[18]

Relative stability was apparently not a determining factor in selecting rehabilitation clients. In six areas there were relatively more migrants to the county among farm operators on rehabilitation than on relief. Only in the Cotton and Corn Belts did natives of the county appear to be preferred as rehabilitation clients (table 14 and figure 8).

---

[18] The data on movements of farmers and farm laborers to cities, presented in chapter V. indicate that the number of farm laborers migrating to cities was twice as great as that of farm operators.

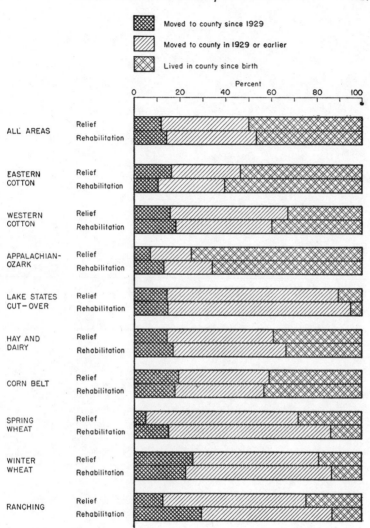

FIG. 8 – MOBILITY OF HEADS OF RURAL RELIEF AND REHABILITATION
HOUSEHOLDS WHO WERE FARM OPERATORS BY
USUAL OCCUPATION, BY AREA
June 1935

AF – 1075, W.P.A.

CHAPTER V

EMPLOYMENT AND RELATION TO THE LAND

MOST OF THE FARM families on relief in June 1935 were still in the open country, although families of laborers lived in villages to a much greater extent than did those of operators. Tenant farmers were more dependent on public aid than were farm owners in June 1935. The overwhelming majority of both tenant farmers (exclusive of croppers) and farm owners on relief received aid while still operating their farms, whereas farm laborers and sharecroppers on relief were largely unemployed or displaced from the land. Laborers and croppers had stayed off relief for very brief periods after losing their usual jobs, while other tenants and owners who had lost their usual occupation had remained off public relief rolls for much longer periods. The great majority of the relief families with farm experience who had left the land had lost their farms during the depression years. While many rural families had left their farms, the influx into agriculture of nonagricultural workers was marked in part-time farming areas.

Rural rehabilitation clients were predominantly selected from the farm operator group. The program had raised the tenure status of nearly one-half of the sharecroppers who became clients, placing them in the tenant category. Laborers and nonagricultural workers on rehabilitation became tenants for the most part, but few tenants or owners changed their tenure status on rehabilitation. The rehabilitation program diverged somewhat from its primary purpose of aiding farm families to become independent of relief, as indicated by the fact that some nonagricultural workers were accepted as clients, and that some of the clients in June 1935 were not operating farms or engaging in any other employment. Almost all of the clients had agricultural experience, however, and farm operators far outnumbered farm laborers and nonagricultural workers on rehabilitation rolls.

RESIDENCE

Of the farm operators by usual occupation [1] on relief in June 1935, 89 percent lived in the open country and 11 percent in villages, the proportions varying greatly from area to area (appendix table 11). Village residents included those currently employed in operating nearby farms, those who had shifted temporarily or permanently to

---

[1] For definition of usual occupation, see Introduction, p. x, and Glossary, p. 210.

nonfarm occupations, and those retired or unemployed for other
reasons.

Most of the farm operators living in villages had evidently come
to the villages from the open country since the beginning of the depression. Unemployment apparently caused much of the movement
of tenant farmers and sharecroppers to villages, as indicated by the
fact that most of those living in villages at the time of the survey
were found to be unemployed. On the other hand, the farm owners
on relief and living in villages were for the most part still engaged
in farming. It cannot be assumed, therefore, that they necessarily
represent retired or unemployed farmers. The type of settlement
prevailing may have favored their location in villages.

Laborers on relief lived in villages to a much greater extent than
did farm operators, unemployment during the depression having
caused many of them to move from the open country.

Of the rehabilitation clients, only 4.4 percent lived in villages
(appendix table 13). Such a small percentage would be expected
since in most cases rehabilitation clients would necessarily have land
to operate in order to obtain rehabilitation loans or grants, and since
the great majority of them were located in the Cotton Areas where
farmers generally live in the open country.

USUAL TENURE STATUS

Farm operators (by usual occupation) made up about three-fourths
of the rural farm relief load in June 1935, while farm laborer heads
of households accounted for slightly more than one-fourth. The
proportions of farm operators were as high as 93 and 86 percent in
the two self-sufficing areas, Appalachian-Ozark and Lake States Cut-
Over, and 90 percent in the Spring Wheat Area. In the Corn Belt,
on the other hand, farm operator and farm laborer households were
about equally represented and among Negroes in the Eastern Cotton
Belt more than one-half of the rural relief households were those of
farm laborers (appendix table 15). These differences reflect variations in type of agriculture in the nine areas.

Of the farm operators, 35 percent were owners by usual occupation
while tenants accounted for 65 percent (including croppers, 11 percent) (appendix table 12). The proportion of owners ranged by
areas, however, from 12 percent in the Western Cotton Area to 78
percent in the Lake States Cut-Over Area.

Proportionately more farm tenants by usual occupation than farm
owners were receiving relief in all areas in both February and June
(table 16 and figure 9).[2] This was to be expected because the eco-

---

[2] In comparing February and June relief rates, the June rate for relief and rehabilitation combined is more nearly comparable to the February relief rate than is the
June rate for relief only, since between February and June many former relief cases
had been transferred to the rural rehabilitation program.

nomic position of tenants is, on the whole, less secure than that of owners.

The Negro farm operators on relief in the two Cotton Areas differed from the whites in tenure distribution. The proportion of owners in the Negro relief group was considerably smaller than in the white group in the Eastern Cotton Belt and slightly greater in the Western Cotton Area (appendix table 15).

TABLE 16.—RATIO OF FARM OPERATORS [1] RECEIVING RELIEF GRANTS IN FEBRUARY AND JUNE 1935 AND OF FARM OPERATORS RECEIVING RELIEF GRANTS OR REHABILITATION ADVANCES IN JUNE 1935 TO ALL FARM OPERATORS IN JANUARY 1935

Area and tenure	Percent of all farm operators on relief		Percent of all farm operators on relief or rehabilitation,[2] June 1935	Area and tenure	Percent of all farm operators on relief		Percent of all farm operators on relief or rehabilitation, June 1935
	February 1935	June 1935			February 1935	June 1935	
All areas:				Hay and Dairy:			
Farm operators....	10.0	5.4	8.8	Farm operators....	6.2	2.8	4.9
Owners...........	6.0	3.5	5.4	Owners...........	3.8	1.7	3.2
Tenants [3].........	14.8	8.2	12.2	Tenants..........	15.1	7.0	11.6
Croppers..........	14.4	5.3	14.3	Corn Belt:			
Eastern Cotton:				Farm operators....	7.0	2.8	4.7
Farm operators....	4.8	2.3	7.6	Owners...........	2.9	1.3	2.0
Owners...........	2.6	1.4	5.0	Tenants..........	11.8	4.5	7.9
Tenants..........	3.9	1.9	8.6	Spring Wheat:			
Croppers..........	8.1	3.6	9.3	Farm operators....	31.5	20.0	28.2
Western Cotton:				Owners...........	19.2	13.3	17.9
Farm operators....	19.5	5.5	9.3	Tenants..........	51.7	31.0	45.3
Owners...........	10.1	1.7	3.1	Winter Wheat:			
Tenants..........	20.4	6.4	11.1	Farm operators....	13.3	6.2	9.7
Croppers..........	36.2	11.2	17.8	Owners...........	8.1	2.6	4.3
Appalachian-Ozark:				Tenants..........	19.1	10.0	15.6
Farm operators....	12.2	12.1	13.4	Ranching:			
Owners...........	6.9	7.1	8.0	Farm operators....	9.4	6.1	8.1
Tenants.........	23.5	22.8	25.2	Owners...........	7.5	4.9	6.1
Lake States Cut-Over:				Tenants..........	15.7	9.9	14.3
Farm operators....	22.0	10.7	18.4				
Owners...........	20.0	9.9	17.6				
Tenants..........	33.2	15.4	22.8				

[1] By usual occupation.
[2] Unduplicated. Cases that received both relief and rehabilitation were considered rehabilitation cases.
[3] Exclusive of croppers in the 2 Cotton Areas.

Sources: *United States Census of Agriculture: 1935,* and Survey of Current Changes in the Rural Relief Population.

Sharecroppers made up a smaller part of the Negro relief load than of the white relief load in the Eastern Cotton Belt, while the situation was reversed in the Western Cotton Area. It is possible that Negro croppers were more likely to be retained by the landlords in the Eastern Cotton Belt where tradition is in their favor,[3] but it seems still more probable that the local officials in the old Cotton South were more reluctant to take Negro sharecroppers on relief than in the Western Cotton Area. Differences between the two areas in distribution of tenants other than croppers by color

[3] Hoffsommer, Harold, *Landlord-Tenant Relations and Relief in Alabama,* Research Bulletin. Series II, No. 9, Division of Research, Statistics, and Finance, Federal Emergency Relief Administration, November 14, 1935, p. 8.

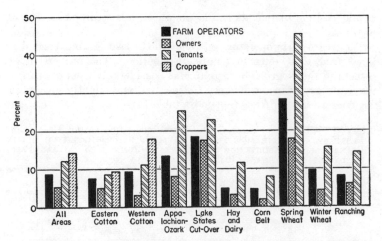

FIG. 9 – PERCENT OF ALL FARM OPERATORS* RECEIVING RELIEF GRANTS
OR REHABILITATION ADVANCES, BY AREA
June 1935

*Reported in the United States
Census of Agriculture: 1935   AF-1071, W.P.A.

is also significant in this connection. Such tenants were represented
among Negro relief families in slightly larger proportions than
among whites in the Eastern Cotton Belt and in much smaller proportions than among whites in the Western Cotton Area.

CURRENT EMPLOYMENT STATUS

More than nine-tenths of the farm owners on relief were still
on their farms in the spring of 1935,[4] and were therefore recorded
as being employed at their usual occupation (appendix table 14).
The percentages of such farmers were highest in the Lake States
Cut-Over, Spring Wheat, and Appalachian-Ozark Areas (96–98
percent) and lowest in the Corn Belt (73 percent). The high percentages in the Appalachian-Ozark and Lake States Cut-Over Areas
are easily understood, since both areas are characterized by small
self-sufficing or part-time farms, and the economic resources of many
farm owners had always been inadequate.[5] Among reasons frequently given on the case records for these families receiving relief
were "farm too small," "loss of supplementary occupation," and "poor
land," all indicating the inadequacy of their farming enterprise even
in good times.

---

[4] For definition of *current employment,* see Introduction, pp. x–xi.
[5] Reports from various sources, for instance the county reports of this survey, agree
that, in those areas, relief clients were not much worse off than the corresponding nonrelief groups and in some instances had even improved their standard of living since
going on relief.

In the Spring Wheat Area, many of the farm owners still on their own farms while receiving relief had been substantial farmers before they lost their crops and livestock in the drought of 1934, and their need for relief was, therefore, of recent origin.[6]

The small proportion of farm owners by usual occupation still on their farms in the Corn Belt is probably related to widespread foreclosures forcing many farmers to leave their farms. Some retired farm owners, whose assets became depleted during the depression and who thus became dependent on public assistance, may also be included in the large proportion of former farm owners no longer on their farms in this area.

Tenant farmers had been unable to remain on their farms to the same degree as had owners, only 85 percent of tenants (exclusive of croppers) on relief being still employed as tenants in June 1935. The Corn Belt again showed the smallest proportion (66 percent) of any area, a possible indication that the return of retired farm owners to their farms in this area during the depression may have displaced some tenants.[7] As in the case of owners, high rates of employment at usual occupation among tenants were found in the Appalachian-Ozark and Spring Wheat Areas (96 and 90 percent, respectively).

Sharecroppers had the lowest employment rate at usual occupation of all farm operators: 63 percent in the Western Cotton Area and only 35 percent in the Eastern Cotton Belt. Even though there were many chronically dependent cases among the croppers on relief, the conclusion seems inevitable that the restriction of employment opportunities as a result of the A. A. A. program was partly responsible for the low rate of employment in the Eastern Cotton Belt.

Employment rates at usual occupation were higher for Negroes than for whites among croppers and other tenants on relief in both Cotton Areas. This finding might be taken as evidence confirming earlier observations that landlords often prefer the more docile Negro tenant to the white.

Only 14 percent of the farm laborer heads of households[8] on relief were employed at their usual occupation (appendix table 14). This low rate would be expected since farm laborers resemble industrial

---

[6] Wynne, Waller, Jr. and Blackwell, Gordon W., *Survey of Rural Relief Closed for Administrative Reasons in South Dakota*, Research Bulletin, Series II, No. 12, Division of Social Research, Works Progress Administration, p. 2.

[7] Report from Federal Emergency Relief Administration Survey of the Rural Relief Situation, October 1934, Whiteside County, Illinois, p. 15.

[8] In order to get an accurate picture of the employment situation, the figures for farm laborers who were heads of households are shown separately. No such division was necessary for farm operators, as practically all operators (98.6 percent) were heads of households.

workers in their employment situation, being entirely dependent
on the actual demand for farm labor. If compelled to reduce costs,
the farmer will first reduce his labor costs since this reduction is
most easily effected. He may either decide to increase his own
or his children's working hours or he may take recourse to trading
help with his neighbors.[9]

The data for all members of farm laborer families show a higher
rate of employment than for heads alone, owing to the inclusion of
unpaid family labor. Even so, the rate of employment at usual
occupation was lower for farm laborers (54 percent) than for any
other agricultural group except sharecroppers.

<h2 style="text-align:center">CHANGES IN OCCUPATION</h2>

Changes in occupation played an important part in the farm relief
situation. Although rural workers migrating into the city and
remaining there are outside the scope of this study, farm to rural-
nonfarm and nonfarm to rural-farm movements are included.

Influx into Agriculture.

While a number of farm families gave up farming either before
or after going on relief, the ranks of active farmers experienced an
influx of nonagricultural workers. Miners, lumbermen, and sub-
urban laborers attempted to shift to farming and, under the impact
of the depression, industrial workers went back to the land and took
up farming in an attempt to tide themselves over the period of
unemployment. Heads of households usually engaged in nonagricultural industry constituted 48 percent of the rural relief load in
June (appendix table 17). As far as these workers found another
occupation after they lost their usual one, such change, in the majority
of cases, involved a shift into agriculture (appendix table 16).
Skilled, semiskilled, and unskilled workers tended to go into agriculture to a considerably greater extent than did the white collar
workers.

The influx into agriculture was most marked in the Appalachian-
Ozark and the Lake States Cut-Over Areas (involving 27 and 20 percent of all nonagricultural workers, respectively), where loss of a
job in lumbering or mining led the workers to devote full time to
farming. Also, access to the land was comparatively easy for those
industrial workers who either came into these areas from the industrial centers for the first time, or who returned to the areas. How-

---

[9] Such substitution of neighbor help has been frequent during the depression, according
to Josiah C. Folsom, Bureau of Agricultural Economics, U. S. Department of Agriculture.
See also report from Hand County, South Dakota, p. 10 (files of Division of Social
Research, Works Progress Administration).

ever, they found the soil usually of such poor quality that it was difficult to eke out a living and many were forced on relief.

In the other areas, where part-time farming is less widespread, the shift into agriculture did not reach any significant proportions, involving only from 2 to 10 percent of the nonagricultural workers (appendix table 16). These variations reflect not only differing possibilities for nonagricultural employment, but also varying opportunities for getting back onto the land.

Findings in this study thus confirm those made in the survey of six rural problem areas [10] in 1934. A pronounced shift from non-agricultural to agricultural employment was found in the same two areas—Appalachian-Ozark and Lake States Cut-Over. Many such heads of families in shifting occupations had made no radical change either in their residence or their mode of living. This was because they had already been living on small farms, while working in nearby industries, and the shift in occupation merely represented a failure of their industrial employment and a consequent major attention to farming their small pieces of land. The farm, formerly only an incidental source of income, became the family's sole source of income and subsistence, and hence a shift in occupation and industry was recorded.

Leaving the Farm.

For farm families, loss of usual occupation in most cases involved leaving the farm. In all areas the great majority of the heads of families with farm experience,[11] but not currently engaged in agriculture, left the farm during the 5-year period coinciding with the depression (table 17). The conclusion seems justified that the depression was the immediate cause for this migration. Leaving the farm does not necessarily mean migration from the open country to a village or urban center. Many of those who had to give up agriculture as their usual occupation remained in the open country after discontinuing farm operations. In fact, there has been a tendency on the part of landlords, particularly in the South, to let former croppers, tenants, or farm laborers continue to occupy houses on their land.

Within the farm operator group, tenants and croppers were found to have left the farm more recently than owners, over one-half of them having left the farm between July 1, 1934, and July 1, 1935, in comparison with only two-fifths of the owners (appendix table 18).

---

[10] Beck, P. G. and Forster, M. C., *Six Rural Problem Areas, Relief–Resources–Rehabilitation*, Research Monograph I, Division of Research, Statistics, and Finance, Federal Emergency Relief Administration, 1935, pp. 65–66.

[11] Since 16 years of age.

One-fifth of the owners had left the farm prior to the depression period.

TABLE 17.—LENGTH OF TIME SINCE HEADS OF RURAL RELIEF HOUSEHOLDS WITH FARM EXPERIENCE [1] BUT NOT CURRENTLY ENGAGED IN AGRICULTURE LEFT THE FARM, BY AREA, JUNE 1935

[138 counties representing 9 agricultural areas]

Area	Total		1 year	2 years	3–4 years	5–9 years	10 years and over
	Number	Percent					
All areas	10,700	100.0	57.9	18.1	11.0	8.7	4.3
Eastern Cotton	2,530	100.0	56.1	22.8	11.6	7.1	2.4
Western Cotton	2,126	100.0	78.1	11.7	5.3	3.8	1.1
Appalachian-Ozark	762	100.0	52.2	20.2	12.6	7.4	7.6
Lake States Cut-Over	314	100.0	37.6	15.3	15.3	22.3	9.5
Hay and Dairy	1,574	100.0	56.9	15.5	12.8	9.7	5.1
Corn Belt	2,184	100.0	45.5	21.1	15.4	12.3	5.7
Spring Wheat	330	100.0	48.5	26.1	10.9	8.5	6.0
Winter Wheat	312	100.0	62.2	13.5	5.1	15.4	3.8
Ranching	568	100.0	61.6	14.4	7.0	8.5	8.5

[1] Exclusive of heads for whom length of time since farm experience was unknown and exclusive of part-time farm operators.

Farm laborers, the youngest agricultural group, had left the farm even more recently than tenants and croppers. Leaving the farm has, of course, a different aspect for farm laborers than for farm operators in that it is not a phenomenon peculiar to depressions.

Workers who lost their usual occupation during a period of general prosperity were probably victims of more or less "chronic" unfavorable conditions and included individual instances of failure and poverty which were brought to the surface, once public aid became available on a large scale. The high percentage for displaced owners indicates that this group comprised many "chronic" cases, whose need for relief was only partly a result of the depression. It also points to the difficulties in the way of farm owners returning to the land, once they have lost their farms.

It is probable that a large proportion of the heads of families with farm experience but not currently engaged in agriculture who had left the farm in the earlier years were usually engaged in nonagriculture. One-fourth of the heads of relief families with farm experience had been usually engaged in nonagricultural industries (table 18).

TIME BETWEEN LOSS OF JOB AND OPENING OF RELIEF CASE

Although the time which elapsed between loss of job at usual occupation and opening of the relief case is in part indicative of the individual resourcefulness of the relief clients in finding other means of support, it is largely an index of their economic position—savings, credit, salable assets, friends, and relatives who could help—and of economic conditions in general which would permit them to find employment in some other occupation.

TABLE 18.—USUAL OCCUPATION OF HEADS OF RURAL RELIEF HOUSEHOLDS WITH FARM EXPERIENCE[1] BUT NOT CURRENTLY ENGAGED IN AGRICULTURE, BY AREA, JUNE 1935

[138 counties representing 9 agricultural areas]

Area	Total		Usual occupation			
	Number	Percent	Agriculture			Nonagriculture
			Total	Farm operators	Farm laborers	
All areas	10,700	100.0	75.3	24.2	51.1	24.7
Eastern Cotton	2,530	100.0	83.6	34.6	49.0	16.4
Western Cotton	2,126	100.0	85.4	26.7	58.7	14.6
Appalachian-Ozark	762	100.0	63.0	22.0	41.0	37.0
Lake States Cut-Over	314	100.0	42.0	12.1	29.9	58.0
Hay and Dairy	1,574	100.0	65.4	14.9	50.5	34.6
Corn Belt	2,184	100.0	73.9	19.8	54.1	26.1
Spring Wheat	330	100.0	82.4	37.0	45.4	17.6
Winter Wheat	312	100.0	80.8	26.3	54.5	19.2
Ranching	568	100.0	60.9	13.0	47.9	39.1

[1] Exclusive of heads for whom length of time since farm experience was unknown and exclusive of part-time farm operators.

Ten percent of the farm laborers stayed off relief less than a month after they lost their usual occupation, while this was true of only two percent of the owners, five percent of the tenants, and seven percent of the croppers (table 19). The low wage standard prevailing for farm labor usually made it impossible for the laborers to accumulate any reserves, and loss of job, therefore, forced them on relief after a short period. Thus, 62 percent of farm laborer heads of families on relief, who had lost their usual type of job, went on the rolls within 6 months after this loss of job.[12] The croppers showed nearly the same characteristics as the farm laborers: 55 percent were able to stay off relief for not more than 6 months after losing their sharecropper status. In contrast, only 37 percent of the other tenants and 31 percent of the owners were in this category. Correspondingly, much larger percentages of owners and tenants than of croppers and laborers managed to stay off relief for 2 years or more after loss of their usual occupation.

---

[12] This does not necessarily mean that they were unemployed, as some of them may have found work at another occupation.

Table 19.—Length of Time Between End of Job at Last Usual Occupation and Opening of Relief Case of Heads of Farm Households Not Currently Engaged in Usual Occupation, June 1935

[138 counties representing 9 agricultural areas]

Usual occupation	Total		Length of time between loss of job and opening of relief case								
	Number	Percent	After opening of case	Less than 1 month	1 month	2-6 months	7-12 months	13-24 months	25-48 months	More than 48 months	Average number of months [1]
Farm operators	1,420	100.0	10.4	4.8	7.6	30.3	13.0	16.2	10.8	6.9	6.5
Owners	242	100.0	5.8	1.7	6.6	23.1	13.2	19.0	15.7	14.9	12.8
Tenants [2]	652	100.0	14.1	4.6	8.3	24.2	14.4	14.4	12.3	7.7	6.8
Croppers	526	100.0	8.0	6.5	7.2	41.1	11.0	17.1	6.8	2.3	5.4
Farm laborers	3,002	100.0	12.7	10.3	19.0	32.5	10.5	7.2	4.9	2.9	3.2

[1] Median.
[2] Exclusive of croppers in the 2 Cotton Areas.

In some cases, the loss of usual occupation occurred only after the relief case was opened. Tenants (exclusive of sharecroppers) and farm laborers showed the highest percentages of such cases (14 and 13 percent, respectively), whereas only 6 percent of the former farm owners lost their farms after going on relief.

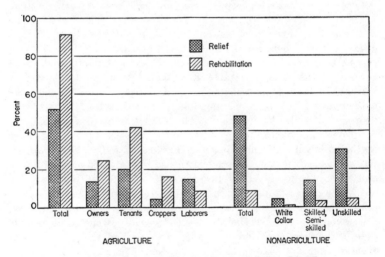

FIG. 10-USUAL OCCUPATION OF HEADS OF RURAL RELIEF AND REHABILITATION HOUSEHOLDS

June 1935

AF-1073, W.P.A.

REHABILITATION CLIENTS

Usual Occupations.

Most of the rehabilitation clients were drawn from relief rolls, but their occupational composition did not parallel that of the relief group. This was because the specific purposes of the rehabilitation program required the selection of clients primarily from the agricultural groups (appendix tables 13 and 19 and figure 10).

For all the sample areas combined, 89 percent of the heads of rehabilitation households in June 1935 were agricultural workers by usual occupation (appendix table 19). Of these, 91 percent belonged to the farm operator group, and 9 percent were farm laborers (table 20).

TABLE 20.—HEADS OF RURAL REHABILITATION HOUSEHOLDS WITH AGRICULTURE AS THE USUAL OCCUPATION, BY COLOR AND BY AREA, JUNE 1935

[138 counties representing 9 agricultural areas]

Area	Total		Usual occupation				
			Farm operators				Farm laborers
	Number	Percent	Total	Owners	Tenants [1]	Croppers	
All areas	12,744	100.0	90.8	27.3	45.0	18.5	9.2
Eastern Cotton:							
Total	5,688	100.0	89.1	20.3	39.7	29.1	10.9
White	3,586	100.0	87.5	21.0	38.4	28.1	12.5
Negro	2,102	100.0	91.7	18.9	41.9	30.9	8.3
Western Cotton:							
Total	2,034	100.0	83.8	11.7	44.7	27.4	16.2
White	1,630	100.0	82.3	9.1	46.1	27.1	17.7
Negro	404	100.0	89.6	22.3	38.6	28.7	10.4
Appalachian-Ozark	730	100.0	97.5	43.0	54.5		2.5
Lake States Cut-Over	618	100.0	98.4	84.2	14.2		1.6
Hay and Dairy	1,168	100.0	96.1	52.6	43.5		3.9
Corn Belt	1,144	100.0	93.2	17.7	75.5		6.8
Spring Wheat	894	100.0	95.7	33.1	62.6		4.3
Winter Wheat	290	100.0	97.9	24.1	73.8		2.1
Ranching	178	100.0	87.6	41.6	46.0		12.4

[1] Exclusive of croppers in the 2 Cotton Areas.

About one-half of the rehabilitation clients were tenants, other than croppers, while owners made up a little more than one-fourth of the group. In comparison with heads of farm families on relief (appendix table 15), owners, tenants, and croppers were overrepresented on rehabilitation while farm laborers showed a marked underrepresentation. These differences varied widely by areas.

The overrepresentation on rehabilitation of Negro owners in the two Cotton Areas, in comparison with Negro owners on relief, was especially noticeable. Negro laborers were much underrepresented on rehabilitation, due probably to their low economic status which caused them to be considered bad risks for a rehabilitation program.

It is obvious that farm operators would be preferred to farm laborers as clients, both because it would be a simpler matter to rehabilitate them "in place," [13] and because they had had greater experience in farm management and therefore would seem, on the whole, to be better risks. Arbitrary policies, however, may also be responsible for this restriction of choice.

About 8 percent of the rehabilitation clients in June were not agricultural workers at all, but belonged to the nonagricultural group (appendix table 19). Half of them (4 percent of the total) were unskilled workers, and another 3 percent came from the skilled and semiskilled workers, while white collar workers made up about 1 percent of the total.

TABLE 21.—USUAL OCCUPATION OF HEADS OF RURAL REHABILITATION HOUSE-
HOLDS, BY CURRENT EMPLOYMENT STATUS, JUNE 1935

[138 counties representing 9 agricultural areas]

Usual occupation	Total		Current employment status									
			Employed in agriculture					Employed in nonagriculture				Unemployed and seeking work
	Number	Percent	Total	Owners	Tenants [1]	Croppers	Farm laborers	Total	White collar [2]	Skilled and semiskilled	Unskilled	
Agriculture	12,744	100.0	95.7	27.5	56.5	10.3	1.4	0.2	(3)	0.1	0.1	4.1
Farm operators	11,574	100.0	97.7	29.8	57.2	10.6	.1	.2	(3)	.1	.1	2.1
Owners	3,480	100.0	99.3	95.7	3.3	.3		.2	0.1	.1		.5
Tenants [1]	5,742	100.0	98.0	1.4	95.4	1.1	.1	.1			.1	1.9
Croppers	2,352	100.0	94.5	1.4	43.7	48.9	.5	.3		.1	.2	5.2
Farm laborers	1,170	100.0	76.3	5.5	49.4	7.9	13.5	.3			.3	23.4
Nonagriculture	1,204	100.0	75.8	20.3	47.7	6.8	1.0	4.6	1.8	.8	2.0	19.6
White collar [2]	128	100.0	64.1	10.9	48.5	3.1	1.6	15.6	15.6			20.3
Skilled and semiskilled	454	100.0	78.4	24.2	45.4	7.9	.9	3.1	.4	2.3	.4	18.5
Unskilled	622	100.0	76.2	19.3	49.2	6.7	1.0	3.5			3.5	20.3

[1] Exclusive of croppers in the 2 Cotton Areas.
[2] Professional, proprietary, and clerical workers.
[3] Less than 0 05 percent.

Employment Status.

As originally set up, the rural rehabilitation program was designed primarily for families that would be actively engaged in farming. However, there were some variations as the program developed. Four percent of all heads of rehabilitation households usually engaged in agriculture were reported as unemployed in June 1935 (table 21). This unemployment figure indicates that not all cases under care of the various rehabilitation agencies could be called rehabilitation cases in the accepted sense of the term. From the fact that these clients were unemployed and seeking work, it must be assumed that they were no longer active rehabilitation cases. They were on the rehabilitation rolls because they once received advances

---

[13] For definition, see p. 17, footnote 10.

A Rehabilitation Client

in some form or other—a cow, some feed, food supplies—from the rehabilitation agency, which they had not yet fully repaid. It is possible that they were later dropped from the rehabilitation rolls as poor risks or for noncompliance with their rehabilitation contracts. But it must also be kept in mind that the rehabilitation program was often regarded not as a program for rehabilitating farmers, but as a special type of general rural relief program which need not apply any definite selective policy with regard to its clients. This was largely the case in the South, for example, where the program had its greatest development.

In some cases nonagricultural workers and farm laborers became rehabilitation clients without actually being settled on the land. Fourteen percent of all clients who were farm laborers by usual occupation were currently employed as farm laborers, whereas five percent of all nonagricultural workers were currently employed at their usual occupations and one percent at farm labor (table 21). Some of these workers were probably engaged in nonfarming aspects of rehabilitation projects.

Advances in Status.

Whereas 96 percent of the owners and 95 percent of the tenants, other than sharecroppers, remained at their usual occupations under the rehabilitation program, 44 percent of the croppers climbed up the agricultural ladder, becoming tenants (table 21). Probably as far as the cropper clients concluded new contracts under the rehabilitation program, tenant agreements were thought more appropriate than the customary sharecropping arrangements for the purposes of actual rehabilitation and were, therefore, furthered by the rehabilitation agencies.

Only 1 percent each of croppers and other tenants on rehabilitation had gone so far up the agricultural ladder as to become owners. The percentage was higher for the farm laborers (6 percent), whereas 20 percent of the nonagricultural workers had become farm owners. Almost one-half of the farm laborers and nonagricultural workers became tenants (exclusive of croppers), however, this being the easiest way to return to the land. It is possible, of course, that some of these had carried out the shift to tenancy before they became rehabilitation clients. This explanation would apply in those cases where nonagricultural workers returned to the open country and took up agriculture again to tide themselves over a period of unemployment.

Only 8 percent of the farm laborers and 7 percent of the nonagricultural workers became croppers. This shift does not involve any capital requirements and may also have occurred before the client entered into a rehabilitation agreement.

Chapter VI

FACTORS IN PRODUCTION

FARM OPERATORS on relief manifestly produced less on the average than their neighbors not on relief. The distinction between those farmers who sank below the subsistence level and those who did not, except in cases of affliction by natural disasters, such as drought, flood, or crop pests, was closely allied to differences in control over the factors of production—land, livestock, experience in farming, and personal ability. This and other relief studies have given definite evidence that the farmers on relief were at a disadvantage in respect to available land and livestock. They were experienced farmers, but their formal education was less than that of farmers who managed to stay off relief.

ACREAGE OPERATED

The average acreage [1] operated by farmers on relief was found to be less than the acreage for all farms [2] in every area surveyed in June 1935; in most areas it was far smaller (table 22).

The owner group showed the greatest difference between the size of relief farms and of all farms (figure 11). In some instances— Western Cotton and Ranching Areas—the farms operated by owners on relief had only about one-fourth of the acreage reported in the 1935 Census for farms operated by all owners in those areas.

TABLE 22.—SIZE OF FARMS OPERATED BY FARMERS ON RELIEF IN JUNE 1935 AND BY ALL FARMERS IN JANUARY 1935,[1] BY TENURE, BY COLOR, AND BY AREA

[138 counties representing 9 agricultural areas]

Area	Average number of acres operated					
	Owners		Tenants [2]		Croppers	
	Relief	Census 1935	Relief	Census 1935	Relief	Census 1935
All areas	86	171	80	126	38	40
Eastern Cotton:						
Total	52	116	33	64	26	37
White	55	123	36	72	29	49
Negro	36	74	29	48	20	30
Western Cotton:						
Total	49	176	79	113	46	52
White	55	192	81	121	50	63
Negro	36	73	70	61	34	35
Appalachian-Ozark	34	83	21	56		
Lake States Cut-Over	40	97	71	110		
Hay and Dairy	60	114	82	134		
Corn Belt	94	157	124	164		
Spring Wheat	338	745	310	483		
Winter Wheat	146	423	115	304		
Ranching	234	899	166	445		

[1] *United States Census of Agriculture: 1935.*   [2] Exclusive of croppers in the 2 Cotton Areas.

[1] The 1935 Census of Agriculture data for computing medians were not yet available at the time the report was prepared; consequently, the arithmetic average is used.

[2] The Census figures include those farms whose operators were on relief. As these relief farms were concentrated in the lower brackets, the difference between relief and nonrelief farms was greater than shown in table 22.

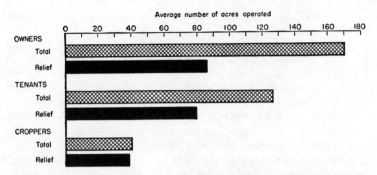

FIG. II – SIZE OF FARMS OPERATED BY FARMERS ON RELIEF IN JUNE 1935
AND BY ALL FARMERS REPORTED IN THE
1935 CENSUS OF AGRICULTURE

AF–2131, W.P.A.

There was less difference in size of farm between tenants (exclusive of croppers) on relief and tenants in the general population. It is probable that since the tenant class was of greater economic homogeneity, it was more uniformly affected by the depression than were the farm owners. Among owners, only the lower stratum, the marginal group, was forced by the depression to seek public aid, while the larger owners, on the whole, could rely on their own resources to weather the storm.

The difference in size of relief and total farms was least pronounced for the croppers, since cropper farms usually have a high percentage of land in cotton or tobacco and are adjusted in size to what one man can cultivate.

Farmers with comparatively large farms apparently found it relatively easy to become self-supporting again. A comparison of the February and June data on the acreage of relief farmers in all tenure groups showed a decided decrease in the median acreage in June as compared with February (table 23).

The differences in average size between February and June are striking because the combined number of farm operators on relief and rehabilitation in June was about seven-eighths of the number on relief in February. Owing to the turn-over in the relief population, however, they were not the same individuals. Some farmers had become self-supporting and had been replaced on relief rolls by others who had exhausted their resources. The change in average size of farms means, roughly, that those with the largest farms became self-supporting, those with the next largest farms were chosen as rehabilitation clients, while those with the smallest farms remained on relief. As recovery in agriculture becomes more general, the relief

TABLE 23.—ACREAGE OPERATED BY FARM OPERATOR HOUSEHOLDS ON RELIEF IN FEBRUARY AND JUNE 1935 AND BY RURAL REHABILITATION HOUSEHOLDS IN JUNE 1935, BY COLOR AND BY AREA

[138 counties representing 9 agricultural areas]

Area	Median acres per household								
	Owners			Tenants [1]			Croppers		
	Relief, February 1935	Relief, June 1935	Rehabilitation, June 1935	Relief, February 1935	Relief, June 1935	Rehabilitation, June 1935	Relief, February 1935	Relief, June 1935	Rehabilitation, June 1935
All areas	66	38	48	62	26	43	26	23	28
Eastern Cotton:									
Total	45	37	38	31	20	33	20	19	27
White	50	39	39	33	21	32	20	20	27
Negro	34	27	36	26	20	30	19	17	26
Western Cotton:									
Total	45	33	33	40	76	31	30	28	33
White	46	38	34	43	79	32	30	29	35
Negro	44	19	32	34	43	27	29	27	28
Appalachian-Ozark	34	24	44	14	10	40			
Lake States Cut-Over	63	29	58	83	45	70			
Hay and Dairy	84	46	58	106	76	92			
Corn Belt	99	77	87	145	103	120			
Spring Wheat	357	348	360	345	332	341			
Winter Wheat	159	144	198	145	96	159			
Ranching	170	162	149	145	120	160			

[1] Exclusive of croppers in the 2 Cotton Areas.

group will probably contain a larger proportion of chronic or marginal cases as measured by size of holdings.

Acreage alone is a crude measure of farm production. Unfortunately, the relationship between the quality of the land and farm relief incidence has not been accurately appraised. General evidence of this relationship is apparent from the high relief incidence in the poor land areas, such as the Appalachian-Ozark and Lake States Cut-Over, but this is not entirely conclusive, as other factors, such as size of farms and loss of supplementary employment, are also operating in these areas.

FARM EXPERIENCE

Farm families were not forced on relief by lack of agricultural experience. The great majority of the heads of farm families on relief had had 10 years or more of farm experience (table 24), indicating that the farm relief group was composed mostly of persons. for whom agriculture had been the lifelong job. The length of farm experience varied, however, with tenure status, partly due to existing age differences among the various agricultural groups. Of the farm owners, 82 percent had had 10 years or more of farm experience. Only 57 percent of the farm laborers had had as much experience. Nearly 70 percent of the tenants other than croppers and 63 percent.

of the croppers reported farm experience of 10 years and over. On the other hand, 29 percent of the farm laborers and 23 percent of the croppers had been engaged in agriculture for not more than 6 years, whereas only 11 percent of the owners and 19 percent of the other tenants fell into this category.

TABLE 24.—LENGTH OF FARM EXPERIENCE OF HEADS [1] OF RURAL RELIEF AND REHABILITATION HOUSEHOLDS, JUNE 1935

[138 counties representing 9 agricultural areas]

Usual occupation	Total		Years engaged in agriculture [2]			
	Number	Percent	1-3	4-6	7-9	10 and over
RELIEF						
Farm operators	18,026	100.0	5.7	10.8	10.6	72.9
Owners	6,396	100.0	4.0	6.5	7.2	82.3
Tenants [3]	8,586	100.0	6.5	12.2	12.0	69.3
Croppers	3,044	100.0	7.1	15.9	13.8	63.2
Farm laborers	6,722	100.0	10.4	18.6	13.8	57.2
REHABILITATION						
Farm operators	13,102	100.0	6.5	11.7	11.2	70.6
Owners	3,732	100.0	4.6	7.7	6.6	81.1
Tenants [3]	7,970	100.0	7.3	12.4	12.7	67.6
Croppers	1,400	100.0	6.7	18.6	14.6	60.1
Farm laborers	540	100.0	9.6	19.3	17.4	53.7

[1] With agriculture as the usual occupation.
[2] Since age 16.
[3] Exclusive of croppers in the 2 Cotton Areas.

A farm background was practically universal among the rehabilitation clients, and length of farm experience had evidently been a determining factor in their selection. Although only 89 percent of the rehabilitation clients were agricultural workers by usual occupation (appendix table 19), 98 out of 100 clients reported having had some farm experience since they were 16 years of age.

As in the case of heads of relief households, the length of farm experience of rehabilitation clients differed considerably among the various occupational groups, partly because of the differences in average age of these groups. Eighty-one percent of the farm owners who were rehabilitation clients had had 10 years or more of farm experience, while among the farm laborers only fifty-four percent had had such extensive experience. Of the tenants and croppers, 68 and 60 percent, respectively, reported at least 10 years of experience (table 24).

Whereas 29 percent of the farm laborers and 25 percent of the croppers on the rehabilitation program had had only 1 to 6 years of experience, only 20 percent of the other tenants and 12 percent of the owners had had so little experience.

OWNERSHIP OF LIVESTOCK

Many farm operators with adequate land resources were hampered in their efforts at self-support by lack of sufficient livestock. Some had lost their work stock and food animals through chattel mortgage foreclosure. Others had sold or eaten their domestic animals and were without breeding stock.

TABLE 25.—PERCENT OF RURAL RELIEF AND NONRELIEF HOUSEHOLDS THAT OWNED NO LIVESTOCK, JANUARY 1, 1934, BY SEX OF HEAD AND BY OCTOBER 1933 OCCUPATION OF MALE HEAD

Sex of head and October 1933 occupation of male head	Percent of households					
	Without cows		Without hogs		Without poultry	
	Relief	Nonrelief	Relief	Nonrelief	Relief	Nonrelief
All heads	68	47	72	65	45	34
Male heads	65	45	69	63	42	33
Farm owner	31	13	[1] 53	[1] 45	17	9
Cropper	50	54	44	39	20	10
Other tenant	27	15	35	29	12	7
Farm laborer	86	83	85	87	47	48
Nonagriculture	84	85	85	93	57	67
Unemployed	87	76	88	87	61	52
Female heads	89	72	91	84	72	53

[1] The smaller percentages for croppers and tenants than for owners are due to the concentration of owners in areas where few hogs were kept, especially the Dairy Area.

Source: McCormick, T. C., *Comparative Study of Rural Relief and Non-Relief Households*, Research Monograph II, Division of Social Research, Works Progress Administration, 1935, table Q.

Although no information on ownership of livestock was obtained in this study, data for January 1, 1934, are available from a survey of relief and nonrelief households.[3] Relatively fewer relief than nonrelief households were found owning livestock, and the relief families owning livestock had fewer animals than did families not on relief (tables 25 and 26 and appendix table 20).

TABLE 26.—AVERAGE NUMBER OF LIVESTOCK OWNED BY RURAL RELIEF AND NONRELIEF HOUSEHOLDS REPORTING SUCH LIVESTOCK, JANUARY 1, 1934, BY SEX OF HEAD AND BY OCTOBER 1933 OCCUPATION OF MALE HEAD

Sex of head and October 1933 occupation of male head	Average number of cows		Average number of hogs		Average number of poultry	
	Relief	Nonrelief	Relief	Nonrelief	Relief	Nonrelief
All heads	3.0	5.7	3.7	11.1	37	81
Male heads	3.0	6.2	3.8	11.4	38	81
Farm owner	3.5	6.8	4.6	13.0	49	110
Cropper	1.4	1.8	2.6	3.9	23	26
Other tenant	3.9	5.8	4.7	10.8	52	79
Farm laborer	1.8	1.6	1.8	2.9	32	34
Nonagriculture	1.4	1.9	2.1	6.0	23	32
Unemployed	1.4	2.4	1.9	4.3	27	40
Female heads	2.2	4.2	2.5	8.2	23	66

Source: McCormick, T. C., *Comparative Study of Rural Relief and Non-Relief Households*, Research Monograph II, Division of Social Research, Works Progress Administration, 1935, table R.

[3] McCormick, T. C., *Comparative Study of Rural Relief and Non-Relief Households*, Research Monograph II, Division of Social Research, Works Progress Administration, 1935, pp. 45–50, 98–99. Beck, P. G. and Forster, M. C., *Six Rural Problem Areas Relief—Resources—Rehabilitation*, Research Monograph I, Division of Research, Statistics, and Finance, Federal Emergency Relief Administration, 1935, pp. 129–130, also present data on ownership of livestock of relief families in six areas of high relief intensity.

Part of the differences in livestock ownership between relief and nonrelief farmers was associated with differences in size of farm between the two groups, the relief group being concentrated on the smaller farms. Size of farm, however, cannot explain all of the difference between relief and nonrelief farmers in the extent of livestock ownership. In all but one acreage class smaller proportions of relief than nonrelief farmers owned work animals and in most acreage classes the relief operators owned fewer animals than the nonrelief (table 27).

TABLE 27.—PERCENT OF RURAL RELIEF AND NONRELIEF FARM OPERATORS, OTHER THAN CROPPERS, WHO OWNED NO WORK STOCK, AND THE AVERAGE NUMBER OF WORK STOCK OWNED ON JANUARY 1, 1934, BY FARM OPERATORS WITH WORK STOCK, BY ACREAGE GROUPS

Acreage	Percent of farm owners and tenants without work stock		Average number of work stock owned by farm operators with work stock	
	Relief	Nonrelief	Relief	Nonrelief
All acreage groups	34	18	3. 6	4. 2
Under 10 acres	80	72	1. 6	1. 6
10 to 19 acres	71	52	1. 4	1. 5
20 to 49 acres	48	39	1. 9	2. 1
50 to 99 acres	29	15	2. 3	2. 9
100 to 174 acres	18	12	3. 2	3. 7
175 to 259 acres	13	6	4. 5	4. 4
260 to 379 acres	12	7	6. 0	5. 9
380 to 499 acres	5	9	6. 8	7. 2
500 to 749 acres	35	13	6. 4	8. 7
750 to 999 acres	23	10	9. 1	9. 9
1,000 to 4,999 acres	(¹)	12	(¹)	11. 7
5,000 acres and over	(¹)	(¹)	(¹)	(¹)

¹ Less than 10 cases. Average not computed.

Source: McCormick, T. C., *Comparative Study of Rural Relief and Non-Relief Households*, Research Monograph II, Division of Social Research, Works Progress Administration, 1935, table P.

Relatively more farm owners than tenants owned cows, hogs, and poultry in most areas surveyed. In both tenures more nonrelief than relief farmers owned such livestock, and greater numbers of all three types of livestock were owned by nonrelief farmers (tables 25 and 26 and appendix tables 21 and 22).

In the case of sharecroppers, who owned less livestock than other southern farmers, there was little difference between relief and nonrelief groups in the number reporting livestock. Relief status also made little difference in the ownership of livestock among farm laborer heads of families.

The extent of ownership of livestock varied considerably from area to area, depending on the prevalent type of farming and size of farm. In such part-time or truck farming regions as California, Oregon, and Massachusetts, at least three-fourths of the farmers on relief and about half or more of the nonrelief group had no work animals, whereas in the Wheat, Cash Grain, New Mexico, and

Tobacco Regions, at least five out of six of both relief and nonrelief groups had horses or mules (appendix table 20).

The difference between relief and nonrelief groups in the proportion owning work stock was particularly marked in the Old South Cotton, Corn-and-Hog, Cut-Over, and Dairy Regions. Only in the Tobacco Area did relatively more relief than nonrelief farmers own work animals.

Generally in areas where high percentages of farm operators owned work animals, the average number of animals owned was also large (appendix table 20). Farm operators on relief in most areas who owned any work stock at all usually had one team, but in the Mountain, Cash Grain, and Wheat Areas they averaged more than three animals each, while the nonrelief farmers in these and the Corn-and-Hog and Southwest Cotton Areas averaged four or more work animals apiece. In most areas nonrelief operators owned an average of at least one more work animal than did relief operators.

EDUCATION

It is readily understandable that farm tenants and laborers could become dislocated from the land and thus lose their ability to earn a living, but it is more difficult to conceive why, except in case of crop failure, an owner of land with a house for shelter and with work stock, cows, pigs, and poultry should become dependent upon public aid. However, even when such measurable factors of difference between relief and nonrelief farmers are accounted for, there still remains the intangible complex of personality traits which determine success and failure.

One of the few measurable indices of difference in the quality of the relief and nonrelief populations is the difference in educational attainment. This is shown by data from the relief and nonrelief study previously referred to (table 28). These percentages are used for comparison of relief and nonrelief groups in the whole

TABLE 28.—GRADE ATTAINMENT OF HEADS OF RURAL RELIEF AND NONRELIEF HOUSEHOLDS, OCTOBER 1933

Grade attainment	Percent distribution	
	Relief	Nonrelief
Total	100	100
No schooling	8	3
Partial grade school only	46	31
Completed grade school only	29	36
Partial high school only	12	15
Completed high school only	3	8
College	2	7

Source: McCormick, T. C., *Comparative Study of Rural Relief and Non-Relief Households.*, Research Monograph II, Division of Social Research, Works Progress Administration, 1935, tables J and K.

rural population, however, and are not indicative of the grade attainment of the farm operator group on relief.

The grade attainment of heads of open country households receiving relief in October 1935 is shown in table 29 and figure 12. Since most of these are agricultural households, the data may be considered as representative of the educational status of the farm group.

TABLE 29.—GRADE ATTAINMENT OF HEADS OF OPEN COUNTRY HOUSEHOLDS ON RELIEF, OCTOBER 1935

[138 counties representing 9 agricultural areas]

Grade attainment	Percent distribution	Grade attainment	Percent distribution
Number_____	23, 530	Completed grade school only_____	22. 0
Percent_____	100. 0	Partial high school only_____	5. 8
		Completed high school only_____	1. 5
No schooling_____	10. 7	College_____	. 6
Partial grade school only_____	59. 4		

When the heads of families on relief, 35 years of age and over, in the open country in October 1935 are considered, the educational attainments appear even lower (appendix table 23). Of the heads 35–44 years of age, 10 percent had never completed a grade in school, while 14 percent of those 45–54 years of age and 21 percent of those 55–64 years of age had had no schooling. The better grade attainment record of the heads 16–24 years of age and 25–34 years of age reflects the improvement in rural educational opportunities in the past generation.

On the average, heads of open country relief households had completed at least the seventh grade in all areas except the Appalachian-Ozark and Cotton Areas (appendix table 24). In four areas—

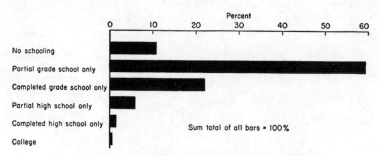

FIG. 12 – GRADE ATTAINMENT OF HEADS OF OPEN COUNTRY HOUSEHOLDS ON RELIEF
October 1935

AF-2125, W.P.A.

Rural School

Spring and Winter Wheat, Ranching, and Corn Belt—the average head of an open country relief household had completed the eighth grade.

Differences in grade attainment by areas reflect well-known differences in educational opportunity. Negroes in the Eastern Cotton Belt had received just half as much education, on the average, as the whites. White heads of open country families had not completed the sixth grade, while Negro heads had not finished the third year of school on the average. In the Western Cotton Area the average school attainment of Negroes was about a year less than that of whites.

CHAPTER VII

RELIEF TRENDS, 1933 THROUGH 1935

WHEN THE Federal Emergency Relief Administration was established in the spring of 1933,[1] provision was made for extending unemployment relief to farm operators who could not make a living on their farms as well as to unemployed farm laborers and to farmers who had lost their land.

In October 1933, 5 months after the inauguration of the Federal Emergency Relief Administration, an estimated 417,000 farm operators (over 6 percent of all farmers in 1935), plus an undetermined number of farm laborers, were receiving Federal-State assistance through the Emergency Relief Administrations (table 30). During the next 12 months, which witnessed the widespread drought of 1934, the number of farmers on general relief or rehabilitation rolls increased 58 percent, the estimated number rising from 417,000 to 659,000.

Both drought and depression effects were cumulative during the months following October 1934. In spite of the fact that all indices of rural prosperity were showing an upward trend from their low point in 1932, the peak period for Federal assistance to farm families came during the winter of 1934–35. From October 1934 to February 1935 the estimated number of farmers receiving general relief grants or rehabilitation loans increased about 4 percent, reaching a peak of 685,000 cases, more than 10 percent of all farmers in the United States at that time [2] (table 30 and figure 13). These included 598,000 farm operators on general relief rolls and 87,000 farm operators receiving aid in the form of rehabilitation loans. In addition, an estimated 279,000 farm laborer families were on general relief rolls making a total of 964,000 agricultural families in rural areas receiving assistance.[3]

---

[1] See chapter II.

[2] *United States Census of Agriculture: 1935.*

[3] For an estimate including farmers or farm laborers living in cities and total rural rehabilitation clients under care, see chapter I.

TABLE 30.—NUMBER OF FARM OPERATORS IN RURAL AREAS RECEIVING FEDERAL ASSISTANCE, BY TYPE OF ASSISTANCE, OCTOBER 1933 THROUGH DECEMBER 1935 [1]

Month	Number				Percent			
	Total [2]	General relief [3]	Rehabilitation [4]	Works Program [5]	Total	General relief	Rehabilitation	Works Program
October 1933	417,000	417,000			100	100		
October 1934	659,000	613,000	46,000		100	93	7	
February 1935	685,000	598,000	87,000		100	87	13	
June 1935	594,000	390,000	204,000		100	66	34	
October 1935	382,000	290,000	58,000	34,000	100	76	15	9
December 1935	396,000	54,000	[6] 156,000	186,000	100	14	39	47

[1] General relief and Works Program cases as estimated; rehabilitation cases as reported.
[2] Cases that received general relief and Works Program earnings during the same month are as a general rule allocated to the Works Program category exclusively in this table. A few such duplicated cases are, however, counted in both categories. Likewise, cases that received both general relief and rehabilitation advances during the same month are generally allocated to the rehabilitation category exclusively but a few duplications of this type are counted in both categories.
[3] Slightly less than 2 percent of these farm operators lived in small towns of 2,500 to 5,000 population. Data are estimated as of end of month.
[4] Number of clients receiving advances during the month. Prior to July 1, 1935, rehabilitation clients were included in the Federal Emergency Relief Administration program. On that date they were taken over by the Resettlement Administration. The relatively small number of clients to whom State rehabilitation corporations continued to make advances after July 1 are not included.
[5] Exclusive of Civilian Conservation Corps.
[6] Loan cases 26,000; grant cases 130,000.

Sources: Survey of Current Changes in the Rural Relief Population; *Monthly Reports of the Federal Emergency Relief Administration;* and Resettlement Administration.

After February 1935, the number of farmers receiving aid began to decline. By June, the estimated number of clients stood at 594,000, about 13 percent less than in February. During the 4 months following June 1935, the rate of decrease was accelerated as a result of several factors, the most important of which were: (a) curtailment

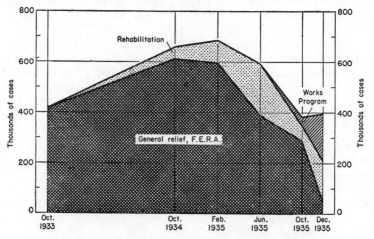

FIG. 13—NUMBER OF FARM OPERATORS BY USUAL OCCUPATION
RECEIVING FEDERAL ASSISTANCE
IN RURAL AREAS
October 1933 – December 1935

AF-2137, W.P.A.

of the number receiving rehabilitation loans as Resettlement slowly got under way (see pp. 21 and 22); (b) restriction of general relief funds as plans got under way for abandoning the general relief program and for inaugurating a works program; and (c) the progress of economic recovery.

During the last months of 1935, the number of farmers receiving Federal assistance rose again. Many families that were able to support themselves during the summer months needed aid with the approach of the winter season. The Works Program employed some, the Emergency Relief Administrations continued to extend general assistance to others, and the Resettlement Administration made a limited number of loans. These means of assistance proved inadequate to meet winter needs, and in November 1935, the Resettlement Administration began to make emergency subsistence grants which were comparable to general relief grants under the F. E. R. A.

The combined number of farm operators aided under these several programs was estimated at 396,000 in December 1935, an increase of about 4 percent since October (table 30 and figure 13).

CHARACTERISTICS OF THE FEBRUARY 1935 GENERAL RELIEF LOAD

First Receipt of Relief.

The bulk of the February 1935 cases had come on relief in 1934 or 1935. Ten percent of all employable [4] rural cases on relief in February sought aid for the first time during January or February of 1935, and about fifty-five percent first received relief in 1934. Twenty-four percent, however, had first received relief in 1933, and eleven percent had first received aid prior to that year (table 31).[5]

TABLE 31.—YEAR OF FIRST RECEIPT OF RELIEF BY EMPLOYABLE [1] RURAL HOUSEHOLDS,[2] BY RESIDENCE, FEBRUARY 1935

[138 counties representing 9 agricultural areas]

Year of first accession to relief	Number			Percent		
	Rural	Open country	Village	Rural	Open country	Village
Total	71, 898	49, 202	22, 696	100. 0	100. 0	100. 0
1935	7, 286	4, 745	2, 541	10. 1	9. 6	11. 2
1934	39, 435	27, 880	11, 555	54. 9	56. 7	50. 9
1933	17, 407	11, 792	5, 615	24. 2	24. 0	24. 7
1932	7, 770	4, 785	2, 985	10. 8	9. 7	13. 2

[1] A case was classified as employable if it contained 1 or more members, 16–64 years of age, working or seeking work.
[2] Exclusive of cases whose relief history was not determined.

[4] A case was classified as employable if it had one or more members, 16–64 years of age, working or seeking work.
[5] Data are presented by "open country" and "village" due to lack of information on time of accession by "agricultural" and "nonagricultural" groups. These two methods

Geographical Location.

Agricultural cases on relief in February 1935 were concentrated in drought-stricken and poor land areas.

In the Spring Wheat Area, the section hardest hit by drought, nearly one-third of all farm operators were on relief in February 1935 (table 37). The relief intensity rate for this area was three times greater than that for all areas for which information was collected. Other areas hard hit by the 1934 drought also had high proportions of farmers on relief, notably the Western Cotton and Winter Wheat Areas.

Areas of concentration outside the major drought sections were the poor land areas—Lake States Cut-Over and Appalachian-Ozark. On the other hand, the proportion of farmers on relief was below average in the Corn Belt and in the Hay and Dairy Area, relatively prosperous regions, and in the Eastern Cotton Belt, where the rural rehabilitation program had had its greatest development.

Reasons for Accessions.

Drought was the largest single factor forcing farm families on relief during the months preceding February 1935. More than 37 percent of the open country cases were farmers who were known to have sought relief as a direct result of crop failure or loss of livestock (table 32).

About 17 percent of all open country cases on relief in February were households whose breadwinners had lost their jobs within 4 months of the accession date and had been forced to apply for relief for this reason. This group was made up for the most part of unemployed farm laborers, although it included some farm operators who had lost their off-the-farm employment.

Loss of job was given as a reason for accession only in instances where such loss represented the most recent change in economic status which cost the household its self-sufficiency. In those instances where the wage earner had been unemployed more than 4 months before his household used up its savings and sought relief, the reason given for accession was "loss or depletion of assets." About 24 percent of all open country cases receiving relief in February 1935 had sought relief after loss or depletion of assets. Among these were farm operators who had lost their farms as well as laborers who had lost their jobs.

An additional 10 percent of the cases had been accepted for relief because their current income had been reduced to a point where it

---

of classifying heads of relief cases do not give identical results since some agricultural workers reside in villages and some nonagricultural workers reside in the open country. Moreover, not all open country and village heads are gainful workers. However, the great bulk of open country heads are agricultural workers and the great bulk of village heads are nonagricultural workers.

was insufficient to meet minimum budget needs. The remaining 11 percent consisted of cases that had sought relief only when the household lost its last or only breadwinner, due to old age, death, disability, or separation, and of cases opened for such miscellaneous reasons as illness and loss of support from relatives and friends (table 32).

TABLE 32.—REASONS FOR ACCESSION TO RELIEF OF RURAL HOUSEHOLDS, BY RESIDENCE, FEBRUARY AND JUNE 1935

[138 counties representing 9 agricultural areas]

Reason for accession	February			June			Percent change February to June		
	Rural	Open country	Village	Rural	Open country	Village	Rural	Open country	Village
Number	84,101	56,736	27,365	58,516	35,802	22,714			
Percent	100.0	100.0	100.0	100.0	100.0	100.0	−30.4	−36.9	−17.0
Loss or depletion of assets	26.6	24.2	31.9	32.6	31.7	33.9	−15.2	−17.5	−11.6
Crop failure or loss of livestock	26.3	37.3	3.4	14.6	22.1	2.7	−61.4	−62.6	−34.8
Loss of job	24.3	17.2	39.1	24.4	17.7	35.0	−30.1	−35.0	−25.6
Insufficient income	10.3	10.0	11.0	12.2	13.1	10.9	−17.8	−17.0	−17.4
Became unemployable	4.7	4.2	5.6	5.1	4.7	5.8	−23.5	−29.0	−14.8
Other reasons	7.8	7.1	9.0	11.1	10.7	11.7	−0.6	−5.3	+7.1

First-Period Cases in the February Load.

About two-thirds of all open country households receiving relief in February had remained continuously on the relief rolls since they first received aid. The proportion was about the same for cases added because of crop failure or loss of livestock and those added because of loss or depletion of assets. Of those households receiving relief as a result of loss of job, a larger proportion had been on and off relief rolls since they first received aid, whereas, among households added because they became unemployable, nearly three-fourths had received relief continuously since they first went on the rolls (table 33).

TABLE 33.—REASONS FOR ACCESSION TO RELIEF OF OPEN COUNTRY HOUSEHOLDS IN THEIR FIRST RELIEF PERIOD, FEBRUARY AND JUNE 1935

[138 counties representing 9 agricultural areas]

Reason for accession	February			June		
	Total cases	First-period cases		Total cases	First-period cases	
		Number	Percent		Number	Percent
Total	56,736	36,197	63.8	35,802	19,890	55.6
Loss or depletion of assets	13,713	8,952	65.3	11,312	6,558	58.0
Crop failure or loss of livestock	21,171	13,992	66.0	7,928	4,390	55.4
Loss of job	9,754	5,662	58.0	6,338	3,344	52.8
Insufficient income	5,649	3,313	58.6	4,686	2,386	50.9
Became unemployable	2,390	1,736	72.6	1,696	1,134	66.9
Other reasons	4,059	2,542	62.6	3,842	2,078	54.1

CHANGES FROM FEBRUARY THROUGH JUNE 1935

Farm families left the relief rolls rapidly after February 1935. Of all agricultural cases on relief in February, only 42 percent remained on relief through the month of June, while 58 percent were either closed or transferred to the rural rehabilitation program before June 30 (table 34 and appendix table 25). These proportions were true of farm owners and farm tenants other than sharecroppers, but among sharecroppers only 27 percent of the February cases were carried through June on general relief rolls. One-half of the farm laborers remained on relief through June. In contrast, the majority (63 percent) of the nonagricultural cases on rural relief rolls in February still received assistance in June.

TABLE 34.—ACCESSION, SEPARATION, AND CARRY-OVER RATES [1] OF RURAL HOUSEHOLDS RECEIVING RELIEF, BY USUAL OCCUPATION OF THE HEAD, FEBRUARY THROUGH JUNE 1935

[138 counties representing 9 agricultural areas]

Usual occupation	February cases	Percent of February cases		Accessions March–June per 100 cases in February		
		Carried through June	Separated prior to June [2]	Total	New	Reopened
Total	71,340	49.9	50.1	17.6	7.5	10.1
Agriculture	44,651	42.3	57.7	13.6	5.1	8.5
Owners	10,995	42.7	57.3	15.6	5.3	10.3
Tenants [3]	17,432	42.1	57.9	13.5	4.8	8.7
Croppers	5,486	27.2	72.8	9.7	3.7	6.0
Laborers	10,738	50.1	49.9	13.7	6.3	7.4
Nonagriculture	26,689	62.5	37.5	24.2	11.5	12.7

[1] Cases opened and closed in the interim, March through June, but which did not receive relief in February or June, are not included in the rates as here computed. Separations include cases on relief in February only and accessions include cases on relief in June only.
[2] Including transfers to rural rehabilitation.
[3] Exclusive of croppers in the 2 Cotton Areas.

In the Western Cotton Area, where large numbers of clients were transferred from general relief to the rural rehabilitation program, only 28 percent of the February farm relief families remained on general relief in June. At the other extreme was the Appalachian-Ozark Area where relatively few rehabilitation transfers occurred. Here more than two-thirds of the February cases remained on relief in June (table 35).

Few farm families that left relief during the spring months returned to the rolls before the end of June.[6] Reopenings were more numerous among nonagricultural heads (table 34). Extension of

---

[6] Not all June cases that were reopened during the months March through June received relief in February. Some were closed prior to February and reopened after February. A few were opened, closed, and reopened after February.

special aid under the rural rehabilitation program, and a favorable planting season in most of the country in 1935 probably accounted largely for the greater ability of farm families to remain independent of general public aid.

TABLE 35.—CARRY-OVER RATES OF RURAL HOUSEHOLDS RECEIVING RELIEF, BY USUAL OCCUPATION OF THE HEAD AND BY AREA, FEBRUARY THROUGH JUNE 1935

[138 counties representing 9 agricultural areas]

Area	Percent of February cases carried through June						
	All heads	Agricultural heads					Nonagricultural heads
		Total	Owners	Tenants [1]	Croppers	Laborers	
All areas	49. 9	42. 3	42. 7	42. 1	27. 2	50. 1	62. 5
Eastern Cotton:							
Total	40. 7	35. 5	35. 4	32. 2	28. 0	43. 9	54. 6
White	38. 6	32. 6	37. 7	29. 1	27. 7	38. 5	54. 2
Negro	45. 3	41. 7	27. 8	39. 7	29. 1	51. 0	55. 5
Western Cotton:							
Total	32. 6	28. 1	13. 8	25. 1	26. 5	43. 5	53. 8
White	35. 7	31. 4	15. 5	28. 0	29. 1	49. 3	54. 2
Negro	25. 0	20. 5	10. 7	16. 6	21. 3	31. 2	52. 7
Appalachian-Ozark	71. 1	68. 5	70. 7	69. 0		54. 8	73. 7
Lake States Cut-Over	56. 9	42. 9	39. 6	38. 3		89. 7	70. 1
Hay and Dairy	50. 2	43. 3	36. 6	39. 1		55. 0	55. 6
Corn Belt	48. 3	39. 6	31. 9	29. 1		58. 6	60. 6
Spring Wheat	54. 6	51. 7	53. 5	50. 2		54. 2	68. 2
Winter Wheat	47. 1	39. 8	26. 0	41. 1		55. 1	66. 3
Ranching	48. 6	47. 7	46. 3	49. 1		48. 1	50. 1

[1] Exclusive of croppers in the 2 Cotton Areas.

TABLE 36.—PERCENT CHANGE IN THE NUMBER OF EMPLOYABLE [1] RURAL RELIEF HOUSEHOLDS, BY USUAL OCCUPATION OF THE HEAD AND BY AREA, FEBRUARY THROUGH JUNE 1935

[138 counties representing 9 agricultural areas]

Area	Usual occupation of head						
	All heads	Agricultural heads					Nonagricultural heads
		Total	Owners	Tenants [2]	Croppers	Laborers	
All areas	−32. 5	−44. 1	−41. 7	−44. 4	−64. 1	−36. 2	−13. 3
Eastern Cotton:							
Total	−38. 7	−49. 1	−45. 2	−51. 4	−55. 6	−43. 4	−10. 7
White	−39. 1	−51. 0	−40. 4	−56. 1	−55. 7	−46. 8	−7. 9
Negro	−37. 9	−45. 1	−61. 5	−39. 9	−55. 1	−39. 2	−17. 4
Western Cotton:							
Total	−58. 7	−65. 7	−82. 7	−68. 7	−69. 0	−46. 8	−25. 1
White	−54. 1	−61. 4	−80. 5	−65. 1	−65. 8	−38. 8	−22. 7
Negro	−69. 7	−75. 6	−86. 7	−79. 3	−75. 3	−63. 8	−32. 8
Appalachian-Ozark	+1. 1	−1. 1	+3. 0	−2. 8		−7. 0	+3. 3
Lake States Cut-Over	−22. 0	−47. 3	−50. 7	−53. 7		+5. 9	+2. 0
Hay and Dairy	−36. 4	−47. 7	−55. 1	−53. 7		−33. 3	−27. 5
Corn Belt	−38. 0	−49. 6	−55. 7	−61. 5		−29. 1	−21. 7
Spring Wheat	−33. 0	−36. 3	−30. 6	−40. 1		−33. 9	−17. 4
Winter Wheat	−38. 2	−47. 0	−67. 5	−47. 5		−17. 4	−14. 8
Ranching	−27. 4	−34. 3	−34. 5	−37. 1		−32. 5	−16. 6

[1] A case was classified as employable if it contained 1 or more members, 16-64 years of age, working or seeking work.
[2] Exclusive of croppers in the 2 Cotton Areas.

Not only did greater proportions of agricultural than of non-agricultural cases leave relief rolls in the spring of 1935, but relatively fewer agricultural than nonagricultural cases came on relief during the period (appendix table 25). As a result, the farm group declined 44 percent from February through June, while the nonfarm group declined only 13 percent (table 36).

Relatively more owners than tenants came on relief during the season. Croppers not only left the relief rolls faster than any other group but they also came on the rolls at a slower rate. While farm laborers in the February case load went off relief less rapidly than did other agricultural heads, they came on relief during the 4 months following February at about the same rate as did owners and tenants.

REDISTRIBUTION OF THE GENERAL RELIEF LOAD, JUNE 1935

As a result of different rates at which various groups in the rural relief population left the rolls or came on relief, the relief population changed considerably between February and June in both its geographical and its occupational distribution.

Geographical Redistribution.

In the Western Cotton Area, as an extreme example, the number of farmers on general relief in June was less than one-third of the number on relief in February. This area, which had contained 24 percent of all farmers on relief in the nine areas sampled in February, contained only 13 percent of them in June (table 37).

TABLE 37.—ESTIMATED NUMBER OF FARM OPERATORS RECEIVING RELIEF IN NINE AGRICULTURAL AREAS, FEBRUARY AND JUNE 1935, AND THEIR RATIO TO ALL FARM OPERATORS IN JANUARY 1935

[138 counties representing 9 agricultural areas]

Area	Farm operators on relief				Farm operators on relief as percent of all farm operators in 1935 [1]	
	Number		Percent			
	February	June	February	June	February	June
All areas	404,000	214,000	100	100	10.0	5.4
Western Cotton	96,000	28,000	24	13	19.5	5.5
Appalachian-Ozark	74,000	73,000	18	34	12.2	12.1
Eastern Cotton	69,000	33,000	17	16	4.8	2.3
Corn Belt	54,000	22,000	13	10	7.0	2.8
Hay and Dairy	36,000	16,000	9	8	6.2	2.8
Spring Wheat	29,000	19,000	7	9	31.5	20.0
Lake States Cut-Over	26,000	13,000	7	6	22.0	10.7
Winter Wheat	16,000	7,500	4	3	13.3	6.2
Ranching	4,000	2,500	1	1	9.4	6.1

[1] *United States Census of Agriculture: 1935.*

The Appalachian-Ozark Area showed the opposite tendency. As a result of lack of movement off relief rolls, the proportion of all farmers on relief in this area nearly doubled, increasing from 18 percent in February to 34 percent in June.

The total farm operator general relief load declined from 10.0 percent of all farm operators in the United States in February to 5.4 percent in June.[7]

Occupational Redistribution.

Farmers and farm laborers accounted for 63 percent of all employable heads of February rural relief cases with occupational experience, nonagricultural workers accounting for only 37 percent. Due in large measure to transfers of farmers to the rural rehabilitation program, the agricultural proportion of the total decreased to 52 percent in June, while the nonfarm proportion increased to 48 percent. The proportions of sharecroppers and other tenants in the rural relief load showed the greatest reductions between February and June (table 38).

TABLE 38.—USUAL OCCUPATION OF EMPLOYABLE HEADS [1] OF RURAL RELIEF HOUSEHOLDS, FEBRUARY AND JUNE 1935

[138 counties representing 9 agricultural areas]

| Usual occupation | Rural relief cases | | | |
| | Number | | Percent | |
	February	June	February	June
Total	71,340	48,112	100.0	100.0
Agriculture	44,651	24,976	62.6	51.9
Owners	10,995	6,418	15.4	13.3
Tenants[2]	17,432	9,684	24.4	20.2
Croppers	5,486	2,024	7.7	4.2
Laborers	10,738	6,850	15.1	14.2
Nonagriculture	26,689	23,136	37.4	48.1

[1] 16–64 years of age and working or seeking work.
[2] Exclusive of croppers in the 2 Cotton Areas.

---

[7] Farm operators on general relief rolls declined during the spring of 1935 much more rapidly in the nine agricultural areas than outside those areas. Estimates indicate that for the country as a whole farm operators on relief decreased from 598,000 in February to 390,000 in June, a decline of only 35 percent. During this same time farmers on relief in the 9 areas sampled dropped from 404,000 to 214,000, a decline of 47 percent (table 37). This differential rate of change was a result of concentration, within the areas, of loans extended under the rehabilitation program, much of the decline in general relief case loads being due to transfers of farmers to this special program. It is estimated that 67 percent of all farm operators on general relief were located within the nine agricultural areas in February. By June this proportion had declined to 55 percent.

CHARACTERISTICS OF THE JUNE 1935 GENERAL RELIEF LOAD

More than three-fourths of all agricultural cases on general relief in June 1935 had received relief each month since February (table 39). The other 24 percent of the June load was made up of cases added during the 4 months following February. Hence, while the bulk of the June cases were continuous from February, 15 percent were reopened cases and 9 percent were cases that came on relief for the first time during the spring of 1935. The proportions differed little among the various occupational groups.

TABLE 39.—USUAL OCCUPATION OF EMPLOYABLE [1] HEADS OF RURAL RELIEF HOUSEHOLDS, BY PERCENT CARRIED OVER FROM FEBRUARY THROUGH JUNE 1935 AND BY ACCESSSIONS FROM MARCH THROUGH JUNE 1935

[138 counties representing 9 agricultural areas]

Usual occupation	February cases		June cases			
				Percent distribution		
	Number	Percent carried over through June	Number	Carried over from February	Reopened March–June	Opened March–June
Total_____	71,340	49.9	48,112	73.9	14.9	11.2
Agriculture_____	44,651	42.3	24,976	75.7	15.1	9.2
Owners_____	10,995	42.7	6,418	73.2	17.8	9.0
Tenants [2]_____	17,432	42.1	9,684	75.7	15.6	8.7
Croppers_____	5,486	27.2	2,024	73.6	16.3	10.1
Laborers_____	10,738	50.1	6,850	78.5	11.7	9.8
Nonagriculture_____	26,689	62.5	23,136	72.1	14.6	13.3

[1] 16–64 years of age and working or seeking work.
[2] Exclusive of croppers in the 2 Cotton Areas.

Only 22 percent of all June open country cases had come on relief because of crop failure or loss of livestock. The proportions that were opened or reopened because of loss or depletion of assets, insufficient income, and miscellaneous reasons showed gains over February (table 32).

CHARACTERISTICS OF THE GENERAL RELIEF LOAD, JULY THROUGH DECEMBER 1935

At the end of June 1935, plans were under way for getting the new Federal Works Program into operation and for tapering off the activities of the Federal Emergency Relief Administration. At that time it is estimated that 390,000 farm operator heads and 147,000 farm laborer heads of rural households were receiving general relief.

During the last 6 months of 1935, about 215,000 farm operator families were accepted for general relief by agencies expending F. E. R. A. funds (table 40). About 41,000 (19 percent) of these additions were families not previously known to the accepting agencies. The other 174,000 were families which were forced to return to relief after a period of self-maintenance.

Some light is thrown on the type of family represented by the 41,000 farm operator families who were new to relief agencies by figures available for the cases opened from July through October. In those 4 months, 21 percent of all accessions of farm families and 30 percent of nonfarm families came on relief for the first time. A higher proportion of such cases was found among farm laborers (22 percent) and croppers (42 percent) than among owners (15 percent) and tenants (16 percent). The smallest proportion of cases coming on relief for the first time was found in the northern States,[8] where only 10 percent of the farm operators and 20 percent of the farm laborers had not previously received relief. The highest proportions were in the New England States of Connecticut and Massachusetts[9] (appendix table 26).

The accession of 215,000 farm families during the last 6 months of 1935 was more than offset by about 551,000 farm families that left the relief rolls of agencies financed by the F. E. R. A., making a net decrease of 336,000 farm families (table 40 and figures 14 and 15).[10]

TABLE 40.—FARM OPERATOR ACCESSIONS TO, AND SEPARATIONS FROM, THE RELIEF ROLLS OF AGENCIES EXPENDING FEDERAL EMERGENCY RELIEF ADMINISTRATION FUNDS, JULY THROUGH DECEMBER 1935

Item	Number		Percent
	Sample counties [1]	Estimate for United States	
All accessions	19,970	215,000	100
New cases	3,764	41,000	19
Reopened cases	16,206	174,000	81
All separations	55,890	551,000	100
To Works Program	18,661	186,000	34
To Resettlement Administration [2]	3,690	37,000	6
Other reasons	33,539	328,000	60

[1] The 300 counties and 83 New England townships included in the State sample contained 8.8 percent of all rural families in the United States in 1930 and 10.0 percent of all farm operators in 1935.
[2] Whereas only an estimated 37,000 cases were transferred directly from general relief rolls to rehabilitation during the period, an undetermined number of cases which had gone off relief for other reasons were given loans or grants.

Only 54,000 farmers and their families remained on F. E. R. A. relief rolls at the end of December 1935 (appendix table 27).

Reasons for Accessions, July Through October.

It may seem paradoxical that during the time when the Federal Government was completing plans for getting out of the business of direct relief, a fifth of a million farm operator families should

[8] Analysis is made by regional groups of States in this section rather than by agricultural areas in order to have the advantage of a larger sample, first available in June 1935. See appendix B.
[9] The number of cases in the sample was very small, however.
[10] Also, see appendix tables 38 and 39.

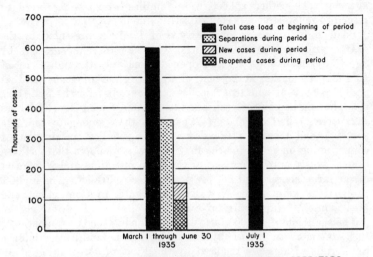

FIG. 14 – CHANGES IN ESTIMATED NUMBER OF FARM OPERATORS
RECEIVING GENERAL RELIEF*

March through June 1935**

(Estimated from survey of 138 counties)

*From agencies expending F. E. R. A. funds
**Exclusive of those cases that were opened or reopened
and also closed during the four months' period   AF – 2149, W.P.A.

be accepted for direct relief. It appears, however, that the same
factors which brought families onto relief in the earlier periods
were still operating in the last half of 1935.

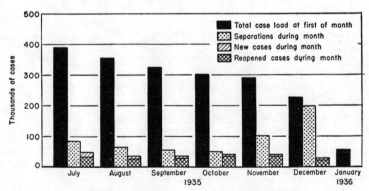

FIG. 15 – CHANGES DURING MONTH IN ESTIMATED NUMBER OF FARM
OPERATORS RECEIVING GENERAL RELIEF*

July through December 1935

(Estimated from survey of 300 counties and 83 New England townships)

*From agencies expending F. E. R. A. funds   AF – 2151, W.P.A.

TABLE 41.—REASONS FOR ACCESSION TO RURAL RELIEF OF FARM HOUSE-
HOLDS, JULY THROUGH OCTOBER 1935

[300 counties and 83 New England townships]

Reason for accession	Usual occupation of head				
	Farm operators				Farm laborers
	Total	Owners	Tenants[1]	Croppers	
Number	13,384	4,294	6,488	2,602	7,806
Percent	100.0	100.0	100.0	100.0	100.0
Loss or depletion of assets	10.3	13.0	8.7	9.8	6.3
Crop failure or loss of livestock	32.3	36.9	34.4	19.1	1.8
Loss of employment:					
Private employment	11.3	9.9	10.8	14.8	63.3
Works Program	.6	.9	.7	.1	.7
Decreased earnings	16.4	17.7	17.2	12.3	12.5
Increased needs	9.8	10.3	9.9	8.8	8.0
Administrative ruling	9.4	6.6	12.4	6.6	5.0
All others	9.9	4.7	5.9	28.5	2.4

[1] Exclusive of croppers in the Southern States.

Crop failure and livestock loss were the most important factors
responsible for farm operator families going on relief during the 4
months July through October 1935.[11] They accounted for 37 percent of all farm owners and 34 percent of all tenants who went on
relief during the period (table 41).

The States where the largest proportions of cases came on relief
because of crop failure or loss of livestock were North Dakota and

TABLE 42.—FARM OPERATOR ACCESSIONS TO RURAL RELIEF ROLLS, FOR ALL
REASONS AND BECAUSE OF CROP FAILURE OR LOSS OF LIVESTOCK, BY STATE,
JULY THROUGH OCTOBER 1935

[300 counties and 83 New England townships]

State	Total accessions	Cases added because of crop failure or loss of livestock	
		Number	Percent
Total, 32 States	13,384	4,322	32.3
North Dakota	1,362	1,174	86.2
Missouri	856	550	64.3
South Dakota	406	252	62.1
Montana	196	120	61.2
Louisiana	830	440	53.0
Tennessee	218	112	51.4
Nebraska	208	86	41.3
Texas	678	274	40.4
Colorado	200	80	40.0
Ohio	234	74	31.6
South Carolina	494	146	29.6
Florida	366	108	29.5
Georgia	260	66	25.4
19 other States	7,076	840	11.9

[11] Data not complete for November and December.

Missouri. In seven additional States, however, at least 40 percent of all farm cases added from July through October were accepted for this reason (table 42).

Other major factors causing farm families to seek relief during the period July through October 1935 were loss of employment or decreased earnings (table 41 and appendix table 28). These factors affected farm owners, tenants, and croppers about equally (27 to 29 percent). They were much more important in the case of farm laborers [12]—more than 63 percent of all farm laborers added to relief rolls during the period had recently lost their jobs, and an additional 13 percent applied for relief to supplement decreased earnings. Loss or depletion of assets and administrative rulings reinstating families previously declared ineligible for relief each accounted for about one-tenth of the reopenings of farm operators and 5 to 6 percent of the reopenings of farm laborers. Nearly 15 percent of all reopenings of farm tenant families (other than cropper families) were due to administrative ruling.[13] A few cases were enrolled as new cases due to the administrative practice of transferring certain cases from State and local agencies to the Emergency Relief Administration and to the formation of new relief units within the general relief population.

Increased needs with the approach of the winter season, loss of assistance from relatives and friends, and other reasons accounted for about 20 percent of the farm operator and 10 percent of the farm laborer additions to relief rolls.

Reasons for Separations, July Through October.

Of farm operator families who left the relief rolls from July through October 1935, 42 percent became self-supporting through their own efforts (table 43 and appendix table 33), largely through the sale of farm produce (71 percent), and to a smaller degree because of sufficient earnings from employment off the farm (29 percent). Such employment opportunities were greatest during July and August, declining very rapidly in the fall months.

Approximately 22 percent of all farm families who left the relief rolls up to the end of October did so because of employment of a member under the Works Program. Another 6 percent of the farmers became clients of the Resettlement Administration, 6 percent found other sources of income or relief, and 9 percent were declared ineligible for relief on the basis of reinvestigation and administrative rulings.

---

[12] For data by regions, see appendix tables 29–32.

[13] This high ratio was a result of a large number of cases in the State of Oklahoma that had received no relief during the preceding month and hence by definition were closed and reopened.

TABLE 43.—REASONS FOR SEPARATIONS OF FARM HOUSEHOLDS FROM RURAL RELIEF ROLLS, JULY THROUGH OCTOBER 1935

[300 counties and 83 New England townships]

Reason for separation	Usual occupation of head				
	Farm operators				Farm laborers
	Total	Owners	Tenants[1]	Croppers	
Number	26,091	9,293	13,032	3,766	13,694
Percent	100.0	100.0	100.0	100.0	100.0
Sufficient means for self-support	41.9	48.3	42.0	25.5	48.8
Private employment [2]	12.1	12.8	10.9	14.6	47.5
Crops marketed	29.8	35.5	31.1	10.9	1.3
Works Program employment	21.8	20.1	17.2	42.0	21.5
Civilian Conservation Corps	8.6	9.5	7.3	10.9	5.6
Works Progress Administration and other	13.2	10.6	9.9	31.1	15.9
Transferred to Resettlement Administration	6.1	6.5	7.4	.9	.7
Other income [3]	5.9	5.6	6.1	6.1	3.5
Administrative policy	8.8	8.0	9.4	8.5	8.3
Moved or failed to report	7.2	5.6	7.8	9.0	8.5
All others	8.3	5.9	10.1	8.0	8.7

[1] Exclusive of croppers in the southern States.
[2] Including regular government employment.
[3] Assistance from local relief agencies, relatives, and friends, and from miscellaneous sources.

Sale of farm produce and Works Program employment accounted for the greater part of the farm owner and tenant closings, and private or Works Program employment was chiefly responsible for removing farm croppers and laborers. Private employment was relatively most effective in making farm operator families self-supporting in Connecticut and Massachusetts, where Works Program employment was of less importance than in any other area in 1935.[14]

Whereas about 13 percent of all farmers who went off relief during the period July through October left to take jobs under the Works Program (exclusive of C. C. C.), the great bulk of relief closings due to Works Program employment took place during November and December. It is estimated that 34,000 farmers received their first Works Program wages during July, August, September, and October, while an additional 152,000 farmers received their first Works Program checks during November and December (table 44).

Industries Responsible for Closing Agricultural Cases.

Approximately one-fourth (24 percent) of all agricultural cases closed during the months July through October received sufficient earnings from private or regular government employment to support themselves (appendix table 33). Only about two-thirds (65 percent) of these workers were reemployed in agriculture, however. More than one-tenth (11 percent) obtained employment on street and road construction projects, and an additional one-tenth were employed in rural manufacturing industries, such as building con-

---

[14] For data by regions, see appendix tables 34–37.

TABLE 44.—SEPARATIONS FROM RURAL RELIEF BECAUSE OF EMPLOYMENT
UNDER THE WORKS PROGRAM, JULY THROUGH DECEMBER 1935

[300 counties and 83 New England townships]

Month	Sample counties			Estimate for United States		
	All heads	Farm operators	All others	All heads	Farm operators	All others
July-December	57, 460	18, 661	38, 799	653, 000	186, 000	467, 000
July	116	26	90	1, 000		1, 000
August	1, 817	402	1, 415	21, 000	4, 000	17, 000
September	3, 547	1, 014	2, 533	40, 000	10, 000	30, 000
October	6, 529	2, 024	4, 505	74, 000	20, 000	54, 000
November	16, 772	5, 391	11, 381	191, 000	54, 000	137, 000
December	28, 679	9, 804	18, 875	326, 000	98, 000	228, 000

struction, canning factories, and lumber and furniture factories.
About 5 percent were employed in mining, in forestry, or in fishing.
Nearly 3 percent went into trade; about 1 percent entered the field
of public and professional service; and somewhat more than 1
percent became domestic and personal servants (table 45).

TABLE 45.—INDUSTRY OF REEMPLOYMENT [1] RESPONSIBLE FOR CLOSING RURAL
RELIEF CASES, BY REGION, JULY THROUGH OCTOBER 1935

[300 counties]

Industry of reemployment [1]	Total 30 States [2]	11 northern States	13 southern States	6 western States
Number	5, 062	1, 764	2, 364	934
Percent	100. 0	100. 0	100. 0	100. 0
Agriculture	65. 3	63. 3	67. 5	63. 6
Forestry and fishing	2. 8	2. 7	2. 9	3. 0
Extraction of minerals	2. 4	2. 0	2. 5	2. 8
Manufacturing and mechanical industries	10. 4	9. 5	9. 5	14. 1
Building construction	3. 0	4. 1	1. 6	4. 3
Food and allied industries	2. 2	1. 8	1. 1	5. 9
Auto factories and repair shops	. 6	1. 0	. 4	
Lumber and furniture	2. 2	1. 0	3. 1	2. 4
Textile	. 3	. 2	. 4	
Other and not specified	2. 1	1. 4	2. 9	1. 5
Transportation and communication	13. 8	18. 5	11. 8	10. 1
Street and road construction	11. 1	14. 6	10. 2	7. 1
Other transportation and communication	2. 7	3. 9	1. 6	3. 0
Trade	2. 8	2. 3	2. 8	4. 1
Public and professional service	1. 0	. 9	1. 0	. 8
Domestic and personal service	1. 5	. 8	2. 0	1. 5

[1] Of workers usually engaged in agriculture.
[2] Exclusive of cases for which industry of reemployment was unknown.

CHAPTER VIII

PROGRAMS OF RECONSTRUCTION

THE RECONSTRUCTION of American agriculture demands the conservation of the human values in rural life as specifically as it calls for the conservation of soil and natural resources.

Households whose breadwinners had been chiefly experienced in agriculture constituted at one time about 20 percent of the national relief burden and included a wide variety of people. Farm families on relief varied in many respects: in their distance from the land—some living on the farm and unsuccessfully attempting to make a living, while some, for various reasons, had migrated from the land and had not successfully adapted themselves to village and town occupations; in their previous relation to the land—some having been owners, some tenants, some laborers; in the extent to which they had been subject to loss of supplementary occupations and to the impact of natural disasters such as drought and flood; in the extent of their unemployability because of old age, physical handicap, and absence of a male worker in the family group; and in the type of farming they practiced. They likewise varied widely with respect to ownership of land, livestock, and equipment, and in the possession of personal qualifications essential to success in agriculture.

The differing combinations of these varying factors produce strikingly different situations in the major agricultural regions, indicating the necessity of sufficient regional variations in constructive programs to make possible their adaptation to peculiar regional needs. In some areas tenancy is the paramount problem, in others drought, in others small farms and pressure of population, and in still others, loss of supplementary occupation.

Examination of the problems of farmers on relief calls attention to the need of programs both to assist recovery and to prevent widespread rural distress in future crises. These measures are concerned both with the economic well-being of farm families and the social structure of rural communities. They must involve the improvement of farming both as a source of income and as a way of living.

ECONOMIC RECONSTRUCTION

Part-Time Farming.

The promotion of part-time farm and part-time industrial employment has been suggested as a partial remedy for farm depression problems. It is true that the combination of agricultural and industrial enterprise has been successful in keeping some families off the relief rolls, but the most authoritative studies show that the majority of these families were those with regular income from industrial employment, and that the commercial farmer is seldom successful in supplementing his income with industrial employment.[1] Such studies also indicate that there is little prospect of marked increase in the number of part-time farmers (excepting among those industrial workers already employed who may supplement their wages with the products from a garden or a cow) unless there is a fundamental change in the geographical distribution and the hours of industry.

Submarginal Land Retirement.

The necessity of removing submarginal lands from agricultural production is one of the most evident long-time needs, as there are many families which have drifted to these lands under the impression that they will yield a livelihood, and many others which have remained while productivity declined below the economic margin.

The following methods of retirement have been suggested:

(*a*) Purchase by the Federal Government and transfer from agricultural use to other uses, such as forestry, public grazing, game preserves, recreation. The acquisition of all lands which have been judged submarginal would, however, prove prohibitive in cost and would again build up a vast public domain.

(*b*) A legal zoning process in rural areas which would operate similarly to restrictive zoning in cities. This is a process which would have to be carried out State by State and county by county, and which would encounter many legislative and constitutional snags.

(*c*) A zoning process without legal sanctions which would designate lands unfit for commercial agriculture, and by a process of education guide settlers away from these and toward other areas. Such a movement would be supplemented by such measures as the withdrawal of public services from the proscribed areas, the curtailment of road extension and repairs, and the abandonment of schools.

---

[1] Allen, R. H.; Cottrell, L. S., Jr.; Troxell, W. W.; Herring, Harriet L.; and Edwards, A. D., *Part-time Farming in the Southeast*, Research Monograph IX, Division of Social Research, Works Progress Administration, 1937.

Eroded Cropland

Soil Conservation.

Soil conservation programs propose to restore fertility to those lands which through erosion or soil exhaustion have been greatly impaired in productivity but which are still in some measure productive. As long as rivers are clouded with silt, the farmers on their tributaries are losing the natural fertility of the land faster than they can replace it. Only when the streams run clear will the account with nature be balanced.

Soil conservation measures are, therefore, a sound basis for human conservation.

Crop Control.

Measures to control surplus production have proved their worth both in keeping people off relief and to a limited extent in removing people from relief during the depression. Future security for the farmer and parity in prices depend upon the continuation of crop controls to be evolved from the present program which ties together soil conservation and crop control.

It is clear, however, that the planning of agricultural production must be adjusted to rural population trends, or such measures as may be inaugurated will be defeated at the outset.

TENANCY PROBLEMS

For some areas the reform of the tenant system and the arrest of the spread of tenancy are of paramount importance.[2] Tenancy proves a stumbling block in the path of other constructive efforts, such as the promotion of diversification, soil conservation, and cooperative marketing. Constructive measures suggested in this field include proposals for reform within the tenant system and proposals to promote the ownership of family-sized farms to replace tenancy.

Suggestions for improving tenant relationships within the system include proposals for stronger protective State laws, especially those relating to the leasing system; improvement of tenant living conditions through better housing; diversification of crops; reform of the crop and credit system; a more thorough and realistic system of rural education; and supervision of the type provided by the rural rehabilitation program.

The promotion of land ownership has been widely discussed for years and has been the subject of much investigation. No concrete governmental programs designed to accomplish this goal have been put into effect, however. In the light of the experience of European nations, progress along this line will be slow, requiring a generation or two to accomplish large-scale results.

---

[2] Woofter, T. J., Jr., *Landlord and Tenant on the Cotton Plantation*, Research Monograph V, Division of Social Research, Works Progress Administration, 1936.

The essentials of a land ownership program are:

(*a*) Making available to the tenant small family-sized tracts of *good* land. Usually the best commercial cropland is concentrated in the larger holdings which, when sold, are kept in as large tracts as possible and not cut up into family-sized farms. New land brought into cultivation through clearing and stumping, irrigation or drainage, must usually be developed in large tracts for economy, and it is beyond the means of the small farmer to carry on such operations unaided.

(*b*) Providing long-time credit on easy terms. The usual period of 3 or 6 years for repayment of mortgages is too short a time for the prospective purchaser to acquire full equity, especially under the unstable conditions faced by the cotton farmers or by farmers in areas subject to drought or crop failure.

The small cash incomes produced on family-sized cotton farming units emphasize the need of keeping initial costs of these tracts low. Even a 40-year amortization of a $4,000 farm would require payments on the principal of $100 per year, which would constitute a heavy drain on a cash income such as the 1934 tenant average of about $200.

(*c*) Provision of supervision in the nature of adult education which will not only give the farmer the benefit of improved agricultural practices but will train him in the habits necessary for successful management of his own enterprise.

SOCIAL RECONSTRUCTION

Measures intended to secure economic parity for the farmer, such as those embodied in carefully planned control and marketing programs, are necessary to safeguard agricultural income, but equally important is the need for programs which will take into account human and social factors in safeguarding rural values in future crises.

To meet the needs of diverse farm groups, a variety of programs has been evolved from the single program of the dole offered in the early days of the F. E. R. A. Rehabilitation was early set up as a goal for those cases whose head was employable and judged capable of agricultural success. During the summer and fall of 1935, the unemployables were gradually transferred back to State and local care, and in 1936 the Social Security program rapidly assumed responsibility for the aged, for the blind, and for dependent children.

The rehabilitation program was soon limited to those whose success in regaining a self-supporting status seemed most assured. The concrete test applied in acceptance of a client on the rehabilitation program was whether or not, in the opinion of the supervisor and local committee, he was a promising enough risk to warrant the judgment that he would be able to repay such loans as might be necessary for his return to successful agricultural production.

The removal of the handicapped farmers to local relief and of the better prospects to rehabilitation left a group of employable persons whose prospects were not sufficiently bright to make them good loan risks. These remained on Federal relief. Almost 200,000 farm operators and over 200,000 farm laborers from this group were assigned to W. P. A. projects early in 1936. Also, late in 1935 and early in 1936 the Resettlement Administration began to care for a number of these cases on a grant rather than a loan basis.

Thus, the emergency has evolved a three-fold program for meeting the needs of distressed farm families.

1. Support of the unemployables through general relief and aid to Social Security classes.

2. Rehabilitation of farmers by Government loans made on the basis of a farm plan adapted to the family size and land type of the client and carried out under supervision.

3. For farm families with able-bodied members, not considered prospects for rehabilitation, financial aid either in the form of work relief or grants which would provide the necessary cash with the minimum time taken from farm work in busy seasons. Placing members of these families other than the head on programs such as the C. C. C. should be a chief reliance of such a program. This type of aid needs to be accompanied by special educational and retraining efforts to bring these families up to the rehabilitation level.

Direct Relief.

Often the full time of the farmer and his family is needed on the farm and direct relief programs are the most advantageous method of extending aid. However, to neither the farmer nor the community do lasting values accrue from the dole.

Work Relief.

Work programs have been used to advantage both for maintaining family morale and contributing social utility to the community. These have been especially adaptable where crop failures have made farm work unprofitable. Building of farm-to-market roads, development of soil and water conservation projects, processing surplus commodities, and improvement of rural institutions have all been accomplished by work relief. The following conditions need to be observed, however, in such a program:

(a) A work program is not well adapted to conserving agricultural assets unless it is concentrated in off-seasons or unless

137296°—37——8

members of farm families other than the operators are available for employment. Because of efforts to operate on marginal lands, because of large families, or because of natural disaster, such as drought or flood, many farm families need cash when the loan of such cash would be economically unsound. Still every effort should be made to provide this cash through grants to families temporarily in need, in order that farmers may remain on their farms and preserve their agricultural assets.

(*b*) This points to the consideration that in many instances direct relief, such as Resettlement emergency grants, is most suited to the needs of the farmer. Though perhaps less calculated to preserve his self respect, such grants, nevertheless, leave him free to devote his full time to recouping his farm assets.

(*c*) Work projects which tend to draw farmers into towns and villages should be minimized.

Rural Rehabilitation.

Loans for productive goods were early substituted for subsistence relief for farmers. It is evident that if many of the disadvantaged farmers are to be put back on their feet some such aid is necessary. The essentials of the rehabilitation program are:

That it provides the necessary credit at a reasonable rate of interest.

That it provides an individual farm plan worked out to fit the land, family, and situation of the farmer.

That it provides advice and supervision in the execution of this plan.

These are proving basic measures for restoring thousands of disheartened farmers to self-sufficiency.

Population Policy.

A definite population policy should be stressed as basic to any system of agrarian reform. It must be recognized that the farm's most important crop is its children and that the farm homes are rearing people for the cities. There is also a tendency for natural increase to be greatest in those areas least capable of supporting increased population. It is from these blighted areas that people move to cities most rapidly in times of industrial expansion and to which they return in times of industrial deflation; and it is in these areas that large numbers of youth mature without substantial opportunity. It is apparent, therefore, that guided migration is a basic need in rural reconstruction. Such guidance must take the form of an intensive search for areas of opportunity wherever they exist, or can be created. The advice of the agricultural expert should be substituted for that of the speculator in worthless and semiworthless farm lands.

Building a Farm-to-Market Road

A recent report on migration and economic opportunity in regional analyses of the population situation asserts:[3]

Though it is suggested that the Cut-Over Region might, by migration within the region, take care of all but a few thousand of its present population, the three other chapters present very different conclusions. In the case of the Great Plains, it is argued that the minimum exodus "consistent with the safe use of the land" would be a quarter of a million people, and that the ideal economy would require the removal of nearly three times as many. Similarly, the authors of the chapter on the Coal Plateaus of the Southern Appalachians suggest that some three hundred and fifty thousand people should leave their crowded region, and describe this figure as a minimum which would by no means bring living levels in the area up to the average rural standards of the rest of the nation. Even more staggering figures are suggested for the Old Cotton Belt and its dependent areas, with estimates of the need of migration ranging, on various hypotheses, from one and one-half to six or seven millions. If these analyses are sound, they indicate that each of these three regions is doomed not only to continuing but to increasing poverty unless it is relieved of large numbers of people.

Although these figures are based on the minimum of assumptions favorable to retention of population in these areas, and the picture may be, therefore, somewhat exaggerated, the magnitude of present population maladjustment is apparent. Coupled with the rapid natural increase in population in these areas, the future difficulties of adjusting manpower to resources assume the aspect of a major national problem.

It is, of course, not advisable for a democratic government to go into the wholesale movement of people. On the other hand, when a farmer wishes voluntarily to leave an area in which he cannot support himself, the minimum service he should have is advice and counsel as to where better locations are to be found, education in the type of farming best suited to his new location, and possibly loans which will enable him to make the desired move.

Cooperation.

The stimulation of mutual aid among farmers can, in many respects, give to the American rural social fabric the strength of the agrarian organization of European countries. In marketing and in purchasing, cooperation is gradually being recognized as one of the hopes of the smaller farmer.

---

[3] Goodrich, Carter, and Others, *Migration and Economic Opportunity*, Philadelphia: University of Pennsylvania Press, 1936, p. 495.

Many of the advantages of large-scale mechanized operations can be made available to the operator of the family-sized farm if expensive heavy farm machinery and pasture lands are held in common.

Also, in meeting the everyday problems of planting and harvesting, purchasing and processing, and problems of diet and health, mutual aid would prove beneficial, particularly to the youngest farmers and to those with the fewest resources.

Higher Standard of Living.

One incentive to increased production is the increase in the number of things wanted. Fundamental improvements in rural housing, diet, sanitation, and education will never be thorough until the desire for these improvements is widespread and strong among the farm families, especially among the farm women. The improvement of production alone does not automatically raise the standard of living. The benefits of increased production have to be converted into better living through the process of education.

Rural Institutions and Services.

Interwoven with the problems of increasing the opportunity for rural employment, raising the standard of living, and the general strengthening of the foundations of rural life is the necessity for strengthening rural institutions and services, particularly the institutions of education and health and the service relating to technical advice in farm problems.

Sounder financial support of rural institutions is dependent upon equalization between the country and the city of opportunities afforded by publicly financed agencies. Surplus wealth, regardless of where it is produced, is so greatly concentrated in the cities that the tax base of public services in rural areas is comparatively meager. This points to the need of equalization funds for health, education, and public welfare which will smooth out the financial inequalities between rural States and States which contain points of financial concentration—between rural counties and industrial cities.

NEED FOR A LONG-RANGE COORDINATED PROGRAM

Hitherto, farmers have been confused by the numerous programs and the rapidity of administrative changes. Aid to farmers has evolved through the stages of direct relief, work relief, rehabilitation, and Works Program employment. The inauguration of each new program necessitated a period of adjustment and experiment during which administrative policies and procedures were not always clear. The destitute farmer has often been left with a marked feeling of insecurity. Successful rehabilitation is not to be accomplished in a few months; it is a step-by-step process. To accomplish it there must be continuity of administration, guided by a consistent policy.

Furthermore, the lines of administration in the local unit—the county—have not always been clearly demarcated, with the result that changes in policy in Federal, regional, or State headquarters have often left the local administration, as well as the client, bewildered regarding the proper course to pursue.

In other words, the administration has been groping ,through an unprecedented situation without an adequate chart or compass. The experience of the past 3 years has marked the course for the Federal Government to pursue. Definite, enduring accomplishment in alleviating rural distress will, however, depend on coordination from Washington down to the county, and a continuing course of action uninterrupted by sudden shifts in policy.

The more fundamental measures for building an agrarian civilization of the highest order in the United States are evidently long-time measures, not planned for quick results. This is especially true of tenancy reform, of programs for crop control, of the development of a population policy, and of the improvement of the rural standard of living and rural institutions.

The broad regional incidence of some of the measures of agrarian reform emphasizes the necessity for national coordination of constructive programs, and the need for equalization of opportunity emphasizes the need for Federal funds in support of these programs. National neglect of these problems probably costs more in the long run than their constructive solution. If future financial crises are not again to plunge millions of farm families into distress, it is along these lines that Federal and State Governments should proceed.

Appendix A
SUPPLEMENTARY TABLES

TABLE 1.—TYPE OF RELIEF RECEIVED BY RURAL HOUSEHOLDS, BY CURRENT OCCUPATION OF THE HEAD, BY COLOR, AND BY AREA, FEBRUARY 1935

[138 counties representing 9 agricultural areas]

Type of relief	All areas	Eastern Cotton Total	White	Negro	Western Cotton Total	White	Negro	Appalachian-Ozark	Lake States Cut-Over	Hay and Dairy	Corn Belt	Spring Wheat	Winter Wheat	Ranching
FARM OPERATORS														
Number	30,266	2,957	2,163	794	7,274	4,982	2,292	7,703	1,876	2,872	3,320	2,834	799	631
Percent	100.0	100.0	100.0	100.0	100.0	100.0	100.0	100.0	100.0	100.0	100.0	100.0	100.0	100.0
Drought only	20.7				41.0	38.8	45.6	2.0	27.0	31.0	24.0	4.8	83.1	21.1
Work only	38.6	41.8	47.1	27.3	33.8	35.9	29.0	34.4	28.1	31.0	60.8	59.6	12.4	19.6
Direct only	25.4	29.8	23.3	47.4	17.5	16.5	19.9	41.1	28.9	29.5	7.4	15.1	1.1	47.4
Work and direct	15.3	28.4	29.6	25.3	7.7	8.8	5.5	22.5	16.0	8.5	7.8	20.5	3.4	11.9
OWNERS														
Number	10,727	754	598	156	1,644	1,066	578	2,966	1,460	1,416	727	1,083	276	401
Percent	100.0	100.0	100.0	100.0	100.0	100.0	100.0	100.0	100.0	100.0	100.0	100.0	100.0	100.0
Drought only	19.7				45.8	40.2	56.2	2.8	26.0	27.5	23.9	4.6	80.0	16.0
Work only	36.7	45.6	48.5	34.6	26.2	28.9	21.3	38.9	27.1	29.2	60.2	58.8	16.7	18.5
Direct only	29.1	26.4	22.9	39.8	20.8	22.1	18.3	39.3	29.9	35.0	10.0	17.9	0.4	53.8
Work and direct	14.5	28.0	28.6	25.6	7.2	8.8	4.2	19.0	17.0	8.3	5.9	18.7	2.9	11.7
TENANTS [1]														
Number	16,126	1,031	717	314	3,389	2,494	895	4,737	416	1,456	2,593	1,751	523	250
Percent	100.0	100.0	100.0	100.0	100.0	100.0	100.0	100.0	100.0	100.0	100.0	100.0	100.0	100.0
Drought only	20.9				42.8	38.8	53.6	1.5	30.5	34.3	24.0	5.0	84.8	30.0
Work only	39.8	38.5	44.6	24.5	34.8	37.7	27.0	31.5	31.3	32.8	61.0	60.0	10.1	21.7
Direct only	23.4	32.4	24.1	51.3	14.3	14.4	14.0	42.2	25.7	24.1	6.7	13.3	1.5	36.1
Work and direct	15.9	29.1	31.3	24.2	8.1	9.1	5.4	24.8	12.5	8.8	8.3	21.7	3.6	12.2

CROPPERS

Number	3,413	1,172	848	324	2,241	1,422	819	201	20	251	272	92	33	14
Percent	100.0	100.0	100.0	100.0	100.0	100.0	100.0	100.0	[2]	100.0	100.0	100.0	[2]	[2]
Drought only	22.8				34.7	37.7	29.4		[2]	5.6	2.6	17.4	[2]	[2]
Work only	39.2	42.2	48.2	26.6	37.6	38.1	36.7	40.8	[2]	15.5	32.0	75.0	[2]	[2]
Direct only	23.4	29.6	22.9	47.2	20.1	15.9	27.4	34.8	[2]	75.7	48.1	3.3	[2]	[2]
Work and direct	14.6	28.2	28.9	26.2	7.6	8.3	6.5	24.4	[2]	3.2	17.3	4.3	[2]	[2]

FARM LABORERS

Number	1,593	384	182	202	326	246	80	201						
Percent	100.0	100.0	100.0	100.0	100.0	100.0	100.0	100.0						
Drought only	10.5				30.7	27.6	40.0							
Work only	33.7	21.6	28.0	15.8	47.2	51.3	35.0	40.8						
Direct only	40.4	50.3	33.5	65.4	14.1	13.4	16.2	34.8						
Work and direct	15.4	28.1	38.5	18.8	8.0	7.7	8.8	24.4						

NONAGRICULTURAL WORKERS

Number	14,001	1,850	875	975	2,792	1,675	1,117	2,758	848	2,716	1,797	498	242	500
Percent	100.0	100.0	100.0	100.0	100.0	100.0	100.0	100.0	100.0	100.0	100.0	100.0	100.0	100.0
Drought only	4.9				10.9	12.4	8.7	.9	5.9	2.8	3.1	14.1	40.1	1.6
Work only	19.0	23.5	37.7	10.8	18.3	22.1	12.5	20.2	11.7	7.4	31.7	32.3	27.7	12.2
Direct only	65.9	57.8	39.3	74.3	65.3	59.4	74.2	65.8	73.5	82.6	53.9	43.2	22.3	82.0
Work and direct	10.2	18.7	23.0	14.9	5.5	6.1	4.6	13.1	8.9	7.2	11.3	10.4	9.9	4.2

UNEMPLOYED

Number	30,371	5,219	3,560	1,659	4,741	3,518	1,223	5,157	1,298	5,745	5,411	1,043	665	1,092
Percent	100.0	100.0	100.0	100.0	100.0	100.0	100.0	100.0	100.0	100.0	100.0	100.0	100.0	100.0
Drought only	3.6				9.7	12.6	1.1	.6	1.2	1.1	2.1	13.9	34.7	1.3
Work only	38.9	54.2	58.9	43.8	34.5	32.9	39.0	42.9	15.5	23.0	45.4	54.9	34.9	36.9
Direct only	35.3	20.7	15.1	32.9	33.6	28.9	47.5	32.9	60.2	59.6	27.5	15.6	6.6	42.2
Work and direct	22.2	25.1	26.0	23.2	22.2	25.6	12.4	24.5	23.1	16.3	25.0	15.6	23.8	19.6

[1] Exclusive of croppers in the 2 Cotton Areas.
[2] Percent not computed on a base of less than 50 cases.

TABLE 2.—TYPE OF RELIEF RECEIVED BY RURAL HOUSEHOLDS, BY CURRENT OCCUPATION OF THE HEAD, BY COLOR, AND BY AREA, JUNE 1935

[138 counties representing 9 agricultural areas]

Type of relief	All areas	Eastern Cotton			Western Cotton			Appalachian-Ozark	Lake States Cut-Over	Hay and Dairy	Corn Belt	Spring Wheat	Winter Wheat	Ranching
		Total	White	Negro	Total	White	Negro							
FARM OPERATORS														
Number	17,380	1,074	792	282	1,876	1,448	428	7,894	1,160	1,600	1,074	1,878	404	420
Percent	100.0	100.0	100.0	100.0	100.0	100.0	100.0	100.0	100.0	100.0	100.0	100.0	100.0	100.0
Work only	58.8	41.7	47.5	25.5	69.4	71.4	62.6	69.9	23.1	43.1	72.3	44.3	76.3	20.0
Direct only	25.9	37.6	31.6	54.6	16.3	14.0	24.3	19.6	49.7	47.6	21.6	18.6	7.4	68.1
Work and direct	15.3	20.7	20.9	19.9	14.3	14.6	13.1	10.5	27.2	9.3	6.1	37.1	16.3	11.9
OWNERS														
Number	6,942	352	298	54	288	206	82	3,006	960	800	290	804	94	288
Percent	100.0	100.0	100.0	100.0	100.0	100.0	100.0	100.0	100.0	100.0	100.0	100.0	100.0	100.0
Work only	52.8	46.6	51.0	22.2	54.9	57.3	48.8	69.4	21.2	38.0	72.4	45.8	72.4	14.7
Direct only	32.1	33.5	31.5	44.5	29.9	27.2	36.6	20.9	51.3	55.5	22.1	20.9	8.5	76.8
Work and direct	15.1	19.9	17.5	33.3	15.2	15.5	14.6	9.7	27.5	6.5	5.5	33.3	19.1	8.5
TENANTS [1]														
Number	9,454	376	228	148	950	788	162	4,798	200	800	784	1,074	310	162
Percent	100.0	100.0	100.0	100.0	100.0	100.0	100.0	100.0	100.0	100.0	100.0	100.0	100.0	100.0
Work only	62.9	34.1	40.4	24.3	72.6	73.6	67.9	70.1	32.0	48.3	72.2	43.2	77.4	28.4
Direct only	21.8	43.6	31.6	62.2	13.9	12.7	19.8	18.8	42.0	39.7	21.4	16.9	7.1	54.3
Work and direct	15.3	22.3	28.0	13.5	13.5	13.7	12.3	11.1	26.0	12.0	6.4	39.9	15.5	17.3
CROPPERS														
Number	984	346	266	80	638	454	184							
Percent	100.0	100.0	100.0	100.0	100.0	100.0	100.0							
Work only	62.0	45.1	49.6	30.0	71.2	74.0	64.2							
Direct only	21.3	35.3	31.6	47.5	13.8	10.1	22.8							
Work and direct	16.7	19.6	18.8	22.5	15.0	15.9	13.0							
FARM LABORERS														
Number	1,198	270	134	136	212	176	36	150	34	150	268	66	34	14
Percent	100.0	100.0	100.0	100.0	100.0	100.0	(²)	100.0	(²)	100.0	100.0	100.0	(²)	(²)

Work only	42.1	27.4	44.8	10.3	68.9	69.3	(²)	73.3	(²)	32.0	26.1	36.4	(²)	(²)
Direct only	40.4	50.4	23.9	76.5	9.4	8.0	(²)	12.0	(²)	57.3	64.9	24.2	(²)	(²)
Work and direct	17.5	22.2	31.3	13.2	21.7	22.7	(²)	14.7	(²)	10.7	9.0	39.4	(²)	(²)
NONAGRICULTURAL WORKERS													
Number	2,880	412	246	166	430	308	122	500	148	498	598	122	74	98
Percent.	100.0	100.0	100.0	100.0	100.0	100.0	100.0	100.0	100.0	100.0	100.0	100.0	100.0	100.0
Work only	42.9	36.9	46.3	22.9	56.7	64.3	37.7	62.8	17.5	17.7	42.2	50.8	73.0	44.9
Direct only	42.3	31.6	18.7	50.6	28.4	16.9	57.4	26.8	62.2	74.7	47.8	18.0	16.2	49.0
Work and direct	14.8	31.5	35.0	26.5	14.9	18.8	4.9	10.4	20.3	7.6	10.0	31.2	10.8	6.1
UNEMPLOYED													
Number	12,361	1,978	1,378	600	1,501	1,208	293	2,832	763	2,149	2,016	429	291	402
Percent.	100.0	100.0	100.0	100.0	100.0	100.0	100.0	100.0	100.0	100.0	100.0	100.0	100.0	100.0
Work only	46.8	56.9	56.7	57.5	57.9	59.9	49.5	52.2	20.4	28.2	49.5	63.2	57.4	28.4
Direct only	36.0	20.9	19.0	25.2	27.8	25.7	36.9	31.8	55.3	58.6	35.0	14.0	19.6	54.5
Work and direct	17.2	22.2	24.3	17.3	14.3	14.4	13.6	16.0	24.3	13.2	15.5	22.8	23.0	17.1

1 Exclusive of croppers in the 2 Cotton Areas.
2 Percent not computed on a base of less than 50 cases.

TABLE 3.—AVERAGE AMOUNT OF RELIEF RECEIVED BY RURAL HOUSEHOLDS, BY TYPE OF RELIEF, BY CURRENT OCCUPATION OF THE HEAD, BY COLOR, AND BY AREA, FEBRUARY 1935 [1]

[138 counties representing 9 agricultural areas]

Type of relief	All areas	Eastern Cotton			Western Cotton			Appalachian-Ozark	Lake States Cut-Over	Hay and Dairy	Corn Belt	Spring Wheat	Winter Wheat	Ranching
		Total	White	Negro	Total	White	Negro							
FARM OPERATORS														
Total	$15.00	$10.50	$11.71	$7.21	$9.76	$10.19	$8.81	$10.27	$23.18	$25.41	$19.00	$23.60	$14.81	$22.93
Drought only	15.85	----	----	----	9.93	10.64	8.62	11.27	21.31	28.78	16.91	32.90	15.01	26.75
Work only	15.95	11.84	12.25	9.92	9.41	9.46	9.27	11.66	25.24	26.87	19.19	22.26	13.28	23.48
Direct only	9.94	5.73	7.06	3.96	8.18	8.64	7.35	6.68	16.61	18.06	13.08	15.91	8.56	18.16
Work and direct	19.85	13.51	14.51	10.34	13.91	14.11	13.23	14.64	34.59	33.29	29.60	30.96	17.48	34.23
OWNERS														
Total	16.23	12.73	13.95	8.04	10.31	11.00	9.06	9.82	24.28	24.56	16.45	21.60	14.10	22.20
Drought only	17.48	----	----	----	10.02	10.92	8.84	12.46	22.20	29.50	14.75	22.48	14.20	25.47
Work only	16.99	15.92	16.92	10.56	9.29	12.11	10.35	11.29	26.91	25.29	16.87	21.21	13.76	22.35
Direct only	11.69	5.39	5.66	4.77	8.70	8.97	8.08	6.29	17.39	17.75	11.01	15.05	9.00	18.59
Work and direct	21.69	14.45	15.57	9.70	12.14	12.79	9.58	13.74	35.34	34.44	28.33	28.86	13.87	34.09
TENANTS [2]														
Total	15.41	9.90	11.01	7.36	10.02	10.23	9.46	10.56	19.32	26.23	19.71	24.84	15.18	24.19
Drought only	16.28	----	----	----	10.09	10.59	13.26	9.88	18.63	28.22	17.51	38.88	15.41	27.94
Work only	16.59	11.18	11.23	10.99	9.07	8.98	9.45	11.94	20.16	28.23	19.83	22.89	12.87	25.14
Direct only	9.40	5.31	6.76	3.75	8.62	8.73	8.28	6.90	13.44	18.50	13.95	16.63	8.50	17.04
Work and direct	20.16	13.31	13.97	11.36	16.20	16.20	16.21	15.07	31.00	32.23	29.86	32.07	19.00	34.46
CROPPERS														
Total	9.17	9.59	10.71	6.65	8.95	9.53	7.94	----	----	----	----	----	----	----
Drought only	9.54	----	----	----	9.54	10.50	7.40	----	----	----	----	----	----	----
Work only	9.05	9.53	9.73	8.57	8.76	8.80	8.69	----	----	----	----	----	----	----
Direct only	6.89	6.34	8.30	3.86	7.32	8.15	6.48	----	----	----	----	----	----	----
Work and direct	12.54	13.10	14.27	9.73	11.46	11.14	12.19	----	----	----	----	----	----	----
FARM LABORERS														
Total	13.09	7.65	10.42	5.15	6.77	6.83	6.60	12.79	31.95	21.64	15.54	22.45	13.52	23.21
Drought only	13.82	----	----	----	7.05	7.35	6.41	----	29.50	30.50	11.43	35.75	----	36.50
Work only	13.18	10.13	12.02	7.13	6.92	6.52	8.75	11.44	25.00	25.92	16.62	19.22	8.95	18.25
Direct only	11.74	4.73	7.56	3.42	6.74	8.09	3.31	10.41	41.50	19.79	11.08	26.33	----	14.40
Work and direct	15.90	10.96	11.76	9.50	4.88	4.84	5.00	18.43	20.00	29.25	26.55	22.00	19.71	35.67

	12.70	9.15	12.44	6.20	7.31	7.54	6.97	11.34	15.95	18.55	14.44	17.80	14.73	13.82
NONAGRICULTURAL WORKERS														
Total	12.70	9.15	12.44	6.20	7.31	7.54	6.97	11.34	15.95	18.55	14.44	17.80	14.73	13.82
Drought only	13.60	----	----	----	8.27	8.37	8.05	9.12	26.44	18.08	14.27	24.96	12.76	14.25
Work only	15.54	15.24	17.38	8.53	8.45	8.15	9.26	13.27	21.78	29.28	17.57	15.84	19.79	17.98
Direct only	10.65	5.67	6.49	5.28	6.54	6.79	6.25	9.23	11.51	16.63	10.45	14.41	10.19	12.72
Work and direct	20.15	12.25	14.53	9.08	10.73	10.89	10.39	19.11	37.80	29.55	24.71	28.27	18.79	23.14
UNEMPLOYED														
Total	15.39	11.13	12.38	8.46	10.88	11.65	8.69	14.29	23.48	12.28	21.86	27.44	19.03	21.59
Drought only	18.69	16.00	----	16.00	9.82	9.80	10.43	10.90	47.50	16.29	17.70	43.25	20.60	27.00
Work only	15.95	12.01	12.59	10.33	11.24	12.14	9.04	14.25	26.25	13.14	22.79	24.64	17.59	21.02
Direct only	11.15	6.36	7.70	5.05	8.03	8.31	7.54	9.25	17.17	10.91	14.54	18.91	11.27	18.01
Work and direct	20.65	13.17	14.61	9.71	15.12	15.69	11.78	21.21	36.78	15.77	28.58	31.71	21.01	30.02

[1] Exclusive of cases which were opened, reopened, or closed during the month.
[2] Exclusive of croppers in the 2 Cotton Areas.

Type of relief	All areas	Eastern Cotton			Western Cotton			Appalachian-Ozark	Lake States Cut-Over	Hay and Dairy	Corn Belt	Spring Wheat	Winter Wheat	Ranching
		Total	White	Negro	Total	White	Negro							
FARM OPERATORS														
Total	$15.02	$12.64	$14.16	$8.38	$10.82	$11.24	$9.41	$11.59	$24.46	$22.92	$15.02	$21.48	$14.48	$19.79
Work only	13.54	16.14	17.14	10.92	10.53	10.88	9.19	11.54	21.41	25.35	13.36	17.44	13.29	20.05
Direct only	13.25	6.93	8.38	4.57	8.52	9.05	7.50	9.16	20.63	18.47	15.97	13.65	16.73	17.61
Work and direct	23.67	15.96	16.10	15.57	14.89	15.12	14.00	16.49	34.03	34.50	31.21	30.24	19.03	31.84
OWNERS														
Total	16.49	15.20	16.26	9.41	11.37	12.61	8.24	12.01	24.30	22.45	13.50	21.03	16.53	19.53
Work only	14.75	19.73	20.58	9.00	13.06	14.71	8.20	11.88	21.26	26.01	12.41	17.47	16.12	21.58
Direct only	14.93	7.41	8.23	4.17	6.84	6.96	6.60	9.40	21.09	18.68	14.56	14.81	17.25	17.49
Work and direct	25.85	17.74	18.12	16.67	14.14	14.75	12.50	18.55	32.61	33.81	23.50	29.83	17.78	34.27
TENANTS [1]														
Total	14.41	11.57	14.19	7.54	11.09	11.23	10.42	11.32	25.26	23.39	15.58	21.81	13.86	20.21
Work only	13.12	16.25	17.67	12.61	10.44	10.58	9.71	11.32	21.88	24.83	13.71	17.42	12.48	18.78
Direct only	11.99	6.12	8.81	4.02	9.79	9.86	9.56	9.00	17.95	18.18	16.50	12.58	16.55	17.86
Work and direct	23.14	15.10	15.25	14.60	15.94	15.98	15.70	15.32	41.23	34.88	33.68	30.50	19.50	29.93
CROPPERS														
Total	10.53	11.19	11.78	9.23	10.18	10.64	9.03							
Work only	10.42	12.28	12.82	9.33	9.78	10.04	9.03							
Direct only	7.86	7.56	8.19	6.16	8.27	9.83	6.57							
Work and direct	14.40	15.21	15.08	15.56	13.83	14.00	13.33							
FARM LABORERS														
Total	13.10	7.61	10.45	4.82	8.98	9.03	8.72	11.35	21.21	20.31	15.33	20.85	14.94	19.71
Work only	11.75	9.11	9.40	7.86	7.89	7.69	8.92	9.65	29.33	21.13	15.63	17.58	13.42	4.00
Direct only	12.31	4.93	9.00	3.67	8.40	9.14	6.67	10.44	16.00	18.05	14.21	16.50	23.00	23.00
Work and direct	18.18	11.87	13.05	9.11	12.70	13.10	10.00	20.55	28.25	30.00	22.58	26.54	15.67	19.00

	15.86	13.68	16.36	9.71	9.76	11.09	6.39	11.47	24.91	21.90	16.54	23.74	19.43	13.20
NONAGRICULTURAL WORKERS														
Total	15.86	13.68	16.36	9.71	9.76	11.09	6.39	11.47	24.91	21.90	16.54	23.74	19.43	13.20
Work only	16.27	19.05	21.14	12.79	10.30	10.89	7.78	11.80	22.38	30.18	18.29	23.90	19.70	13.64
Direct only	13.54	7.03	7.52	6.76	6.34	8.15	5.00	8.97	20.65	18.31	13.10	17.55	15.33	11.92
Work and only	21.31	14.05	14.74	12.68	14.19	14.41	12.00	15.92	40.13	37.89	25.57	27.05	23.75	20.33
UNEMPLOYED														
Total	17.94	12.79	14.28	9.36	10.53	11.00	8.55	14.56	24.32	26.23	20.63	23.20	17.48	19.69
Work only	17.44	13.76	15.35	10.16	11.62	11.93	10.06	13.32	25.76	31.49	21.82	21.81	15.49	19.70
Direct only	14.85	6.85	7.88	5.08	6.39	6.74	5.42	12.58	17.61	21.07	14.52	14.17	12.61	16.14
Work and direct	25.81	15.88	16.80	12.92	14.15	14.75	11.55	22.49	38.41	37.95	30.62	32.58	26.61	30.94

[1] Exclusive of cases which were opened, reopened, or closed during the month.
[2] Exclusive of croppers in the 2 Cotton Areas.

Farmers on Relief and Rehabilitation

TABLE 5.— AMOUNT OF RELIEF RECEIVED BY RURAL HOUSEHOLDS WITH AGRICULTURE AS THE USUAL OCCUPATION OF THE HEAD, BY COLOR AND BY AREA, JUNE 1935 [1]

[138 counties representing 9 agricultural areas]

Area	Total		Amount of relief						
	Number	Percent	$1 to $9	$10 to $19	$20 to $39	$40 to $59	$60 to $79	$80 to $99	$100 and over
All areas	23,394	100.0	38.8	37.7	19.0	3.7	0.7	0.1	(²)
Eastern Cotton:									
Total	3,308	100.0	53.2	37.2	7.4	1.8	.4		
White	2,184	100.0	46.8	39.8	10.1	2.7	.6		
Negro	1,124	100.0	65.5	32.0	2.3	.2			
Western Cotton:									
Total	3,764	100.0	57.7	35.5	6.0	.6	.2		
White	2,946	100.0	55.7	36.4	6.9	.7	.3		
Negro	818	100.0	64.8	32.3	2.9				
Appalachian-Ozark	6,622	100.0	48.0	43.1	8.0	.8	.1	(²)	
Lake States Cut-Over	952	100.0	16.8	32.2	35.7	11.3	2.9	1.1	
Hay and Dairy	2,370	100.0	12.0	31.8	42.9	11.1	2.1	.1	
Corn Belt	2,778	100.0	26.2	35.9	32.6	4.5	.5	.2	0.1
Spring Wheat	2,212	100.0	20.9	34.7	33.8	8.2	1.8	.3	.3
Winter Wheat	666	100.0	37.3	35.1	21.6	6.0			
Ranching	722	100.0	10.0	45.7	40.4	2.8	1.1		

[1] Exclusive of cases which were opened, reopened, or closed during the month.
[²] Less than 0.05 percent.

TABLE 6.—AGE OF HEADS OF RURAL REHABILITATION HOUSEHOLDS WITH AGRICULTURE AS THE USUAL OCCUPATION, BY AREA, JUNE 1935

[138 counties representing 9 agricultural areas]

Area and usual occupation	Total		Age in years				
	Number	Percent	16–24	25–34	35–44	45–54	55–64
All areas:							
Owners	3,468	100.0	2.8	12.5	31.0	33.2	20.5
Tenants [1]	5,878	100.0	6.4	31.0	28.3	22.7	11.6
Croppers	2,214	100.0	9.1	33.9	28.9	18.7	9.4
Farm laborers	1,170	100.0	18.3	42.1	20.2	13.2	6.2
Eastern Cotton:							
Owners	1,152	100.0	4.2	13.7	29.0	32.3	20.8
Tenants	2,258	100.0	7.0	29.7	25.6	24.4	13.3
Croppers	1,656	100.0	9.2	34.3	29.6	17.5	9.4
Farm laborers	622	100.0	21.2	41.2	16.7	13.2	7.7
Western Cotton:							
Owners	238	100.0	4.2	8.4	27.7	35.3	24.4
Tenants	908	100.0	7.9	30.4	30.4	19.4	11.9
Croppers	558	100.0	9.0	32.6	26.9	22.2	9.3
Farm laborers	330	100.0	13.4	41.5	26.3	14.0	4.8
Appalachian-Ozark:							
Owners	314	100.0	3.8	11.5	38.9	24.8	21.0
Tenants	398	100.0	8.5	30.7	31.2	19.1	10.5
Farm laborers	18	(2)	(2)	(2)	(2)	(2)	
Lake States Cut-Over:							
Owners	510	100.0	1.6	9.8	27.5	42.7	18.4
Tenants	86	100.0		30.2	34.9	23.3	11.6
Farm laborers	10	(2)	(2)	(2)	(2)		
Hay and Dairy:							
Owners	612	100.0	1.9	10.5	35.0	31.4	21.2
Tenants	508	100.0	3.5	32.3	25.6	24.8	13.8
Farm laborers	46	(2)	(2)	(2)	(2)	(2)	
Corn Belt:							
Owners	202	100.0	2.9	12.9	32.7	32.7	18.8
Tenants	864	100.0	6.7	29.9	31.0	24.1	8.3
Farm laborers	78	100.0	12.8	53.9	20.5	12.8	
Spring Wheat:							
Owners	296	100.0	.6	17.6	29.7	31.8	20.3
Tenants	560	100.0	4.9	37.5	31.2	18.9	7.5
Farm laborers	38	(2)	(2)	(2)		(2)	(2)
Winter Wheat:							
Owners	70	100.0		14.3	31.4	31.4	22.9
Tenants	214	100.0	1.9	38.3	27.1	20.6	12.1
Farm laborers	6	(2)	(2)	(2)			
Ranching:							
Owners	74	100.0		24.3	32.4	32.5	10.8
Tenants	82	100.0		17.1	34.1	36.6	12.2
Farm laborers	22	(2)	(2)	(2)	(2)		(2)

[1] Exclusive of croppers in the 2 Cotton Areas.
[2] Percent not computed on a base of less than 50 cases.

TABLE 7.—FAMILY COMPOSITION OF RURAL RELIEF HOUSEHOLDS, BY USUAL OCCUPATION OF THE HEAD, BY COLOR, AND BY AREA, JUNE 1935

[138 counties representing 9 agricultural areas]

Family composition	All areas	Eastern Cotton Total	Eastern Cotton White	Eastern Cotton Negro	Western Cotton Total	Western Cotton White	Western Cotton Negro	Appalachian-Ozark	Lake States Cut-Over	Hay and Dairy	Corn Belt	Spring Wheat	Winter Wheat	Ranching
FARM OPERATORS														
Number	18,126	2,170	1,606	564	2,496	1,956	540	6,514	846	1,488	1,564	2,076	496	476
Percent	100.0	100.0	100.0	100.0	100.0	100.0	100.0	100.0	100.0	100.0	100.0	100.0	100.0	100.0
Husband—wife	9.1	11.2	9.1	17.4	10.2	10.3	10.0	7.9	9.7	6.5	12.4	7.1	17.3	6.7
Husband—wife—children	74.8	66.3	68.5	60.3	75.1	78.0	64.4	75.5	68.1	80.0	76.3	80.3	69.0	74.4
Nonfamily man	7.0	5.3	4.6	7.1	6.7	5.3	11.5	6.4	10.4	8.2	6.4	8.4	9.3	9.7
Nonfamily woman	1.2	2.6	2.5	2.8	.9	.4	3.0	1.3	1.4	.8	.3	.3	---	2.5
Father—children	2.6	3.9	4.6	1.8	2.9	2.6	4.1	2.3	2.8	2.1	3.3	2.2	2.0	2.1
Mother—children	5.3	10.7	10.7	10.6	4.2	3.4	7.0	6.6	7.6	2.4	1.3	1.7	2.4	4.6
OWNERS														
Number	6,418	458	386	72	300	218	82	2,610	662	726	394	864	110	294
Percent	100.0	100.0	100.0	100.0	100.0	100.0	100.0	100.0	100.0	100.0	100.0	100.0	100.0	100.0
Husband—wife	8.0	8.3	6.2	19.5	11.3	9.2	17.1	7.3	10.0	6.3	12.2	5.8	18.2	8.2
Husband—wife—children	66.9	54.6	53.9	58.3	56.0	61.5	41.4	67.4	62.8	71.6	69.5	74.3	52.7	70.8
Nonfamily man	11.2	8.3	8.3	8.3	13.3	10.1	22.0	10.1	12.7	13.0	12.7	12.3	18.2	12.7
Nonfamily woman	2.4	7.9	7.8	8.3	4.0	3.7	4.9	2.5	1.8	.8	1.0	.7	---	2.7
Father—children	3.0	2.6	2.6	2.8	4.0	2.7	7.3	2.7	3.6	4.2	2.0	3.0	3.6	2.7
Mother—children	8.5	18.3	21.2	2.8	11.4	12.8	7.3	10.0	9.1	4.1	4.6	3.9	7.3	5.4
TENANTS [1]														
Number	9,684	646	410	236	1,238	1,028	210	3,904	184	762	1,170	1,212	386	182
Percent	100.0	100.0	100.0	100.0	100.0	100.0	100.0	100.0	100.0	100.0	100.0	100.0	100.0	100.0
Husband—wife	9.0	8.7	7.3	11.0	8.7	9.2	6.7	8.4	8.7	6.5	12.5	8.1	17.1	4.4
Husband—wife—children	80.9	73.4	76.6	67.8	80.5	81.3	76.2	81.0	86.9	87.9	78.6	84.5	73.6	80.2
Nonfamily man	4.7	4.3	2.4	7.6	5.8	5.3	8.6	3.9	2.2	3.7	4.9	5.6	6.7	8.8
Nonfamily woman	.4	1.2	1.5	.9	.3	---	1.9	.4	---	.8	---	---	---	2.2
Father—children	2.1	3.4	4.9	.8	2.3	1.9	3.8	2.0	---	.3	3.8	1.6	1.6	1.1
Mother—children	2.9	9.0	7.3	11.9	2.4	2.3	2.8	4.3	2.2	.8	.2	.2	1.0	3.3

	1	2	3	4	5	6	7	8	9	10	11	12	13	14
CROPPERS [1]														
Number	2,024	1,066	810	256	958	710	248	516	144	1,004	1,454	244	204	334
Percent	100.0	100.0	100.0	100.0	100.0	100.0	100.0	100.0	100.0	100.0	100.0	100.0	100.0	100.0
Husband—wife	13.0	14.1	11.4	22.7	11.9	12.4	10.5	15.9	19.4	13.1	14.0	14.8	24.5	13.8
Husband—wife—children	70.5	67.2	71.3	53.9	74.1	78.3	62.1	69.4	44.5	75.5	72.8	63.1	66.7	71.8
Nonfamily man	5.0	4.5	4.0	6.3	5.6	3.9	10.5	11.2	34.7	8.2	10.9	18.0	8.8	10.8
Nonfamily woman	1.0	1.1	.5	3.1	.8	-	-	.4	-	-	-	3.3	-	-
Father—children	4.1	4.7	5.4	2.3	3.4	3.4	3.2	2.7	1.4	3.2	2.2	.8	-	2.4
Mother—children	6.4	8.4	7.4	11.7	4.2	2.0	10.5	.4	-	-	.1	-	-	1.2
FARM LABORERS														
Number	6,850	1,502	810	692	1,448	1,130	318	-	-	-	-	-	-	-
Percent	100.0	100.0	100.0	100.0	100.0	100.0	100.0	-	-	-	-	-	-	-
Husband—wife	13.6	10.2	10.6	9.8	13.7	13.8	13.2	-	-	-	-	-	-	-
Husband—wife—children	64.2	46.5	59.3	31.5	64.4	67.6	52.8	-	-	-	-	-	-	-
Nonfamily man	9.8	7.3	7.4	7.2	7.9	7.8	8.2	-	-	-	-	-	-	-
Nonfamily woman	1.9	7.1	2.2	12.7	1.4	.9	3.1	-	-	-	-	-	-	-
Father—children	2.9	3.6	3.2	4.1	3.4	3.4	3.8	-	-	-	-	-	-	-
Mother—children	7.6	25.3	17.3	34.7	9.2	6.5	18.9	-	-	-	-	-	-	-
NONAGRICULTURAL WORKERS														
Number	23,136	2,416	1,746	670	1,798	1,418	380	7,458	2,016	4,412	3,312	644	424	656
Percent	100.0	100.0	100.0	100.0	100.0	100.0	100.0	100.0	100.0	100.0	100.0	100.0	100.0	100.0
Husband—wife	12.4	14.5	12.8	18.8	13.2	13.1	13.7	11.9	11.6	12.5	12.1	9.9	15.1	11.6
Husband—wife—children	65.0	55.6	61.9	43.0	54.3	61.2	28.4	68.7	60.4	70.3	65.5	68.0	62.2	57.0
Nonfamily man	11.1	7.2	7.3	6.9	8.1	6.8	13.2	10.5	21.8	10.0	10.8	10.0	10.4	16.8
Nonfamily woman	2.7	6.9	5.5	10.4	4.0	4.6	11.1	1.5	1.0	1.8	3.9	3.7	1.9	4.0
Father—children	2.7	1.7	1.8	1.5	2.5	2.3	3.2	3.3	3.1	2.1	2.4	2.8	5.7	1.5
Mother—children	5.9	13.1	10.7	19.4	15.9	12.0	30.4	4.1	2.1	3.3	4.9	5.6	4.7	9.1

[1] Exclusive of croppers in the 2 Cotton Areas.

TABLE 8.—FAMILY COMPOSITION OF RURAL REHABILITATION HOUSEHOLDS, BY USUAL OCCUPATION OF THE HEAD, BY COLOR, AND BY AREA, JUNE 1935

[138 counties representing 9 agricultural areas]

Family composition	All areas	Eastern Cotton Total	Eastern Cotton White	Eastern Cotton Negro	Western Cotton Total	Western Cotton White	Western Cotton Negro	Appalachian-Ozark	Lake States Cut-Over	Hay and Dairy	Corn Belt	Spring Wheat	Winter Wheat	Ranching
FARM OPERATORS														
Number	11,566	5,066	3,138	1,928	1,704	1,342	362	712	600	1,122	1,066	856	284	156
Percent	100.0	100.0	100.0	100.0	100.0	100.0	100.0	100.0	100.0	100.0	100.0	100.0	100.0	100.0
Husband—wife	10.0	9.6	6.3	14.9	13.7	12.6	17.7	5.9	10.3	10.3	11.4	6.8	9.9	9.0
Husband—wife—children	79.8	80.3	85.3	72.3	77.0	80.2	65.2	85.4	72.7	76.7	81.4	84.8	79.6	76.9
Nonfamily man	5.3	4.0	3.6	4.8	4.5	3.9	6.6	3.4	11.0	9.6	4.4	6.5	5.6	6.4
Nonfamily woman	.2	.3	.1	.5	.6	.2	.6			.2	.4			
Father—children	2.5	2.8	2.2	3.8	2.1	2.1	4.4	3.1	2.7	1.8	1.5	1.4	4.2	2.6
Mother—children	2.2	3.0	2.5	3.7	2.1	1.2	5.5	2.2	3.3	1.4	.4	.5	.7	5.1
OWNERS														
Number	3,472	1,152	754	398	238	148	90	314	512	614	202	296	70	74
Percent	100.0	100.0	100.0	100.0	100.0	100.0	100.0	100.0	100.0	100.0	100.0	100.0	100.0	100.0
Husband—wife	10.1	11.4	8.0	18.1	9.2	6.7	13.3	5.1	10.2	12.1	12.9	5.4	11.4	5.4
Husband—wife—children	74.9	72.6	76.9	65.4	72.4	81.1	57.8	82.2	71.5	73.6	79.2	83.8	68.6	78.4
Nonfamily man	7.5	9.6	5.3	6.0	5.0	4.1	6.7	4.4	12.1	10.4	5.9	8.8	5.7	5.4
Nonfamily woman	.5	.5	.1	1.5	.8		2.2				1.0			
Father—children	3.1	3.8	3.7	4.0	5.9	2.7	11.1	3.2	2.7	2.0	1.0	.7	11.4	2.7
Mother—children	3.9	3.4	5.6	5.0	6.7	5.4	8.9	5.1	3.5	1.6		1.3	2.9	8.1
TENANTS[1]														
Number	5,880	2,258	1,378	880	908	752	156	398	88	508	864	560	214	82
Percent	100.0	100.0	100.0	100.0	100.0	100.0	100.0	100.0	100.0	100.0	100.0	100.0	100.0	100.0
Husband—wife	9.6	8.6	5.7	13.2	13.7	13.3	15.4	6.5	11.4	8.3	11.1	7.5	9.3	12.2
Husband—wife—children	81.6	81.4	87.1	72.5	77.8	79.8	67.9	88.0	79.5	80.3	82.0	85.4	83.2	75.7
Nonfamily man	4.6	3.3	2.9	4.1	5.0	4.0	10.3	2.5	4.5	8.6	4.6	5.3	5.6	7.3
Nonfamily woman														
Father—children	2.4	3.3	2.0	5.2	2.2	2.1	2.6	2.0	2.3	1.6	1.6	1.8	1.9	2.4
Mother—children	1.7	3.2	2.3	4.5	1.3	.8	3.8	1.0	2.3	1.2	.5			2.4

CROPPERS														
Number	2,214	1,656	1,006	650	558	442	116	18	10	46	78	38	6	22
Percent	100.0	100.0	100.0	100.0	100.0	100.0	100.0	(2)	(2)	(2)	100.0	(2)	(2)	(2)
Husband—wife	11.2	9.6	6.0	15.4	15.8	13.6	24.1	(2)	(2)	(2)	23.1	(2)	(2)	(2)
Husband—wife—children	82.4	83.9	89.0	76.1	77.8	80.5	67.3	(2)	(2)	(2)	61.5	(2)	(2)	(2)
Nonfamily man	3.7	3.9	3.2	4.9	3.2	3.6	1.7	(2)	(2)	(2)	12.8	(2)	(2)	(2)
Nonfamily woman								(2)	(2)	(2)		(2)	(2)	(2)
Father—children	1.6	1.6	1.4	1.8	1.8	1.8	1.7	(2)	(2)	(2)	2.6	(2)	(2)	(2)
Mother—children	1.1	1.0	.4	1.8	1.4	.5	5.2	(2)	(2)	(2)		(2)	(2)	(2)
FARM LABORERS														
Number	1,170	622	448	174	330	288	42	(2)	(2)	(2)	(2)	(2)	(2)	(2)
Percent	100.0	100.0	100.0	100.0	100.0	100.0	(2)	(2)	(2)	(2)	(2)	(2)	(2)	(2)
Husband—wife	14.9	15.1	14.3	17.3	10.9	10.4	(2)	(2)	(2)	(2)	(2)	(2)	(2)	(2)
Husband—wife—children	72.1	70.4	74.1	61.0	84.3	84.7	(2)	(2)	(2)	(2)	(2)	(2)	(2)	(2)
Nonfamily man	6.8	4.2	4.5	3.4	3.0	3.5	(2)	(2)	(2)	(2)	(2)	(2)	(2)	(2)
Nonfamily woman	.2	.3		1.1			(2)	(2)	(2)	(2)	(2)	(2)	(2)	(2)
Father—children	2.1	2.6	1.8	4.6	1.8	1.4	(2)	(2)	(2)	(2)	(2)	(2)	(2)	(2)
Mother—children	3.9	7.4	5.3	12.6			(2)	(2)	(2)	(2)	(2)	(2)	(2)	(2)
NONAGRICULTURAL WORKERS														
Number	1,206	482	380	102	184	168	16	158	104	114	106	24	10	24
Percent	100.0	100.0	100.0	100.0	100.0	100.0	(2)	100.0	100.0	100.0	100.0	(2)	(2)	(2)
Husband—wife	12.3	12.0	10.5	17.6	10.9	11.9	(2)	8.9	15.4	8.8	20.8	(2)	(2)	(2)
Husband—wife—children	78.3	77.3	83.2	55.0	78.3	79.8	(2)	81.0	76.9	86.0	75.4	(2)	(2)	(2)
Nonfamily man	5.0	5.8	2.1	19.6	4.3	4.8	(2)	5.0	5.8	3.5	1.9	(2)	(2)	(2)
Nonfamily woman	.2						(2)	1.3				(2)	(2)	(2)
Father—children	3.1	4.1	4.2	3.9	4.3	3.5	(2)	1.3	1.9		1.9	(2)	(2)	(2)
Mother—children	1.1	.8		3.9	2.2		(2)	2.5		1.7		(2)	(2)	(2)

1 Exclusive of croppers in the 2 Cotton Areas.
2 Percent not computed on a base of less than 50 cases.

TABLE 9.—NUMBER OF GAINFUL WORKERS IN RURAL RELIEF HOUSEHOLDS, BY USUAL OCCUPATION OF THE HEAD AND BY SIZE OF HOUSEHOLD, JUNE 1935

[138 counties representing 9 agricultural areas]

Number of gainful workers	Number of persons per household												
	Total	1	2	3	4	5	6	7	8	9	10	11	12 or more
OWNERS													
Number	6,418	228	640	904	980	890	862	616	514	368	210	106	100
Percent	100.0	100.0	100.0	100.0	100.0	100.0	100.0	100.0	100.0	100.0	100.0	100.0	100.0
0													
1	51.4	100.0	84.1	61.5	53.7	47.4	45.0	42.2	38.1	28.8	23.8	17.0	12.0
2	25.4		15.9	32.5	29.0	28.1	27.6	27.9	24.5	26.1	21.0	11.3	14.0
3	13.4			6.0	13.4	15.0	17.4	16.9	19.5	20.6	29.5	20.8	26.0
4	6.4				3.9	8.8	7.2	6.8	13.2	15.8	8.6	24.5	20.0
5 or more	3.4					.7	2.8	6.2	4.7	8.7	17.1	26.4	28.0
TENANTS [1]													
Number	9,684	114	812	1,532	1,774	1,524	1,240	968	700	506	246	164	104
Percent	100.0	100.0	100.0	100.0	100.0	100.0	100.0	100.0	100.0	100.0	100.0	100.0	100.0
0													
1	64.9	100.0	89.4	80.7	70.9	65.6	61.5	56.6	43.7	39.1	35.0	22.0	11.5
2	20.7		10.6	17.5	21.1	23.5	21.1	21.1	28.3	26.9	21.1	31.7	9.6
3	8.7			1.8	7.4	6.8	10.5	13.2	16.6	17.4	22.0	17.0	32.7
4	4.0				.6	3.8	5.8	5.6	6.8	11.9	13.8	18.3	23.1
5 or more	1.7					.3	1.1	3.5	4.6	4.7	8.1	11.0	23.1
CROPPERS													
Number	2,024	24	274	398	366	290	236	178	110	78	36	22	12
Percent	100.0	(2)	100.0	100.0	100.0	100.0	100.0	100.0	100.0	100.0	(2)	(2)	(2)
0													
1	68.9	(2)	85.4	81.9	73.3	63.4	69.5	58.5	51.0	25.6	(2)	(2)	
2	19.6		14.6	15.6	16.9	23.5	20.2	23.6	35.9	(2)	(2)	(2)
3	7.3			2.5	8.2	6.9	7.6	13.5	14.5	23.1	(2)		(2)
4	3.1				1.6	2.1	3.4	5.6	7.3	12.8	(2)	(2)	(2)
5 or more	1.1					.7		2.2	3.6	2.6	(2)	(2)	(2)
FARM LABORERS													
Number	6,850	302	1,076	1,392	1,214	956	714	516	324	180	98	44	34
Percent	100.0	100.0	100.0	100.0	100.0	100.0	100.0	100.0	100.0	100.0	100.0	(2)	(2)
0													
1	74.2	100.0	85.3	83.8	76.2	70.5	63.9	62.0	52.5	52.2	28.6	(2)	(2)
2	17.1		14.7	14.1	17.3	18.4	20.7	24.4	21.0	22.2	30.6	(2)	(2)
3	6.5			2.1	5.3	9.2	13.1	8.5	20.4	16.7	24.5	(2)	(2)
4	1.7				1.2	1.7	2.0	4.3	3.7	7.8	12.2	(2)	(2)
5 or more	.5					.2	.3	.8	2.4	1.1	4.1	(2)	(2)
NONAGRICULTURAL WORKERS													
Number	23,136	1,712	3,428	4,236	4,146	3,246	2,406	1,606	1,004	634	400	196	122
Percent	100.0	100.0	100.0	100.0	100.0	100.0	100.0	100.0	100.0	100.0	100.0	100.0	100.0
0		.2		.1									
1	74.7	99.8	87.4	81.6	76.0	70.8	65.6	60.4	57.0	50.5	37.0	28.6	27.9
2	17.4		12.6	16.7	18.5	20.8	21.9	21.4	22.1	26.2	28.5	27.5	14.7
3	5.6			1.6	4.9	6.3	9.0	12.8	13.7	14.2	23.5	20.4	18.0
4	1.8				.6	2.0	2.6	4.7	5.8	6.9	8.0	10.2	27.9
5 or more	.5					.1	.9	.7	1.4	2.2	3.0	13.3	11.5

[1] Exclusive of croppers in the 2 Cotton Areas.
[2] Percent not computed on a base of less than 50 cases.

Supplementary Tables

TABLE 10.—NUMBER OF GAINFUL WORKERS IN RURAL REHABILITATIOI HOLDS, BY USUAL OCCUPATION OF THE HEAD AND BY SIZE OF HOUSEH(1935

[138 counties representing 9 agricultural areas]

Number of gainful workers	Number of persons per household										
	Total	1	2	3	4	5	6	7	8	9	10
OWNERS											
Number	3,472	102	354	488	574	554	360	370	272	168	122
Percent	100.0	100.0	100.0	100.0	100.0.	100.0	100.0	100.0	100.0	100.0	100.0
0											
1	58.1	100.0	88.7	74.2	58.2	56.0	52.2	50.3	43.4	31.0	24.6
2	23.2	------	11.3	23.4	26.8	28.5	25.6	22.1	25.0	29.8	27.9
3	12.2			2.4	13.6	11.2	12.2	18.4	20.6	25.0	24.6
4	3.5				1.4	3.2	6.7	6.5	5.1	7.1	6.5
5 or more	3.0					1.1	3.3	2.7	5.9	7.1	16.4
TENANTS [1]											
Number	5,880	82	498	908	994	972	738	586	448	292	182
Percent	100.0	100.0	100.0	100.0	100.0	100.0	100.0	100.0	100.0	100.0	100.0
0											
1	64.4	100.0	88.4	78.9	73.3	68.3	61.0	52.3	46.9	39.0	33.0
2	20.5		11.6	18.9	20.3	20.2	21.1	25.6	24.6	24.7	24.2
3	9.8			2.2	5.6	9.2	11.7	14.0	17.4	23.3	20.9
4	3.1				.8	2.3	4.9	6.1	5.8	8.2	6.6
5 or more	2.2						1.3	2.0	5.3	4.8	15.3
CROPPERS											
Number	2,214		204	340	356	366	296	244	164	116	64
Percent	100.0		100.0	100.0	100.0	100.0	100.0	100.0	100.0	100.0	100.0
0											
1	62.4		77.5	79.4	66.3	63.9	64.9	59.1	45.1	36.3	43.8
2	22.5		22.5	20.0	24.7	24.2	18.2	17.2	31.7	31.0	21.9
3	9.4			.6	8.4	9.3	10.1	16.4	14.6	17.2	21.9
4	3.8				.6	3.3	5.4	5.7	3.7	8.6	6.2
5 or more	1.9					1.1	1.4	1.6	4.9	6.9	6.2
FARM LABORERS											
Number	1,170	8	158	272	228	190	144	80	38	24	18
Percent	100.0	(2)	100.0	100.0	100.0	100.0	100.0	100.0	(2)	(2)	(2)
0											
1	73.2	(2)	73.4	87.5	73.7	73.7	69.5	70.0	(2)	(2)	-----
2	18.8		26.6	9.6	21.9	20.0	19.4	17.5	(2)	(2)	(2)
3	5.5			2.9	3.5	5.3	6.9	5.0	(2)	(2)	(2)
4	2.2				.9	1.0	2.8	7.5	(2)	(2)	(2)
5 or more	.3						1.4				(2)
NONAGRICULTURAL WORKERS											
Number	1,206	6	132	196	226	212	160	120	74	42	24
Percent	100.0	(2)	100.0	100.0	100.0	100.0	100.0	100.0	100.0	(2)	(2)
0											
1	72.0	(2)	93.9	76.6	76.1	70.8	70.0	58.4	64.9	(2)	(2)
2	18.4		6.1	21.4	14.2	19.8	17.5	33.3	16.2	(2)	(2)
3	6.5			2.0	8.0	7.5	7.5	3.3	13.5	(2)	(2)
4	2.3				1.7	1.9	3.8	1.7	5.4	(2)	(2)
5 or more	.8						1.2	3.3		(2)	-----

[1] Exclusive of croppers in the 2 Cotton Areas.
[2] Percent not computed on a base of less than 50 cases.

TABLE 11.—CURRENT EMPLOYMENT STATUS OF HEADS [1] OF FARM FAMILIES RECEIVING RELIEF, BY RESIDENCE AND BY AREA, JUNE 1935

[138 counties representing 9 agricultural areas]

Area	Percent residing in open country	Percent of open country residents				Percent residing in village	Percent of village residents			
		Total	Currently employed at—		Currently unemployed		Total	Currently employed at—		Currently unemployed
			Usual occupation	Other occupation				Usual occupation	Other occupation	
FARM OPERATORS										
All areas	88.8	100.0	90.1	1.3	8.6	11.2	100.0	40.4	7.3	52.3
Eastern Cotton	86.4	100.0	61.7	4.1	34.2	13.6	100.0	26.4	4.1	69.5
Western Cotton	87.3	100.0	82.4	3.3	14.3	12.7	100.0	25.3	13.3	61.4
Appalachian-Ozark	93.1	100.0	98.1	.1	1.8	6.9	100.0	85.8	.4	13.8
Lake States Cut-Over	95.5	100.0	97.3	.5	2.2	4.5	100.0	52.7	10.5	36.8
Hay and Dairy	89.6	100.0	88.6	1.5	9.9	10.4	100.0	33.8	2.6	63.6
Corn Belt	73.9	100.0	88.1	2.4	9.5	26.1	100.0	16.2	13.7	70.1
Spring Wheat	93.9	100.0	98.0	.2	1.8	6.1	100.0	20.6	9.5	69.9
Winter Wheat	85.1	100.0	93.9	.9	5.2	14.9	100.0	10.8	18.9	70.3
Ranching	66.4	100.0	95.6	--------	4.4	33.6	100.0	62.4	1.3	36.3
OWNERS										
All areas	90.3	100.0	95.1	1.7	3.2	9.7	100.0	64.9	4.8	30.3
Eastern Cotton	87.3	100.0	86.5	2.0	11.5	12.7	100.0	51.8	3.4	44.8
Western Cotton	87.3	100.0	93.9	1.5	4.6	12.7	100.0	73.7	15.8	10.5
Appalachian-Ozark	92.3	100.0	98.8	.6	.6	7.7	100.0	89.0	1.0	10.0
Lake States Cut-Over	96.1	100.0	97.2	1.9	.9	3.9	100.0	76.9	7.7	15.4
Hay and Dairy	89.5	100.0	84.6	3.7	11.7	10.5	100.0	42.1	2.6	55.3
Corn Belt	73.6	100.0	87.6	8.3	4.1	26.4	100.0	30.8	11.5	57.7
Spring Wheat	96.5	100.0	98.6	.2	1.2	3.5	100.0	40.0	6.7	53.3
Winter Wheat	92.7	100.0	90.2	3.9	5.9	7.3	100.0	50.0	25.0	25.0
Ranching	72.8	100.0	94.4	2.8	2.8	27.2	100.0	82.5	--------	17.5
TENANTS [2]										
All areas	88.7	100.0	84.6	3.3	12.1	11.3	100.0	25.2	9.7	65.1
Eastern Cotton	89.5	100.0	70.3	6.2	23.5	10.5	100.0	50.0	5.9	44.1
Western Cotton	89.2	100.0	84.5	4.3	11.2	10.8	100.0	17.9	14.9	67.2
Appalachian-Ozark	93.5	100.0	97.0	.4	2.6	6.5	100.0	83.3		16.7
Lake States Cut-Over	93.5	100.0	84.9	8.1	7.0	6.5	100.0	--------	16.7	83.3
Hay and Dairy	89.7	100.0	89.5	2.3	8.2	10.3	100.0	25.6	2.6	71.8
Corn Belt	74.0	100.0	85.2	3.5	11.3	26.0	100.0	10.5	15.1	74.4
Spring Wheat	92.1	100.0	96.6	1.1	2.3	7.9	100.0	14.6	10.4	75.0
Winter Wheat	82.9	100.0	94.4	.6	5.0	17.1	100.0	6.1	18.2	75.7
Ranching	56.0	100.0	90.2	2.0	7.8	44.0	100.0	42.5	2.5	55.0
CROPPERS										
All areas	84.5	100.0	54.6	8.3	37.1	15.5	100.0	11.5	8.9	79.6
Eastern Cotton	84.1	100.0	39.5	9.4	51.1	15.9	100.0	7.0	4.7	88.3
Western Cotton	85.0	100.0	71.3	7.1	21.6	15.0	100.0	16.7	13.9	69.4
Appalachian-Ozark										
Lake States Cut-Over										
Hay and Dairy										
Corn Belt										
Spring Wheat										
Winter Wheat										
Ranching										
FARM LABORERS										
All areas	64.1	100.0	17.0	7.5	75.5	35.9	100.0	7.4	4.6	88.0
Eastern Cotton	79.5	100.0	14.9	3.0	82.1	20.5	100.0	13.6	5.2	81.2
Western Cotton	69.8	100.0	11.7	2.0	86.3	30.2	100.0	5.9	5.0	89.1
Appalachian-Ozark	75.6	100.0	25.6	16.4	58.0	24.4	100.0	11.1	7.9	81.0
Lake States Cut-Over	77.8	100.0	30.4	8.9	60.7	22.2	100.0	6.3	--------	93.7
Hay and Dairy	70.9	100.0	15.4	12.4	72.2	29.1	100.0	2.1	1.4	96.5
Corn Belt	42.8	100.0	21.9	9.6	68.5	57.2	100.0	8.7	6.5	84.8
Spring Wheat	58.2	100.0	33.8	14.1	52.1	41.8	100.0	11.8	2.0	86.2
Winter Wheat	58.8	100.0	15.0	8.3	76.7	41.2	100.0	4.8	7.1	88.1
Ranching	26.3	100.0	6.8	22.7	70.5	73.7	100.0	1.6	--------	98.4

[1] Who were gainful workers.   [2] Exclusive of croppers in the 2 Cotton Areas.

TABLE 12.—PERCENT DISTRIBUTION OF FARM OPERATORS IN THE UNITED STATES IN 1935 AND OF FARM OPERATORS [1] RECEIVING RELIEF GRANTS OR REHABILITATION ADVANCES IN JUNE 1935, BY TENURE AND BY AREA

[138 counties representing 9 agricultural areas]

Area and tenure	United States Census of Agriculture, 1935	General relief, June 1935	Relief and rehabilitation combined, June 1935	Area and tenure	United States Census of Agriculture, 1935	General relief, June 1935	Relief and rehabilitation combined, June 1935
All areas:				Hay and Dairy:			
Farm operators___	100.0	100.0	100.0	Farm operators___	100.0	100.0	100.0
Owners_____	54.4	35.4	33.3	Owners_____	80.0	48.8	51.3
Tenants [2]_____	34.5	53.4	52.4	Tenants_____	20.0	51.2	48.7
Croppers_____	11.1	11.2	14.3	Corn Belt:			
Eastern Cotton:				Farm operators___	100.0	100.0	100.0
Farm operators___	100.0	100.0	100.0	Owners_____	54.1	25.2	22.7
Owners_____	33.8	21.1	22.3	Tenants_____	45.9	74.8	77.3
Tenants_____	35.4	29.8	40.1	Spring Wheat:			
Croppers_____	30.8	49.1	37.6	Farm operators___	100.0	100.0	100.0
Western Cotton:				Owners_____	62.4	41.6	39.6
Farm operators___	100.0	100.0	100.0	Tenants_____	37.6	58.4	60.4
Owners_____	38.1	12.0	12.8	Winter Wheat:			
Tenants_____	43.0	49.6	51.1	Farm operators___	100.0	100.0	100.0
Croppers_____	18.9	38.4	36.1	Owners_____	52.2	22.2	23.1
Appalachian-Ozark:				Tenants_____	47.8	77.8	76.9
Farm operators___	100.0	100.0	100.0	Ranching:			
Owners_____	68.2	40.1	40.5	Farm operators___	100.0	100.0	100.0
Tenants_____	31.8	59.9	59.5	Owners_____	76.4	61.8	58.2
Lake States Cut-Over:				Tenants_____	23.6	38.2	41.8
Farm operators___	100.0	100.0	100.0				
Owners_____	84.9	78.3	81.3				
Tenants_____	15.1	21.7	18.7				

[1] By usual occupation.
[2] Exclusive of croppers in the 2 Cotton Areas.

TABLE 13.—USUAL OCCUPATION OF HEADS OF RURAL REHABILITATION HOUSEHOLDS,[1] BY RESIDENCE, BY COLOR, AND BY AREA, JUNE 1935

[138 counties representing 9 agricultural areas]

Usual occupation	All areas	Eastern Cotton			Western Cotton			Appalachian-Ozark	Lake States Cut-Over	Hay and Dairy	Corn Belt	Spring Wheat	Winter Wheat	Ranching
		Total	White	Negro	Total	White	Negro							
RURAL														
Number	13,950	6,170	3,966	2,204	2,218	1,798	420	888	722	1,282	1,250	918	300	202
Percent	100.0	100.0	100.0	100.0	100.0	100.0	100.0	100.0	100.0	100.0	100.0	100.0	100.0	100.0
Agriculture	91.4	92.2	90.4	95.4	91.7	90.7	96.2	82.2	85.6	91.1	91.5	97.4	96.7	88.1
Farm operators	83.0	82.1	79.1	87.5	76.8	74.7	86.2	80.2	84.2	87.0	85.3	93.2	94.7	77.2
Owners	24.9	18.7	19.0	18.1	10.7	8.3	21.4	35.4	72.0	47.4	16.2	32.2	23.3	36.6
Tenants[2]	42.2	36.6	34.7	39.9	40.9	41.8	37.2	44.8	12.2	39.6	69.1	61.0	71.4	40.6
Croppers	15.8	26.8	25.4	29.5	25.2	24.6	27.6							
Farm laborers	8.4	10.1	11.3	7.9	14.9	16.0	10.0	2.0	1.4	3.6	6.2	4.2	2.0	10.9
Nonagriculture	8.6	7.8	9.6	4.6	8.3	9.3	3.8	17.8	14.4	8.9	8.5	2.6	3.3	11.9
White collar[3]	.9	.6	.9	—	1.1	1.3	—	2.3	1.7	1.0	1.0	.7	.7	—
Skilled and semiskilled	3.2	2.5	3.6	.5	3.1	3.6	.9	5.6	4.4	5.9	4.5	1.3	1.3	2.0
Unskilled	4.5	4.7	5.1	4.0	4.1	4.4	2.9	9.9	8.3	2.0	3.0	.6	1.3	9.9
OPEN COUNTRY														
Number	13,330	5,864	3,780	2,084	2,150	1,742	408	854	690	1,246	1,192	876	296	162
Percent	100.0	100.0	100.0	100.0	100.0	100.0	100.0	100.0	100.0	100.0	100.0	100.0	100.0	100.0
Agriculture	92.0	92.8	91.0	96.0	91.7	90.7	96.1	83.6	87.2	91.5	92.4	99.1	97.3	87.7
Farm operators	83.8	82.8	79.7	88.3	76.6	74.4	86.3	81.7	86.4	88.0	87.2	95.4	95.3	77.8
Owners	25.4	19.0	19.1	18.7	10.8	8.3	21.6	35.8	74.2	48.3	16.8	33.3	23.0	38.3
Tenants[2]	42.4	36.7	34.8	39.9	40.9	42.0	36.3	45.9	12.2	39.7	70.4	62.1	72.3	39.5
Croppers	16.0	27.1	25.8	29.7	24.9	24.1	28.4							
Farm laborers	8.2	10.0	11.3	7.7	15.1	16.3	9.8	1.9	.8	3.5	5.2	3.7	2.0	9.9
Nonagriculture	8.0	7.2	9.0	4.0	8.3	9.3	3.9	16.4	12.8	8.5	7.6	.9	2.7	12.3
White collar[3]	.8	.5	.7	—	1.3	1.4	1.0	2.1	1.5	.8	.8	—	—	—
Skilled and semiskilled	3.0	2.4	3.5	.5	2.9	3.5	—	4.7	4.1	5.8	4.4	.7	.7	1.2
Unskilled	4.2	4.3	4.8	3.5	4.1	4.4	2.9	9.6	7.2	1.9	2.4	.2	2.0	11.1

VILLAGE	40	4	42	58	36	32	34	12	56	68	120	186	306	620
Number	40	4	42	58	36	32	34	12	56	68	120	186	306	620
Percent	(4)	(4)	(4)	100.0	(4)	(4)	(4)	(4)	100.0	100.0	100.0	100.0	100.0	100.0
Agriculture	(4)	(4)	(4)	72.4	(4)	(4)	(4)	(4)	89.3	91.2	85.0	78.5	81.1	76.8
Farm operators	(4)	(4)	(4)	44.8	(4)	(4)	(4)	(4)	82.1	82.4	73.3	67.7	70.0	64.5
Owners	(4)	(4)	(4)	3.4	(4)	(4)	(4)	(4)	7.1	8.8	6.7	17.2	13.1	15.1
Tenants [2]	(4)		(4)	41.4	(4)	(4)	(4)	(4)	35.7	41.2	40.0	33.3	36.0	35.5
Croppers									39.3	32.4	26.6	17.2	20.9	13.9
Farm laborers				27.6					7.2	8.8	11.7	10.8	11.1	12.3
Nonagriculture	(4)	(4)	(4)	27.6	(4)	(4)	(4)	(4)	10.7	8.8	15.0	21.5	18.9	23.2
White collar [3]	(4)	(4)	(4)	3.5	(4)	(4)	(4)					4.3	2.6	8.5
Skilled and semiskilled	(4)	(4)	(4)	6.9	(4)	(4)	(4)		3.6	2.9	3.3	6.5	5.2	8.1
Unskilled	(4)	(4)	(4)	17.2	(4)	(4)	(4)		7.1	5.9	11.7	10.7	11.1	11.6

[1] Exclusive of heads with no usual occupation.
[2] Exclusive of croppers in the 2 Cotton Areas.
[3] Professional, proprietary, and clerical workers.
[4] Percent not computed on a base of less than 50 cases.

TABLE 14.—CURRENT EMPLOYMENT STATUS [1] OF HEADS AND MEMBERS OF RURAL RELIEF HOUSEHOLDS WITH AGRICULTURE AS THE USUAL OCCUPATION, BY COLOR AND BY AREA, JUNE 1935

[138 counties representing 9 agricultural areas]

Current employment status	All areas	Eastern Cotton Total	Eastern Cotton White	Eastern Cotton Negro	Western Cotton Total	Western Cotton White	Western Cotton Negro	Appalachian-Ozark	Lake States Cut-Over	Hay and Dairy	Corn Belt	Spring Wheat	Winter Wheat	Ranching
FARM OPERATORS														
Number	18,378	2,252	1,672	580	2,522	1,972	550	6,574	852	1,502	1,582	2,114	498	482
Percent	100.0	100.0	100.0	100.0	100.0	100.0	100.0	100.0	100.0	100.0	100.0	100.0	100.0	100.0
Employed at usual occupation	84.4	57.3	55.0	63.8	75.0	72.8	82.9	97.2	95.3	83.1	69.4	93.2	81.5	83.4
Employed at other occupation	2.1	4.2	5.0	1.7	4.6	5.4	1.8	.1	.9	1.6	5.5	.8	3.6	1.7
Agriculture	1.0	2.7	3.5	.3	2.0	2.0	1.8	(²)		.7	2.7	.4	1.6	1.3
Nonagriculture	1.1	1.5	1.5	1.4	2.6	3.4		.1	.9	.9	2.8	.4	2.0	.4
Unemployed	13.5	38.5	40.0	34.5	20.4	21.8	15.3	2.7	3.8	15.3	25.1	6.0	14.9	14.9
OWNERS														
Number	6,502	476	402	74	302	220	82	2,642	668	738	396	872	110	298
Percent	100.0	100.0	100.0	100.0	100.0	100.0	100.0	100.0	100.0	100.0	100.0	100.0	100.0	100.0
Employed at usual occupation	92.0	82.0	83.6	73.0	91.4	89.1	97.6	97.9	96.4	80.5	72.7	96.6	87.3	89.9
Employed at other occupation	2.1	2.0	1.0	8.1	3.3	3.6	2.4	.7	2.1	3.5	9.1	.4	5.4	3.4
Agriculture	1.4	1.2	1.0	2.7	2.3	1.8	2.4	.5	1.5	2.2	7.1	.2	1.8	3.4
Tenants [3]	1.0	.8	1.0	2.7	1.0	.9			1.5	1.5				
Croppers	.3				.7						2.5			
Farm laborers	.1				.1					.4				
Nonagriculture	.7	.8		5.4	1.0	1.8		.2	.6	1.3	2.0	.2	3.6	1.4
Unemployed	5.9	16.0	15.4	18.9	5.3	7.3		1.4	1.5	16.0	18.2	3.0	7.3	6.7
TENANTS [3]														
Number	9,806	674	436	238	1,252	1,038	214	3,932	184	764	1,186	1,242	388	184
Percent	100.0	100.0	100.0	100.0	100.0	100.0	100.0	100.0	100.0	100.0	100.0	100.0	100.0	100.0
Employed at usual occupation	84.9	68.3	61.9	79.8	77.1	75.9	83.1	96.1	79.3	83.0	65.9	90.2	79.4	68.5
Employed at other occupation	2.9	6.2	6.4	5.9	5.6	6.0	3.8	.4	8.7	2.3	6.6	1.7	3.6	3.3
Agriculture	1.9	5.0	5.5	4.2	3.5	3.5	3.8	.4	6.5	1.8	6.5	1.2	2.1	2.2
Owners	.8	1.8	1.9	1.7	.8	.8	1.9	.3	6.5	.9	3.5	.6		1.1
Croppers	.3	1.4	.9	2.5	1.4	1.7					.8			
Farm laborers	.8	1.8	2.8		1.1	1.0		.1		.5	2.7	.5	2.1	1.1
Nonagriculture	1.0	1.2	2.9	1.7	1.1	2.5	1.9		2.2	.5	3.1	.6	1.5	1.1
Unemployed	12.2	25.5	31.7	14.3	17.3	18.1	13.1	3.5	12.0	14.7	27.5	8.1	17.0	28.2

CROPPERS														
Number	2,070	1,102	834	268	968	714	254	-	-	-	-	-	-	-
Percent	100.0	100.0	100.0	100.0	100.0	100.0	100.0	-	-	-	-	-	-	-
Employed at usual occupation	48.0	35.0	33.8	38.8	62.8	58.5	74.8	-	-	-	-	-	-	-
Employed at other occupation	8.4	8.7	10.1	4.5	8.1	9.8	3.1	-	-	-	-	-	-	-
Agriculture	5.6	6.7	7.4	4.5	4.3	4.8	3.1	-	-	-	-	-	-	-
Owners	.4	.5	.5	.7	.2	-	.8	-	-	-	-	-	-	-
Tenants [3]	1.3	1.8	1.4	3.1	.6	.8	-	-	-	-	-	-	-	-
Farm laborers	3.9	4.4	5.5	.7	3.5	4.0	2.3	-	-	-	-	-	-	-
Nonagriculture	2.8	2.0	2.7	-	3.8	5.0	-	-	-	-	-	-	-	-
Unemployed	43.6	56.3	56.1	56.7	29.1	31.7	22.1	-	-	-	-	-	-	-
FARM LABORERS														
Number	18,652	3,736	2,118	1,618	3,224	2,356	868	4,792	590	1,872	2,214	1,408	322	494
Percent	100.0	100.0	100.0	100.0	100.0	100.0	100.0	100.0	100.0	100.0	100.0	100.0	100.0	100.0
Employed at usual occupation	53.6	35.7	32.9	39.3	37.6	35.7	42.6	88.9	75.3	39.4	30.6	81.9	27.3	18.2
Employed at other occupation	2.7	1.8	2.0	1.5	1.7	2.1	.9	1.5	2.0	5.7	5.6	1.8	5.0	4.5
Agriculture	1.5	.7	.9	.4	.7	1.0	.2	1.3	2.0	3.8	1.5	1.5	2.5	4.0
Owners	.3	(2)	-	.1	(2)	.1	-	.2	.6	1.7	.2	.1	-	1.6
Tenants [3]	1.0	.3	.4	.2	.1	.2	-	1.1	1.4	2.1	1.3	1.4	2.5	2.4
Croppers	.2	.4	.5	.1	.6	.7	.2	-	-	-	-	-	-	-
Nonagriculture	1.2	1.1	1.1	1.1	1.0	1.1	.7	.2	-	1.9	4.1	.3	2.5	.5
Unemployed	43.7	62.5	65.1	59.2	60.7	62.2	56.5	9.6	22.7	54.9	63.8	16.3	67.7	77.3
FARM LABORERS (HEADS ONLY)														
Number	6,850	1,502	810	692	1,448	1,130	318	516	144	1,004	1,454	244	204	334
Percent	100.0	100.0	100.0	100.0	100.0	100.0	100.0	100.0	100.0	100.0	100.0	100.0	100.0	100.0
Employed at usual occupation	13.6	14.6	9.9	20.2	9.9	10.3	8.8	22.1	25.0	11.5	14.3	24.6	10.8	3.0
Employed at other occupation	6.4	3.5	3.4	3.5	2.9	3.0	2.5	14.3	6.9	9.2	7.8	9.0	7.8	6.0
Agriculture	4.0	1.9	2.4	1.2	1.4	1.6	.6	12.0	6.9	7.2	2.3	8.2	3.9	6.0
Nonagriculture	2.4	1.6	1.0	2.3	1.5	1.4	1.9	2.3	-	2.0	5.5	.8	3.9	-
Unemployed	80.0	81.9	86.7	76.3	87.2	86.7	88.7	63.6	68.1	79.3	77.9	66.4	81.4	91.0

[1] Current employment refers to the February employment of the June cases already on relief in February, or to the employment at date of application of cases that came on relief from March through June.

[2] Less than 0.05 percent.

[3] Exclusive of croppers in the 2 Cotton Areas.

TABLE 15.—Residence of Heads of Rural Relief Households with Agriculture as the Usual Occupation, by Color and by Area, June 1935

[138 counties representing 9 agricultural areas]

Usual occupation	All areas	Eastern Cotton — Total	Eastern Cotton — White	Eastern Cotton — Negro	Western Cotton — Total	Western Cotton — White	Western Cotton — Negro	Appalachian-Ozark	Lake States Cut-Over	Hay and Dairy	Corn Belt	Spring Wheat	Winter Wheat	Ranching
RURAL														
Number	24,976	3,672	2,416	1,256	3,944	3,086	858	7,030	990	2,492	3,018	2,320	700	810
Percent	100.0	100.0	100.0	100.0	100.0	100.0	100.0	100.0	100.0	100.0	100.0	100.0	100.0	100.0
Farm operators	72.6	59.1	66.5	44.9	63.4	63.4	62.9	92.7	85.5	59.7	51.8	89.5	70.9	58.8
Owners	25.7	12.5	16.0	5.7	7.6	7.1	9.5	37.1	66.9	29.1	13.0	37.2	15.7	36.3
Tenants[1]	38.8	17.6	17.0	18.8	31.4	33.3	24.5	55.6	18.6	30.6	38.8	52.3	55.2	22.5
Croppers	8.1	29.0	33.5	20.4	24.3	23.0	28.9							
Farm laborers	27.4	40.9	33.5	55.1	36.7	36.6	37.1	7.3	14.5	40.3	48.2	10.5	29.1	41.2
OPEN COUNTRY														
Number	20,490	3,068	2,108	960	3,190	2,506	684	6,452	920	2,044	1,778	2,092	542	404
Percent	100.0	100.0	100.0	100.0	100.0	100.0	100.0	100.0	100.0	100.0	100.0	100.0	100.0	100.0
Farm operators	78.6	61.1	66.9	48.3	68.3	67.8	70.2	94.0	87.8	65.2	65.0	93.2	77.9	78.2
Owners	28.3	13.0	15.8	6.9	8.2	7.4	11.1	37.4	69.1	31.8	16.3	39.9	18.8	53.0
Tenants[1]	41.9	18.9	17.4	22.0	34.6	36.5	27.5	56.6	18.7	33.4	48.7	53.3	59.1	25.2
Croppers	8.4	29.2	33.7	19.4	25.5	23.9	31.6							
Farm laborers	21.4	38.9	33.1	51.7	31.7	32.2	29.8	6.0	12.2	34.8	35.0	6.8	22.1	21.8
VILLAGE														
Number	4,486	604	308	296	754	580	174	578	70	448	1,240	228	158	406
Percent	100.0	100.0	100.0	100.0	100.0	100.0	100.0	100.0	100.0	100.0	100.0	100.0	100.0	100.0
Farm operators	45.2	49.0	63.6	33.8	41.9	44.1	34.5	78.2	54.3	34.8	32.9	55.3	46.8	39.4
Owners	13.8	9.6	16.9	2.0	5.0	5.5	3.4	34.6	37.1	17.0	8.4	13.2	5.0	19.7
Tenants[1]	24.4	11.3	14.3	8.7	17.8	19.3	12.7	43.6	17.2	17.8	24.5	42.1	41.8	19.7
Croppers	7.0	28.1	32.4	23.1	19.1	19.3	18.4							
Farm laborers	54.8	51.0	36.4	66.2	58.1	55.9	65.5	21.8	45.7	65.2	67.1	44.7	53.2	60.6

[1] Exclusive of croppers in the 2 Cotton Areas.

TABLE 16.—CURRENT EMPLOYMENT STATUS [1] OF HEADS OF RURAL RELIEF HOUSEHOLDS USUALLY ENGAGED IN NONAGRICULTURAL OCCUPATIONS, BY AREA, JUNE 1935

[138 counties representing 9 agricultural areas]

Current employment status	All areas	Eastern Cotton	Western Cotton	Appalachian-Ozark	Lake States Cut-Over	Hay and Dairy	Corn Belt	Spring Wheat	Winter Wheat	Ranching
NONAGRICULTURAL WORKERS										
Number	23,132	2,416	1,796	7,458	2,016	4,412	3,310	644	424	656
Percent	100.0	100.0	100.0	100.0	100.0	100.0	100.0	100.0	100.0	100.0
Employed at usual occupation	10.3	14.7	18.6	6.7	6.2	9.4	11.8	16.8	12.3	14.6
Employed at other occupation	15.7	4.7	7.7	27.2	21.6	11.6	8.9	5.3	4.2	8.5
Agriculture	13.9	2.8	5.0	26.6	20.0	9.6	5.0	3.7	2.3	7.0
Nonagriculture	1.8	1.9	2.7	.6	1.6	2.0	3.9	1.6	1.9	1.5
Unemployed	74.0	80.6	73.7	66.1	72.2	79.0	79.3	77.9	83.5	76.9
WHITE COLLAR [2]										
Number	2,022	320	214	350	108	366	438	118	64	44
Percent	100.0	100.0	100.0	100.0	100.0	100.0	100.0	100.0	100.0	(3)
Employed at usual occupation	16.5	11.3	12.2	16.6	14.8	17.5	17.4	22.0	31.3	(3)
Employed at other occupation	13.7	6.2	9.3	25.1	20.4	15.8	12.3	6.8	12.5	
Agriculture	8.7	1.2	5.6	22.8	14.8	8.2	5.5	5.1	6.3	
Nonagriculture	5.0	5.0	3.7	2.3	5.6	7.6	6.8	1.7	6.2	
Unemployed	69.8	82.5	78.5	58.3	64.8	66.7	70.3	71.2	56.2	(3)
SKILLED AND SEMISKILLED										
Number	6,618	920	420	1,148	518	1,822	1,246	234	130	180
Percent	100.0	100.0	100.0	100.0	100.0	100.0	100.0	100.0	100.0	100.0
Employed at usual occupation	7.6	11.1	9.5	6.1	5.4	7.5	6.3	13.7	4.6	6.7
Employed at other occupation	16.4	5.0	16.2	32.6	24.3	14.2	13.6	6.0	6.2	11.1
Agriculture	12.9	3.5	6.7	31.0	20.5	11.6	7.5	3.4	4.6	7.8
Nonagriculture	3.5	1.5	9.5	1.6	3.8	2.6	6.1	2.6	1.6	3.3
Unemployed	76.0	83.9	74.3	61.3	70.3	78.3	80.1	80.3	89.2	82.2
UNSKILLED										
Number	14,492	1,176	1,162	5,960	1,390	2,224	1,626	292	230	432
Percent	100.0	100.0	100.0	100.0	100.0	100.0	100.0	100.0	100.0	100.0
Employed at usual occupation	10.6	18.4	23.1	6.3	5.8	9.6	14.6	17.1	11.3	16.7
Employed at other occupation	15.6	4.1	4.3	26.3	20.7	8.6	4.3	4.1	.9	8.3
Agriculture	15.0	2.7	4.3	26.0	20.3	8.1	3.0	3.4		7.4
Nonagriculture	.6	1.4		.3	.4	.5	1.3	.7	.9	.9
Unemployed	73.8	77.5	72.6	67.4	73.5	81.8	81.1	78.8	87.8	75.0

[1] Current employment refers to the February employment of the June cases already on relief in February or to the employment at date of application of cases that came on relief from March through June.
[2] Professional, proprietary, and clerical workers.
[3] Percent not computed on a base of less than 50 cases.

TABLE 17.—USUAL OCCUPATION OF EMPLOYABLE HEADS [1] OF RURAL RELIEF HOUSEHOLDS, BY COLOR AND BY AREA, JUNE 1935

[138 counties representing 9 agricultural areas]

Area	Total		Usual occupation									
			Agriculture						Nonagriculture			
				Farm operators							Skilled and semi-skilled	
	Number	Percent	Total	Total	Owners	Tenants [2]	Croppers	Farm laborers	Total	White collar [3]		Unskilled
All areas	48,112	100.0	51.9	37.7	13.3	20.2	4.2	14.2	48.1	4.2	13.8	30.1
Eastern Cotton:												
Total	6,088	100.0	60.3	35.6	7.5	10.6	17.5	24.7	39.7	5.3	15.1	19.3
White	4,162	100.0	58.0	38.6	9.3	9.8	19.5	19.4	42.0	7.4	20.0	14.6
Negro	1,926	100.0	65.2	29.3	3.7	12.3	13.3	35.9	34.8	.7	4.6	29.5
Western Cotton:												
Total	5,742	100.0	68.7	43.5	5.2	21.6	16.7	25.2	31.3	3.7	7.4	20.2
White	4,504	100.0	68.5	43.4	4.8	22.8	15.8	25.1	31.5	4.4	8.9	18.2
Negro	1,238	100.0	69.3	43.6	6.6	17.0	20.0	25.7	30.7	1.3	1.6	27.8
Appalachian-Ozark	14,488	100.0	48.5	45.0	18.0	27.0	------	3.5	51.5	2.4	7.9	41.2
Lake States Cut-Over	3,006	100.0	32.9	28.1	22.0	6.1	------	4.8	67.1	3.6	17.2	46.3
Hay and Dairy	6,904	100.0	36.1	21.6	10.5	11.1	------	14.5	63.9	5.3	26.4	32.2
Corn Belt	6,330	100.0	47.7	24.7	6.2	18.5	------	23.0	52.3	6.9	19.7	25.7
Spring Wheat	2,964	100.0	78.3	70.1	29.2	40.9	------	8.2	21.7	4.0	7.9	9.8
Winter Wheat	1,124	100.0	62.3	44.1	9.8	34.3	------	18.2	37.7	5.7	11.6	20.4
Ranching	1,466	100.0	55.3	32.5	20.1	12.4	------	22.8	44.7	3.0	12.3	29.4

[1] 16 to 64 years of age and working or seeking work.
[2] Exclusive of croppers in the 2 Cotton Areas.
[3] Professional, proprietary, and clerical workers.

TABLE 18.—LENGTH OF TIME SINCE HEADS OF RURAL RELIEF HOUSEHOLDS WITH AGRICULTURE AS THE USUAL OCCUPATION, BUT NOT CURRENTLY ENGAGED IN AGRICULTURE, LEFT THE FARM, BY AREA, JUNE 1935

[138 counties representing 9 agricultural areas]

Area	Total		Length of time since left the farm				
	Number	Percent	1 year	2 years	3 to 4 years	5 to 9 years	10 years and over
FARM OPERATORS							
All areas	2,594	100.0	51.7	24.0	15.3	8.9	0.1
Eastern Cotton	876	100.0	48.0	30.1	16.4	5.5	
Western Cotton	568	100.0	66.2	19.0	10.6	4.2	
Appalachian-Ozark	168	100.0	57.2	22.6	10.7	8.3	1.2
Lake States Cut-Over	38	(¹)	(¹)	(¹)	(¹)	(¹)	
Hay and Dairy	234	100.0	48.7	18.8	23.1	9.4	
Corn Belt	432	100.0	40.8	20.8	20.8	17.6	
Spring Wheat	122	100.0	39.3	34.4	11.5	14.8	
Winter Wheat	82	100.0	39.0	22.0	7.3	31.7	
Ranching	74	100.0	73.0	10.8	10.8	5.4	
OWNERS							
All areas	390	100.0	41.0	19.5	20.0	19.0	.5
Eastern Cotton	76	100.0	39.4	21.1	18.4	21.1	
Western Cotton	20	(¹)	(¹)	(¹)	(¹)	(¹)	
Appalachian-Ozark	32	(¹)	(¹)	(¹)		(¹)	(¹)
Lake States Cut-Over	12	(¹)	(¹)	(¹)	(¹)		
Hay and Dairy	118	100.0	37.4	18.6	27.1	16.9	
Corn Belt	78	100.0	28.2	30.8	17.9	23.1	
Spring Wheat	24	(¹)	(¹)	(¹)	(¹)	(¹)	
Winter Wheat	10	(¹)	(¹)		(¹)	(¹)	
Ranching	20	(¹)	(¹)		(¹)		
TENANTS ²							
All areas	1,270	100.0	53.3	22.8	14.3	9.6	
Eastern Cotton	174	100.0	52.9	28.7	13.8	4.6	
Western Cotton	240	100.0	65.8	20.0	9.2	5.0	
Appalachian-Ozark	136	100.0	58.9	25.0	13.2	2.9	
Lake States Cut-Over	26	(¹)	(¹)	(¹)	(¹)		
Hay and Dairy	116	100.0	60.3	19.0	19.0	1.7	
Corn Belt	354	100.0	43.5	18.6	21.5	16.4	
Spring Wheat	98	100.0	38.8	38.8	10.2	12.2	
Winter Wheat	72	100.0	38.8	25.0	5.6	30.6	
Ranching	54	100.0	70.4	14.8	7.4	7.4	
CROPPERS							
All areas	934	100.0	53.9	27.4	14.8	3.9	
Eastern Cotton	626	100.0	47.7	31.6	16.9	3.8	
Western Cotton	308	100.0	66.9	18.8	10.4	3.9	
FARM LABORERS							
All areas	5,464	100.0	71.5	17.0	8.0	3.4	.1
Eastern Cotton	1,240	100.0	72.3	18.2	6.6	2.7	.2
Western Cotton	1,248	100.0	91.8	6.9	.8	.3	.2
Appalachian-Ozark	312	100.0	60.3	23.7	11.5	4.5	
Lake States Cut-Over	94	100.0	53.3	17.0	19.1	10.6	
Hay and Dairy	796	100.0	72.1	15.6	9.5	2.8	
Corn Belt	1,182	100.0	51.3	26.2	15.2	7.3	
Spring Wheat	150	100.0	66.7	25.3	8.0		
Winter Wheat	170	100.0	82.3	7.1	5.9	4.7	
Ranching	272	100.0	76.6	15.4	5.1	2.9	

¹ Percent not computed on a base of less than 50 cases.
² Exclusive of croppers in the 2 Cotton Areas.

TABLE 19.—USUAL OCCUPATION OF HEADS OF RURAL REHABILITATION HOUSEHOLDS, BY COLOR AND BY AREA, JUNE 1935

[138 counties representing 9 agricultural areas]

Area	Total		Usual occupation										
				Agriculture						Nonagriculture			
					Farm operators								
	Number	Percent	Head not a worker	Total	Total	Owners	Tenants [1]	Croppers	Farm laborers	Total	White collar [2]	Skilled and semiskilled	Unskilled
All areas	14,394	100.0	3.1	88.5	80.4	24.2	40.8	15.4	8.1	8.4	0.9	3.2	4.3
Eastern Cotton:													
Total	6,286	100.0	1.8	90.5	80.6	18.3	35.9	26.4	9.9	7.7	.6	2.5	4.6
White	4,026	100.0	1.5	89.1	78.0	18.8	34.2	25.0	11.1	9.4	.8	3.6	5.0
Negro	2,260	100.0	2.5	93.0	85.3	17.6	38.9	28.8	7.7	4.5	.1	.6	3.8
Western Cotton:													
Total	2,332	100.0	4.9	87.2	73.0	10.2	38.9	23.9	14.2	7.9	1.2	2.8	3.9
White	1,872	100.0	4.0	87.0	71.7	7.9	40.2	23.6	15.3	9.0	1.2	3.4	4.4
Negro	460	100.0	8.7	87.8	78.7	19.6	33.9	25.2	9.1	3.5	.9	------	2.6
Appalachian-Ozark	904	100.0	1.8	80.7	78.7	34.7	44.0	------	2.0	17.5	2.2	5.5	9.8
Lake States Cut-Over	768	100.0	6.0	80.5	79.2	67.7	11.5	------	1.3	13.5	1.6	4.1	7.8
Hay and Dairy	1,362	100.0	5.9	85.7	82.4	45.1	37.3	------	3.3	8.4	.9	5.6	1.9
Corn Belt	1,284	100.0	2.6	89.1	83.0	15.7	67.3	------	6.1	8.3	.9	4.4	3.0
Spring Wheat	942	100.0	2.6	94.9	90.9	31.4	59.5	------	4.0	2.5	.6	1.3	.6
Winter Wheat	310	100.0	3.2	93.6	91.7	22.6	69.1	------	1.9	3.2	.6	1.2	1.4
Ranching	206	100.0	1.9	86.4	75.7	35.9	39.8	------	10.7	11.7	-----	2.0	9.7

[1] Exclusive of croppers in the 2 Cotton Areas.
[2] Professional, proprietary, and clerical workers.

TABLE 20.—PERCENT OF RURAL RELIEF AND NONRELIEF FARM OPERATORS, OTHER THAN CROPPERS, WHO OWNED NO WORK STOCK AND THE AVERAGE NUMBER OWNED ON JANUARY 1, 1934, BY AREA

Area	Percent of farm owners and tenants without work stock		Average number of work stock owned [1]	
	Relief	Nonrelief	Relief	Nonrelief
All areas combined	34	18	3.6	4.2
Old South Cotton	59	18	1.8	2.7
Southwest Cotton	21	13	2.6	4.4
Tobacco	14	16	1.6	3.5
Dairy	59	19	1.8	2.7
Massachusetts	87	56	(2)	(2)
Cut-Over	57	24	1.7	2.1
Corn-and-Hog	56	19	2.3	4.0
Cash Grain	7	4	4.9	6.1
Wheat	17	14	6.2	8.3
Mountain	38	27	3.3	4.4
New Mexico	16	12	2.1	2.7
Oregon	74	47	.7	2.6
California	86	61	1.9	3.2

[1] Averages based on those who owned some work stock.
[2] Less than 10 cases. Average not computed.

Source: McCormick, T. C., *Comparative Study of Rural Relief and Non-Relief Households*, Research Monograph II, Division of Social Research, Works Progress Administration, 1935, table 42.

TABLE 21.—PERCENT OF RURAL RELIEF AND NONRELIEF HOUSEHOLDS THAT OWNED NO LIVESTOCK, JANUARY 1, 1934, BY AREA

Area	Percent of households					
	Without cows		Without hogs		Without poultry	
	Relief	Nonrelief	Relief	Nonrelief	Relief	Nonrelief
All areas combined	68	47	72	65	45	34
Old South Cotton	61	32	45	28	19	11
Southwest Cotton	40	21	49	50	25	18
Tobacco	75	48	63	47	28	19
Dairy	86	49	93	78	64	33
Massachusetts	95	89	97	97	80	71
Cut-Over	58	30	86	76	53	41
Corn-and-Hog	88	66	84	73	59	51
Cash Grain	52	50	59	58	41	40
Wheat	38	31	48	47	22	24
Mountain	58	38	72	68	35	26
New Mexico	94	69	91	71	80	50
Oregon	64	45	87	78	43	42
California	84	75	96	94	47	34

Source: McCormick, T. C., *Comparative Study of Rural Relief and Non-Relief Households*, Research Monograph II, Division of Social Research, Works Progress Administration, 1935, table 43.

TABLE 22.—AVERAGE NUMBERS OF LIVESTOCK OWNED BY RURAL RELIEF AND NON-RELIEF HOUSEHOLDS REPORTING SUCH LIVESTOCK, JANUARY 1, 1934, BY AREA

Area	Average number of cows		Average number of hogs		Average number of poultry	
	Relief	Nonrelief	Relief	Nonrelief	Relief	Nonrelief
All areas combined	3.0	5.7	3.7	11.1	37	81
Old South Cotton	1.5	2.7	2.5	5.7	15	29
Southwest Cotton	2.5	5.5	3.7	9.0	34	100
Tobacco	1.3	2.6	3.4	7.5	19	33
Dairy	1.4	7.6	2.6	3.6	35	87
Massachusetts	2.5	6.2	3.0	[1] 2.7	49	64
Cut-Over	2.6	6.2	1.9	2.6	31	43
Corn-and-Hog	1.6	5.0	2.7	26.0	23	78
Cash Grain	4.8	7.0	5.9	21.6	66	125
Wheat	5.3	7.2	4.8	11.0	61	94
Mountain	2.8	4.4	2.3	4.8	44	82
New Mexico	1.3	1.4	1.6	1.6	16	19
Oregon	2.0	4.0	1.9	7.3	30	52
California	1.2	7.8	1.6	4.5	39	198

[1] Several nontypical cases which raised the average unduly were excluded.

Source: McCormick, T. C., *Comparative Study of Rural Relief and Non-Relief Households*, Research Monograph II, Division of Social Research, Works Progress Administration, 1935, table 44.

TABLE 23.—GRADE ATTAINMENT OF HEADS OF OPEN COUNTRY HOUSEHOLDS ON RELIEF BY AGE GROUPS, OCTOBER 1935

[138 counties representing 9 agricultural areas]

Last grade or year completed	Age in years					
	Total	16 to 24	25 to 34	35 to 44	45 to 54	55 to 64
Number	23,514	2,188	6,640	6,132	5,076	3,478
Percent	100.0	100.0	100.0	100.0	100.0	100.0
Grade school:						
No grade completed	10.7	5.1	5.3	10.1	14.0	20.5
1 to 3 grades	15.1	9.7	12.3	14.6	19.3	18.6
4 to 5 grades	23.2	21.9	21.2	23.0	26.6	22.9
6 grades	11.1	11.1	10.8	13.1	10.4	9.1
7 grades	10.0	10.2	12.6	10.8	7.2	7.2
8 grades	22.0	26.2	27.5	21.6	17.6	16.2
High school:						
1 year	2.8	5.5	4.0	2.6	1.6	1.2
2 years	2.0	3.8	2.7	1.6	1.2	1.8
3 years	1.0	2.7	1.2	.8	.6	.4
4 years	1.5	3.1	1.9	.9	.7	1.7
College:						
1 year or more	.6	.7	.5	.9	.8	.4

TABLE 24.—AVERAGE GRADE ATTAINMENT OF HEADS OF OPEN COUNTRY HOUSE-
HOLDS ON RELIEF, BY AGE GROUPS AND BY AREA, OCTOBER 1935

[138 counties representing 9 agricultural areas]

			Median grade completed										
		Eastern Cotton			Western Cotton									
Age	All areas	Total	White	Negro	Total	White	Negro	Appalachian-Ozark	Lake States Cut-Over	Hay and Dairy	Corn Belt	Spring Wheat	Winter Wheat	Ranching
Total	6.1	5.1	5.6	2.8	6.4	6.7	5.4	5.1	7.2	7.8	8.0	8.1	8.1	8.0
Under 21 years	7.0	6.2	6.6	5.5	8.4	8.5	8.0	6.1	8.4	8.5	10.0	8.9	----	5.0
21 to 24 years	7.3	5.6	6.0	4.4	8.1	8.2	6.3	6.1	8.4	8.4	8.5	8.1	8.6	8.3
25 to 34 years	7.0	5.7	6.3	2.4	7.0	7.1	6.5	5.8	8.2	8.2	8.5	8.2	8.3	8.3
35 to 44 years	6.2	5.1	5.8	3.1	6.3	6.5	5.5	5.2	7.4	8.0	7.7	7.3	7.8	7.2
45 to 64 years	5.1	4.4	4.8	2.0	5.6	5.9	4.4	4.2	5.3	6.8	5.9	8.1	8.0	7.3

TABLE 25.—RURAL RELIEF TURN-OVER, MARCH THROUGH JUNE 1935, PER 100
CASES RECEIVING RELIEF IN FEBRUARY,[1] BY USUAL OCCUPATION OF THE HEAD
AND BY AREA

[138 counties representing 9 agricultural areas]

	Separation rates							Accession rates: All cases						
		Agricultural heads					Nonagricultural heads		Agricultural heads					Nonagricultural heads
Area	All heads	Total	Owners	Tenants[2]	Croppers	Laborers		All heads	Total	Owners	Tenants[2]	Croppers	Laborers	
All areas	50.1	57.7	57.3	57.9	72.8	49.9	37.5	17.6	13.6	15.6	13.5	9.7	13.7	24.2
Eastern Cotton:														
Total	59.3	64.5	64.6	67.8	72.0	56.1	45.4	20.6	15.4	19.4	16.4	16.4	12.7	34.7
White	61.4	67.4	62.3	70.9	72.3	61.5	45.8	22.3	16.4	21.9	14.8	16.6	14.7	37.9
Negro	54.7	58.3	72.2	60.3	70.9	49.0	44.5	16.8	13.2	10.7	20.4	15.8	9.8	27.1
Western Cotton:														
Total	67.4	71.9	86.2	74.9	73.5	56.5	46.2	8.7	6.2	3.5	6.2	4.5	9.7	21.1
White	64.3	68.6	84.5	72.0	70.9	50.7	45.8	10.2	7.2	4.0	6.9	5.1	11.9	23.1
Negro	75.0	79.5	89.3	83.4	78.7	68.8	47.3	5.3	3.9	2.6	4.1	3.4	5.0	14.5
Appalachian-Ozark	28.9	31.5	29.3	31.0	----	45.2	26.3	30.0	30.4	32.3	28.2	----	38.2	29.6
Lake States Cut-Over	43.1	57.1	60.4	61.7	----	10.3	29.9	21.1	9.8	9.7	8.0	----	16.2	31.9
Hay and Dairy	49.8	56.7	63.4	60.9	----	45.0	44.4	13.4	9.0	8.3	7.2	----	11.7	16.9
Corn Belt	51.7	60.4	68.1	70.9	----	41.4	39.4	13.7	10.8	12.4	9.4	----	12.3	17.7
Spring Wheat	45.4	48.3	46.5	49.8	----	45.8	31.8	12.4	12.0	15.9	9.7	----	11.9	14.4
Winter Wheat	52.9	60.2	74.0	58.9	----	44.9	33.7	14.7	13.2	6.5	11.4	----	27.5	18.9
Ranching	51.4	52.3	53.7	50.9	----	51.9	49.9	24.0	18.0	19.2	13.8	----	19.4	33.3

	Accession rates: New cases							Accession rates: Reopened cases						
All areas	7.5	5.1	5.3	4.8	3.7	6.3	11.5	10.1	8.5	10.3	8.7	6.0	7.4	12.7
Eastern Cotton:														
Total	9.5	6.3	5.5	5.7	6.7	6.5	18.0	11.1	9.1	13.9	10.7	9.7	6.2	16.7
White	10.9	6.9	6.5	5.8	6.4	8.4	21.1	11.4	9.5	15.4	9.0	10.2	6.3	16.8
Negro	6.5	4.9	2.1	5.6	7.4	3.9	10.9	10.3	8.3	8.6	14.8	8.4	5.9	16.2
Western Cotton:														
Total	3.6	1.9	1.3	1.4	1.4	3.7	11.4	5.1	4.3	2.2	4.8	3.1	6.0	9.7
White	4.4	2.6	2.0	1.7	1.9	5.0	12.4	5.8	4.6	2.0	5.2	3.2	6.9	10.7
Negro	1.5	.5	----	.4	.4	.9	8.1	3.8	3.4	2.6	3.7	3.0	4.1	6.4
Appalachian-Ozark	11.8	10.4	10.7	9.7	----	13.7	13.3	18.2	20.0	21.6	18.5	----	24.5	16.3
Lake States Cut-Over	8.6	3.6	3.6	2.5	----	7.4	13.4	12.5	6.2	6.1	5.5	----	8.8	18.5
Hay and Dairy	6.9	4.7	3.6	4.1	----	6.4	8.7	6.5	4.3	4.7	3.1	----	5.3	8.2
Corn Belt	7.1	5.8	5.4	5.0	----	7.3	9.0	6.6	5.0	7.0	4.4	----	5.0	8.7
Spring Wheat	3.5	3.4	4.3	2.6	----	4.3	4.1	8.9	8.6	11.6	7.1	----	7.6	10.3
Winter Wheat	4.0	3.2	1.2	2.7	----	7.3	6.0	10.7	10.0	5.3	8.7	----	20.2	12.9
Ranching	9.8	6.5	6.2	6.2	----	6.9	15.0	14.2	11.5	13.0	7.6	----	12.5	18.3

[1] Separations include only cases on relief in February but not on relief in June. Accessions include only
cases on relief in June which were not on relief in February.
[2] Exclusive of croppers in the 2 Cotton Areas.

TABLE 26.—NEW CASES AMONG ACCESSIONS TO RURAL RELIEF ROLLS, BY USUAL OCCUPATION OF THE HEAD AND BY REGION, JULY THROUGH OCTOBER 1935

[300 counties and 83 New England townships]

Usual occupation	32 States	11 northern States [1]	13 southern States [2]	6 western States [3]	2 New England States [4]
ALL ACCESSIONS					
Total	39,152	14,472	20,042	3,746	892
Agricultural heads	21,190	7,588	11,760	1,654	188
Farm operators	13,384	5,176	7,370	750	88
Owners	4,294	2,188	1,610	416	80
Tenants [5]	6,488	2,988	3,158	334	8
Croppers	2,602		2,602		
Farm laborers	7,806	2,412	4,390	904	100
Nonagricultural heads	17,962	6,884	8,282	2,092	704
NEW CASES					
Total	9,923	2,836	5,528	1,224	335
Agricultural heads	4,499	1,018	3,014	408	59
Farm operators	2,751	536	2,050	142	23
Owners	658	216	334	90	18
Tenants [5]	1,005	320	628	52	5
Croppers	1,088		1,088		
Farm laborers	1,748	482	964	266	36
Nonagricultural heads	5,424	1,818	2,514	816	276
NEW CASES PER 100 ACCESSIONS					
Total	25.3	19.6	27.6	32.7	37.6
Agricultural heads	21.2	13.4	25.6	24.7	31.4
Farm operators	20.6	10.4	27.8	18.9	([6])
Owners	15.3	9.9	20.7	21.6	([6])
Tenants [5]	15.5	10.7	19.9	15.6	([6])
Croppers	41.8		41.8		
Farm laborers	22.4	20.0	22.0	29.4	36.0
Nonagricultural heads	30.2	26.4	30.4	39.0	39.2

[1] Iowa, Kansas, Michigan, Minnesota, Missouri, Nebraska, New York, North Dakota, Ohio, South Dakota, and Wisconsin.
[2] Alabama, Arkansas, Florida, Georgia, Kentucky, Louisiana, North Carolina, Oklahoma, South Carolina, Tennessee, Texas, Virginia, and West Virginia.
[3] California, Colorado, Montana, Oregon, Utah, and Washington.
[4] Connecticut and Massachusetts.
[5] Exclusive of croppers in the southern States.
[6] Percent not computed on a base of less than 100 cases.

TABLE 27.—FARM OPERATOR ACCESSIONS TO, AND SEPARATIONS FROM, THE GENERAL RELIEF ROLLS OF AGENCIES EXPENDING F. E. R. A. FUNDS, AND THE TOTAL NUMBER OF FARM OPERATORS AT THE FIRST OF EACH MONTH, JULY 1935 TO JANUARY 1936

[300 counties and 83 New England townships]

Month	Sample counties [1]			Estimate for United States		
	Total case load at first of month	Change during month		Total case load at first of month	Change during month	
		Accessions	Separations		Accessions	Separations
All months		19,970	55,890		215,000	551,000
1935						
July	40,725	4,319	8,667	390,000	48,000	83,000
August	36,377	2,813	6,692	355,000	32,000	64,000
September	32,498	2,770	5,491	323,000	32,000	54,000
October	29,777	3,478	5,283	301,000	39,000	50,000
November	27,972	3,954	9,978	290,000	38,000	102,000
December	21,948	2,636	19,779	226,000	26,000	198,000
1936						
January	4,805			54,000		

[1] The counties and townships contained 8.8 percent of all rural families in 1930 and about 10 percent of all farm operators in 1935.

TABLE 28.—ACCESSIONS TO RURAL RELIEF ROLLS, BY USUAL OCCUPATION OF THE HEAD OF THE CASE AND BY REASON FOR OPENING AND REOPENING, JULY THROUGH OCTOBER 1935

[300 counties and 83 New England townships]

Usual occupation	Total		Crop failure or loss of livestock	Decreased earnings	Loss of employment		Administrative ruling	Loss or depletion of assets	Increased needs	All others
	Number	Percent			Private employment	Works Program				
ALL ACCESSIONS										
Total	44,524	100.0	10.9	12.4	36.8	0.8	6.5	13.3	9.9	9.4
Farm operators	13,384	100.0	32.3	16.4	11.3	.6	9.4	10.3	9.8	9.9
Owners	4,294	100.0	36.9	17.7	9.9	.9	6.6	13.0	10.3	4.7
Tenants [1]	6,488	100.0	34.4	17.2	10.8	.7	12.4	8.7	9.9	5.9
Croppers	2,602	100.0	19.1	12.3	14.8	.1	6.6	9.8	8.8	28.5
Farm laborers	7,806	100.0	1.8	12.5	63.3	.7	5.0	6.3	8.0	2.4
Nonagriculture	17,962	100.0	1.1	11.9	50.4	1.0	4.4	13.7	6.7	10.8
All others [2]	5,372	100.0	3.2	4.3	11.6	.7	8.5	29.7	23.1	18.9
NEW CASES										
Total	11,722	100.0	7.7	9.3	36.7	.9	1.5	18.9	8.2	16.8
Farm operators	2,751	100.0	27.5	11.8	9.2	.7	.5	12.4	6.7	31.2
Owners	658	100.0	36.7	16.4	10.6	.6	1.5	18.7	7.6	7.9
Tenants [1]	1,005	100.0	34.8	15.4	9.0	1.4	.4	13.6	9.1	16.3
Croppers	1,088	100.0	15.3	5.7	8.5			7.4	3.9	59.2
Farm laborers	1,748	100.0	2.3	8.6	62.6	1.7	1.5	11.4	9.0	2.9
Nonagriculture	5,424	100.0	1.2	10.2	49.8	.9	1.7	17.5	5.4	13.3
All others [2]	1,799	100.0	2.3	3.3	8.4	.8	2.3	40.5	17.9	24.5
REOPENED CASES										
Total	32,802	100.0	12.0	13.6	36.9	.7	8.3	11.3	10.5	6.7
Farm operators	10,633	100.0	33.5	17.6	11.8	.6	11.7	9.8	10.6	4.4
Owners	3,636	100.0	36.9	18.0	9.7	1.0	7.5	12.0	10.8	4.1
Tenants [1]	5,483	100.0	34.6	17.5	11.1	.5	14.6	7.8	10.0	3.9
Croppers	1,514	100.0	21.8	17.0	19.3	.1	11.4	11.5	12.3	6.6
Farm laborers	6,058	100.0	1.6	13.6	63.6	.5	6.0	4.8	7.7	2.2
Nonagriculture	12,538	100.0	1.1	12.6	50.8	1.0	5.5	12.0	7.3	9.7
All others [2]	3,573	100.0	3.7	4.9	13.2	.6	11.6	24.2	25.7	16.1

[1] Exclusive of croppers in the southern States.
[2] Includes "Head not a worker" and heads with "No usual occupation."

132   *Farmers on Relief and Rehabilitation*

TABLE 29.—ACCESSIONS TO RURAL RELIEF ROLLS IN NORTHERN STATES,[1] BY USUAL OCCUPATION OF THE HEAD OF THE CASE AND BY REASON FOR OPENING AND REOPENING, JULY THROUGH OCTOBER 1935

[109 counties]

| Usual occupation | Total | | Crop failure or loss of live-stock | De-creased earn-ings | Loss of employment | | Admin-istra-tive ruling | Loss or deple-tion of assets | In-creased needs | All others |
	Num-ber	Per-cent			Pri-vate em-ploy-ment	Works Pro-gram				
ALL ACCESSIONS										
Total	16,968	100.0	15.6	12.6	36.5	1.3	2.7	17.2	9.2	4.9
Farm operators	5,176	100.0	46.2	12.2	10.6	1.1	2.9	12.8	10.4	3.8
Owners	2,188	100.0	44.0	12.2	10.4	1.4	5.0	14.0	9.6	3.4
Tenants	2,988	100.0	47.8	12.3	10.7	.9	1.3	11.9	11.0	4.1
Farm laborers	2,412	100.0	2.2	17.7	60.0	1.4	1.3	7.6	7.4	2.4
Nonagriculture	6,884	100.0	1.2	13.9	55.6	1.6	2.0	15.5	5.8	4.4
All others [2]	2,496	100.0	5.0	4.6	11.1	.7	5.4	39.9	17.5	15.8
NEW CASES										
Total	3,772	100.0	7.9	9.8	38.0	1.9	1.4	25.7	8.8	6.5
Farm operators	536	100.0	42.6	13.8	10.4	2.2	1.1	18.3	9.0	2.6
Owners	216	100.0	47.1	9.3	12.9	1.9	1.9	16.7	7.4	2.8
Tenants	320	100.0	39.3	16.9	8.8	2.5	.6	19.4	10.0	2.5
Farm laborers	482	100.0	2.5	9.5	53.2	4.6	1.2	13.3	12.4	3.3
Nonagriculture	1,818	100.0	1.5	12.2	55.6	1.7	1.2	18.0	5.2	4.6
All others [2]	936	100.0	3.2	2.8	7.7	.6	1.9	51.3	13.9	18.6
REOPENED CASES										
Total	13,196	100.0	17.8	13.4	36.3	1.1	3.0	14.7	9.3	4.4
Farm operators	4,640	100.0	46.6	12.1	10.6	1.0	3.1	12.1	10.6	3.9
Owners	1,972	100.0	43.8	12.5	10.1	1.3	5.4	13.7	9.8	3.4
Tenants	2,668	100.0	48.8	11.8	10.9	.7	1.4	10.9	11.2	4.3
Farm laborers	1,930	100.0	2.1	19.7	61.8	.6	1.3	6.2	6.1	2.2
Nonagriculture	5,066	100.0	1.1	14.5	55.6	1.5	2.3	14.7	6.0	4.3
All others [2]	1,560	100.0	6.0	5.6	13.1	.8	7.4	33.3	19.7	14.1

[1] Iowa, Kansas, Michigan, Minnesota, Missouri, Nebraska, New York, North Dakota, Ohio, South Dakota, and Wisconsin.
[2] Includes "Head not a worker" and heads with "No usual occupation."

TABLE 30.—ACCESSIONS TO RURAL RELIEF ROLLS IN SOUTHERN STATES,[1] BY USUAL OCCUPATION OF THE HEAD OF THE CASE AND BY REASON FOR OPENING AND REOPENING, JULY THROUGH OCTOBER 1935

[145 counties]

Usual occupation	Reason for accession									
	Total		Crop failure or loss of livestock	Decreased earnings	Loss of employment		Administrative ruling	Loss or depletion of assets	Increased needs	All others
	Number	Percent			Private employment	Works Program				
ALL ACCESSIONS										
Total	22,298	100.0	8.2	13.6	33.5	0.3	9.8	9.3	11.5	13.8
Farm operators	7,370	100.0	22.4	19.5	10.5	.4	14.5	7.8	10.0	14.9
Owners	1,610	100.0	29.0	25.6	5.8	.6	9.2	9.7	13.3	6.8
Tenants	3,158	100.0	21.7	22.3	9.4	.5	23.9	5.1	9.4	7.7
Croppers	2,602	100.0	19.1	12.3	14.8	.1	6.6	9.8	8.8	28.5
Farm laborers	4,390	100.0	1.8	11.4	62.6	.4	7.5	4.6	9.4	2.3
Nonagriculture	8,282	100.0	.9	12.0	43.7	.3	6.3	10.5	8.3	18.0
All others [2]	2,256	100.0	1.4	4.3	11.1	.4	11.8	18.8	32.1	20.1
NEW CASES										
Total	6,118	100.0	8.5	9.7	33.6	.3	.9	12.8	8.3	25.9
Farm operators	2,050	100.0	22.8	11.0	8.8	.3	.3	9.3	6.3	41.2
Owners	334	100.0	30.4	20.4	9.0		1.2	15.6	9.6	13.8
Tenants	628	100.0	31.9	15.3	9.2	1.0	.3	9.2	8.9	24.2
Croppers	1,088	100.0	15.3	5.7	8.5			7.4	3.9	59.2
Farm laborers	964	100.0	2.9	9.5	65.8	.2	1.5	9.1	8.7	2.3
Nonagriculture	2,514	100.0	.7	10.0	46.5	.2	.9	13.5	5.5	22.7
All others [2]	590	100.0	.7	4.1	8.8	1.0	2.4	27.8	26.1	29.1
REOPENED CASES										
Total	16,180	100.0	8.2	15.0	33.4	.4	13.2	7.9	12.7	9.2
Farm operators	5,320	100.0	22.2	22.7	11.2	.4	20.0	7.2	11.5	4.8
Owners	1,276	100.0	28.4	27.0	5.0	.8	11.3	8.2	14.3	5.0
Tenants	2,530	100.0	19.2	24.0	9.5	.4	29.6	4.1	9.6	3.6
Croppers	1,514	100.0	21.8	17.0	19.3	.1	11.4	11.5	12.3	6.6
Farm laborers	3,426	100.0	1.5	11.9	61.7	.4	9.2	3.4	9.6	2.3
Nonagriculture	5,768	100.0	1.0	12.9	42.7	.3	8.6	9.1	9.5	15.9
All others [2]	1,666	100.0	1.7	4.4	11.9	.1	15.1	15.6	34.3	16.9

[1] Alabama, Arkansas, Florida, Geórgia, Kentucky, Louisiana, North Carolina, Oklahoma, South Carolina, Tennessee, Texas, Virginia, and West Virginia.
[2] Includes "Head not a worker" and heads with "No usual occupation."

TABLE 31.—ACCESSIONS TO RURAL RELIEF ROLLS IN WESTERN STATES,[1] BY USUAL OCCUPATION OF THE HEAD OF THE CASE AND BY REASON FOR OPENING AND RE-OPENING, JULY THROUGH OCTOBER 1935

[46 counties]

Usual occupation	Total		Crop failure or loss of live-stock	De-creased earn-ings	Loss of employ-ment		Admin-istra-tive ruling	Loss or deple-tion of assets	In-creased needs	All others
	Num-ber	Per-cent			Pri-vate em-ploy-ment	Works Pro-gram				
ALL ACCESSIONS										
Total	4,234	100.0	8.0	6.0	52.5	1.3	4.7	16.2	5.2	6.1
Farm operators	750	100.0	37.4	11.5	20.5		4.5	18.4	3.7	4.0
Owners	416	100.0	35.6	10.6	18.3		5.3	22.6	3.8	3.8
Tenants	334	100.0	39.4	12.6	23.4		3.6	13.2	3.6	4.2
Farm laborers	904	100.0	.7	4.2	76.0	.9	3.1	10.0	2.2	2.9
Nonagriculture	2,092	100.0	1.7	5.6	61.0	1.8	4.5	15.8	5.0	4.6
All others [2]	488	100.0	3.7	2.0	11.9	2.0	9.0	25.9	13.9	31.6
NEW CASES										
Total	1,430	100.0	6.2	6.3	44.8	1.3	4.3	21.5	6.4	9.2
Farm operators	142	100.0	42.3	11.3	7.0		1.4	32.4	2.8	2.8
Owners	90	(3)	(3)	(3)	(3)		(3)	(3)	(3)	
Tenants	52	(3)	(3)	(3)	(3)			(3)	(3)	(3)
Farm laborers	266	100.0		3.8	68.3	2.3	2.3	15.8	3.0	4.5
Nonagriculture	816	100.0	2.5	7.4	50.9	1.2	5.4	20.6	5.9	6.1
All others [2]	206	100.0	3.9	1.9	4.9	1.0	4.9	25.2	15.5	42.7
REOPENED CASES										
Total	2,804	100.0	9.0	5.8	56.4	1.4	4.9	13.4	4.6	4.5
Farm operators	608	100.0	36.2	11.5	23.7		5.3	15.1	3.9	4.3
Owners	326	100.0	34.4	9.8	21.5		6.1	19.0	4.3	4.9
Tenants	282	100.0	38.4	13.5	26.2		4.3	10.6	3.5	3.5
Farm laborers	638	100.0	.9	4.4	79.4	.3	3.4	7.5	1.9	2.2
Nonagriculture	1,276	100.0	1.3	4.5	67.4	2.2	3.9	12.7	4.4	3.6
All others [2]	282	100.0	3.5	2.1	17.0	2.8	12.1	26.3	12.8	23.4

[1] California, Colorado, Montana, Oregon, Utah, and Washington.
[2] Includes "Head not a worker" and heads with "No usual occupation."
[3] Percent not computed on a base of less than 100 cases.

TABLE 32.—ACCESSIONS TO RURAL RELIEF ROLLS IN CONNECTICUT AND MASSACHUSETTS, BY USUAL OCCUPATION OF THE HEAD OF THE CASE AND BY REASON FOR OPENING AND REOPENING, JULY THROUGH OCTOBER 1935

[83 townships]

Usual occupation	Total		Crop failure or loss of livestock	Decreased earnings	Loss of employment		Administrative ruling	Loss or depletion of assets	Increased needs	All others
	Number	Percent			Private employment	Works Program				
ALL ACCESSIONS										
Total	1,024	100.0	0.4	13.2	48.0	0.4	5.2	25.3	4.7	2.8
Farm operators	88	(1)	(1)	(1)	(1)	--------	(1)	(1)	(1)	--------
Owners	80	(1)	(1)	(1)	(1)	(1)	(1)	(1)	(1)	--------
Tenants	8	(1)	(1)	(1)	(1)	(1)	(1)	(1)	(1)	--------
Farm laborers	100	100.0	--------	12.0	59.0	--------	4.0	14.0	10.0	1.0
Nonagriculture	704	100.0	--------	10.2	47.1	.6	4.7	27.4	3.3	6.7
All others [2]	132	100.0	--------	8.3	29.5	--------	9.1	34.1	7.6	11.4
NEW CASES										
Total	402	100.0	.2	9.5	39.5	.5	1.5	39.1	6.7	3.0
Farm operators	23	(1)	(1)	(1)	(1)	(1)	(1)	(1)	(1)	(1)
Owners	18	(1)	(1)	(1)	(1)	(1)	(1)	(1)	(1)	(1)
Tenants	5	(1)	(1)	(1)	(1)	(1)	(1)	(1)	(1)	(1)
Farm laborers	36	(1)	(1)	(1)	(1)	(1)	(1)	(1)	(1)	(1)
Nonagriculture	276	100.0	--------	7.6	36.2	.7	2.2	41.4	5.4	6.5
All others [2]	67	(1)	(1)	(1)	(1)	--------	--------	(1)	(1)	(1)
REOPENED CASES										
Total	622	100.0	.5	15.6	53.5	.3	7.6	16.4	3.4	2.7
Farm operators	65	(1)	(1)	(1)	(1)	(1)	(1)	(1)	(1)	(1)
Owners	62	(1)	(1)	(1)	(1)	(1)	(1)	(1)	(1)	(1)
Tenants	3	(1)	(1)	(1)	(1)	(1)	(1)	(1)	(1)	(1)
Farm laborers	64	(1)	(1)	(1)	(1)	(1)	(1)	(1)	(1)	(1)
Nonagriculture	428	100.0	--------	11.9	54.1	.5	6.3	18.5	1.9	6.8
All others [2]	65	(1)	(1)	(1)	(1)	--------	--------	(1)	(1)	(1)

[1] Percent not computed on a base of less than 100 cases.
[2] Includes "Head not a worker" and heads with "No usual occupation."

TABLE 33.—SEPARATIONS FROM RURAL RELIEF ROLLS, BY USUAL OCCUPATION OF THE HEAD OF THE CASE AND BY REASON FOR CLOSING, JULY THROUGH OCTOBER 1935

[300 counties and 83 New England townships]

Reason for closing	Usual occupation of head							
	Total	Farm operators				Farm labor-ers	Non-agri-culture	All others [2]
		Total	Owners	Ten-ants [1]	Crop-pers			
Number	80,863	26,091	9,293	13,032	3,766	13,694	31,667	9,411
Percent	100.0	100.0	100.0	100.0	100.0	100.0	100.0	100.0
Sufficient means for self-support	43.9	41.9	48.3	42.0	25.5	48.8	52.5	13.6
Private employment [3]	33.3	12.1	12.8	10.9	14.6	47.5	51.4	10.5
Crops marketed	10.6	29.8	35.5	31.1	10.9	1.3	1.1	3.1
Works Program employment	21.1	21.8	20.1	17.2	42.0	21.5	23.0	12.2
Civilian Conservation Corps	6.4	8.6	9.5	7.3	10.9	5.6	5.0	6.2
Works Progress Administration and other	14.7	13.2	10.6	9.9	31.1	15.9	18.0	6.0
Transferred to Resettlement Admin-istration	2.5	6.1	6.5	7.4	.9	.7	.9	.6
Other income [4]	8.5	5.9	5.6	6.1	6.1	3.5	3.4	39.8
Administrative policy	8.0	8.8	8.0	9.4	8.5	8.5	6.5	10.4
Moved or failed to report	8.3	7.2	5.6	7.8	9.0	8.5	8.5	10.3
All others	7.7	8.3	5.9	10.1	8.0	8.7	5.2	13.1

[1] Exclusive of croppers in the southern States.
[2] Includes "Head not a worker" and heads with "No usual occupation."
[3] Including regular government employment.
[4] Assistance from local relief agencies, relatives and friends, and from miscellaneous sources.

TABLE 34.—SEPARATIONS FROM RURAL RELIEF ROLLS IN NORTHERN STATES,[1] BY USUAL OCCUPATION OF THE HEAD OF THE CASE AND BY REASON FOR CLOSING, JULY THROUGH OCTOBER 1935

[109 counties]

Reason for closing	Usual occupation of head						
	Total	Farm operators			Farm laborers	Non-agri-culture	All others [2]
		Total	Owners	Tenants			
Number	31,522	11,440	4,838	6,602	4,274	12,396	3,412
Percent	100.0	100.0	100.0	100.0	100.0	100.0	100.0
Sufficient means for self-support	55.5	57.5	59.5	56.0	60.0	61.9	19.8
Private employment [3]	36.6	10.2	9.9	10.5	57.3	60.2	13.5
Crops marketed	18.9	47.3	49.6	45.5	2.7	1.7	6.3
Works Program employment	13.3	9.0	11.8	7.0	15.1	17.4	10.1
Civilian Conservation Corps	4.0	4.1	5.1	3.3	4.1	3.5	5.3
Works Progress Administration and other	9.3	4.9	6.7	3.7	10.9	13.9	4.8
Transferred to Resettlement Administration	4.4	10.9	8.8	12.5	1.1	.5	1.3
Other income [4]	6.9	3.0	3.6	2.5	2.7	3.0	39.4
Administrative policy	10.0	11.0	7.6	13.5	12.0	8.3	10.4
Moved or failed to report	7.2	6.1	5.3	6.7	6.7	6.8	13.1
All others	2.7	2.5	3.4	1.8	2.4	2.1	5.9

[1] Iowa, Kansas, Michigan, Minnesota, Missouri, Nebraska, New York, North Dakota, Ohio, South Dakota, and Wisconsin.
[2] Includes "Head not a worker" and heads with "No usual occupation."
[3] Including regular government employment.
[4] Assistance from local relief agencies, relatives and friends, and from miscellaneous sources.

TABLE 35.—SEPARATIONS FROM RURAL RELIEF ROLLS IN SOUTHERN STATES,[1] BY USUAL OCCUPATION OF THE HEAD OF THE CASE AND BY REASON FOR CLOSING, JULY THROUGH OCTOBER 1935

[145 counties]

Reason for closing	Usual occupation of head							
	Total	Farm operators				Farm laborers	Non-agriculture	All others[2]
		Total	Owners	Tenants	Croppers			
Number	38,438	12,664	3,226	5,672	3,766	7,606	13,470	4,698
Percent	100.0	100.0	100.0	100.0	100.0	100.0	100.0	100.0
Sufficient means for self-support	30.8	25.6	28.8	23.9	25.5	39.4	38.7	8.3
Private employment[3]	25.5	11.2	10.4	9.3	14.6	38.9	38.0	7.0
Crops marketed	5.3	14.4	18.4	14.6	10.9	.5	.7	1.3
Works Program employment	30.4	34.9	35.0	30.1	42.1	27.4	33.1	15.3
Civilian Conservation Corps	9.9	13.8	19.0	12.7	10.9	7.5	8.3	8.2
Works Progress Administration and other	20.5	21.1	16.0	17.4	31.2	19.9	24.8	7.1
Transferred to Resettlement Administration	1.3	2.1	4.4	1.6	.9	.5	1.4	.3
Other income[4]	9.4	8.4	8.1	10.2	6.1	4.0	3.7	37.2
Administrative policy	6.8	7.3	8.9	5.7	8.5	6.5	5.3	10.5
Moved or failed to report	8.1	7.1	4.1	7.7	8.9	8.6	8.8	7.8
All other reasons	13.2	14.6	10.7	20.8	8.0	13.6	9.0	20.6

[1] Alabama, Arkansas, Florida, Georgia, Kentucky, Louisiana, North Carolina, Oklahoma, South Carolina, Tennessee, Texas, Virginia, and West Virginia.
[2] Includes "Head not a worker" and heads with "No usual occupation."
[3] Including regular government employment.
[4] Assistance from local relief agencies, relatives and friends, and from miscellaneous sources.

TABLE 36.—SEPARATIONS FROM RURAL RELIEF ROLLS IN WESTERN STATES,[1] BY USUAL OCCUPATION OF THE HEAD OF THE CASE AND BY REASON FOR CLOSING, JULY THROUGH OCTOBER 1935

[46 counties]

Reason for closing	Usual occupation of head						
	Total	Farm operators			Farm laborers	Non-agriculture	All others[2]
		Total	Owners	Tenants			
Number	9,136	1,844	1,106	738	1,664	4,540	1,088
Percent	100.0	100.0	100.0	100.0	100.0	100.0	100.0
Sufficient means for self-support	54.3	53.6	52.6	55.3	61.3	61.8	13.2
Private employment[3]	48.2	27.5	28.4	26.3	60.0	61.1	11.4
Crops marketed	6.1	26.1	24.2	29.0	1.3	.7	1.8
Works Program employment	12.0	12.7	15.4	8.7	12.0	12.9	7.2
Civilian Conservation Corps	1.3	2.1	2.4	1.6	1.1	1.0	1.8
Works Progress Administration and other	10.7	10.6	13.0	7.1	10.9	11.9	5.4
Transferred to Resettlement Administration	1.2	4.6	3.3	6.5	.5	.5	
Other income[4]	11.0	7.6	8.0	7.0	3.7	4.1	56.6
Administrative policy	5.3	4.4	6.1	1.9	6.5	5.0	5.9
Moved or failed to report	13.5	14.9	12.1	19.0	12.6	13.7	11.8
All other reasons	2.7	2.2	2.5	1.6	3.4	2.0	5.3

[1] California, Colorado, Montana, Oregon, Utah, and Washington.
[2] Includes "Head not a worker" and heads with "No usual occupation."
[3] Including regular government employment.
[4] Assistance from local relief agencies, relatives and friends, and from miscellaneous sources.

TABLE 37.—Separations From Rural Relief Rolls in Connecticut and Massachusetts, by Usual Occupation of the Head of the Case and by Reason for Closing, July Through October 1935

[83 townships]

Reason for closing	Usual occupation of head						
	Total	Farm operators			Farm laborers	Non-agri-culture	All others[1]
		Total	Owners	Tenants			
Number	1,767	143	123	20	150	1,261	213
Percent	100.0	100.0	100.0	(2)	100.0	100.0	100.0
Sufficient means for self-support	66.0	69.2	69.1	(2)	64.1	71.8	31.3
Private employment [3]	64.0	47.5	47.1	(2)	64.1	71.6	30.8
Crops marketed	2.0	21.7	22.0	(2)		.2	.5
Works Program employment	7.2	4.2	4.1	(2)	8.0	7.9	4.2
Civilian Conservation Corps	.5	1.4	1.6	(2)		.5	
Works Progress Administration and other	6.7	2.8	2.5	(2)	8.0	7.4	4.2
Transferred to Resettlement Administration							
Other income [4]	4.1	2.1	2.4		1.3	2.5	16.9
Administrative policy	11.7	16.1	17.1	(2)	15.3	7.1	33.0
Moved or failed to report	5.3	1.4	1.6		8.0	4.4	11.3
All others	5.7	7.0	5.7	(2)	3.3	6.3	3.3

[1] Includes "Head not a worker" and heads with "No usual occupation."
[2] Percent not computed on a base of less than 100 cases.
[3] Including regular government employment.
[4] Assistance from local relief agencies, relatives and friends, and from miscellaneous sources.

TABLE 38.—Changes in Estimated Number of Farm Operators Receiving General Relief,[1] March Through June 1935 and July Through October 1935

[Estimated from 138 counties]

Period	Total case load at be-ginning of period	Changes during period [2]				
		Accessions			Separa-tions	Carried through period
		Total	Reopened	New		
March–June	598,000	152,000	98,000	54,000	360,000	238,000
July–October	390,000	93,000	78,000	15,000	193,000	197,000

[1] From agencies expending Federal Emergency Relief Administration funds.
[2] Exclusive of cases that were opened or reopened and also closed during the (4 months) period.

TABLE 39.—Changes During Month in Estimated Number of Farm Operators Receiving General Relief,[1] July Through December 1935

[Estimated from 300 counties and 83 New England townships]

Month	Total case load at first of month	Changes during month						
		Accessions			Separations			Carried through month
		Total	Reopened	New	Total	W. P. A.	Other	
July–December		215,000	174,000	41,000	551,000	186,000	365,000	
July	390,000	48,000	31,000	17,000	83,000		83,000	307,000
August	355,000	32,000	27,000	5,000	64,000	4,000	60,000	291,000
September	323,000	32,000	28,000	4,000	54,000	10,000	44,000	269,000
October	301,000	39,000	34,000	5,000	50,000	20,000	30,000	521,000
November	290,000	38,000	33,000	5,000	102,000	54,000	48,000	188,000
December	226,000	26,000	21,000	5,000	198,000	98,000	100,000	28,000

[1] From agencies expending Federal Emergency Relief Administration funds.

METHODOLOGY OF RURAL CURRENT CHANGE STUDIES

CONTENTS

TABLES

142   *Contents*

METHODOLOGY OF RURAL CURRENT CHANGE STUDIES

INTRODUCTION

THE RESULTS of an investigation can be better understood when there is an adequate understanding of the methods by which the results were obtained. During its period of activity the Federal Emergency Relief Administration carried through a series of surveys dealing with the characteristics of the rural relief population. These studies reached their greatest adequacy and reliability during the year 1935. Many of the results of these studies have been published in mimeographed bulletins. Other results are being published in the form of monographic reports. It is proposed here to indicate the kinds of broad studies that were made and to describe in detail the methods by which results were obtained.

The administration early recognized that the relief problem in rural areas differed in important respects from that in urban communities. It was further recognized that such rural-urban differences called for differentiation of programs and policies designed for application to the relief situation in country and in city. In order to formulate and operate a rural program, it was imperative that considerable information concerning the rural relief population be made available. The Rural Unit of the Research Section of the Division of Research, Statistics, and Finance was charged with responsibility for collecting that information.

From its beginning, the F. E. R. A. required the emergency relief administration in each State to submit detailed monthly reports showing the number of families and the number of persons receiving unemployment relief and the amounts of obligations incurred for the various types of assistance. These reports did not classify relief cases by rural and urban residence, but tabulations by counties gave clear evidence that the relief problem was by no means limited to urban or to industrial centers. On the contrary, they revealed that many counties, predominantly rural in character, had one-fifth or more of their families on relief.

Only one complete enumeration of the unemployment relief population by rural and urban residence has ever been made. This

143

enumeration was made as a part of the Unemployment Relief Census
of October 1933.   More than 5,000,000 persons, or 40 percent of all
persons receiving relief at that time, resided in the open country and
in villages of less than 2,500 population, the rural relief population
being equal to about 9.5 percent of the total rural population in 1930.[1]

Following the Relief Census of October 1933, several special investigations of the numbers and characteristics of rural relief families
were undertaken at various times by the Rural Unit of the Research
Section.   These studies led up to and paved the way for the initia-
tion of a more adequate study known as the Survey of Current
Changes in the Rural Relief Population.   This survey was launched
in February 1935 for the purpose of providing current information
concerning the characteristics of, and the changes taking place in,
the rural relief population.

The great bulk of material concerning the phases of rural relief to
be studied, together with limitations on time and funds available
for collecting data, made full investigation prohibitive, and made
sampling necessary.   Highly accurate generalizations about a whole
may be made from a small part of that whole, if the part constitutes
a properly selected sample.   One of the first problems to which attention was given in the development of the Survey of Current Changes
in the Rural Relief Population was that of sampling.   The tech-
niques and procedures used in selecting samples, the type of information collected, and the reliability of the data are discussed in the
following pages.

THE UNITS OF STUDY

For purposes of the survey, the relief case or household was
taken as the unit of study.   Interest centered primarily in the
composition and characteristics of these units.   If lists of all rural
cases had been available, it would have been statistically possible
to select random samples from such lists.   If pertinent information
had been available for these cases, it would have been statistically
possible to classify them and to select stratified samples on the basis
of such information.   However, no such lists of rural relief cases
were available.   Moreover, if they had been available, it would have
been administratively impossible to study a sample selected from
them due to the prohibitive amount of time and expense that would
have been involved in visiting widely scattered units.

It was necessary for practical purposes, then, that the units to be
studied be concentrated in a relatively small number of geographical
localities.   There was no serious theoretical objection to such limita-
tion since the rural relief cases residing in one small geographical

---

[1] *Unemployment Relief Census, October 1933*, Report Number Two, Federal Emergency
Relief Administration, 1934, table A.

division might have many of the characteristics of cases residing in the entire area to be covered by the study and might have them in much the same proportions. A careful selection of a number of such divisions would then provide a representative sample of the entire universe of study. Since the country has been divided into numerous political divisions and subdivisions, as counties, townships, etc., it was possible to use one type of political unit as the unit of sampling. As the county was the unit for administering relief throughout most of the country and because much *a priori* information concerning the population and factors vitally affecting the population of the county was available from the United States Census Bureau publications, this unit was chosen for sampling.

SAMPLING METHOD

For practical purposes, then, the universe to be directly sampled was a number of counties covering as large a proportion of the United States as possible under the limitations imposed by administrative considerations. The aim was to select the counties in such a manner as to insure so far as possible the inclusion of a representative sample of rural relief cases. In selecting the sample counties two methods were available. A strictly random sample might have been drawn from among all counties to be included in the study, the selection being made according to one of the accepted procedures. The random method was not workable, since the counties differed widely with respect to their availability for survey purposes, due to their location or to the accessibility of sources of information concerning aspects of rural relief within their borders. Since pertinent information was available for counties, however, it was possible on the basis of factors related to rural relief to classify them into relatively homogeneous groups and to select usable counties from each group. This involved classification and subclassification of all counties on the basis of factors thought to be relevant to the purposes of the studies to be made and the selection of similar proportions of units from each subgroup. A sample selected in this manner may be called a controlled sample, the classificatory factors constituting the controls.

The procedure adopted for selecting representative counties was based primarily on three generally accepted propositions:

1. When, by classification of units, the variability within classes has been reduced to such an extent that each class may be considered sufficiently homogeneous for the purpose in view, any one unit may be studied as representative of the other units in the same class.

2. If one or more variables are related to or dependent upon a given variable, classification of units into groups homogeneous

with respect to the given variable will tend at the same time to give groups which are relatively homogeneous with respect to the dependent variables. Hence, if farm tenancy in the relief population is closely correlated with farm tenancy in the general population, then counties which are alike with respect to the proportion of tenants in the general population will tend to be alike with respect to the proportion of tenants in the relief population.

3. The units constituting a limited universe to be sampled may be broken down into a number of relatively homogeneous subgroups and each subgroup may be sampled separately. If equal proportions of units are selected from each subgroup, the selected units may be combined to form a properly weighted sample of the entire universe of units.

The attempt to sample the rural relief population was in effect an attempt to sample an unknown population. Little recent or usable information regarding the relief population was available. There was, therefore, no direct approach to the problem of selecting a series of counties containing a representative sample of rural relief cases. An indirect approach was made by selecting counties on the basis of certain background factors assumed to be correlated with various aspects of rural relief. The selection of these background factors was based upon *a priori* reasoning, ordinary logic and common sense, and upon the considered judgment and knowledge of research scholars familiar with the sociology and economics of rural life.

THE AREAS SAMPLED

In classifying counties for the selection of a controlled sample, the major control was introduced by grouping the units according to the dominant type of farming engaged in by the farm population, on the assumption that type of farming was a factor relevant to the rural relief situation in many of its aspects. It was possible by the use of Census data to define a number of large aggregations of counties which possessed a high degree of homogeneity with respect to the major agricultural source of income, and which in general were geographically contiguous areas.

Nine major type of farming areas were delimited for study. The areas and the bases of their delineation were as follows:

Eastern Cotton Area.

This area consisted of 424 counties of the Old South scattered among the States of North Carolina, South Carolina, Georgia, Alabama, Mississippi, Louisiana, Arkansas, Tennessee, and southeastern Missouri. These were counties in which two-fifths or more of the total value of products sold, traded, or used on the farm in 1929 was produced on cotton farms as defined by the United States Census of Agriculture.[2]

Western Cotton Area.

This area consisted of 151 counties in Texas and Oklahoma distinguished by the same basic criterion as the Eastern Cotton Area but separated from the latter on the basis of other factors, such as a smaller proportion of sharecroppers and greater frequency of drought.

Appalachian-Ozark Area.

This area consisted of 265 counties in the self-sufficing farming regions of West Virginia, Virginia, Kentucky, Tennessee, North Carolina, Georgia, Arkansas, Oklahoma, Missouri, and southern Illinois. These were counties in which 20 percent or more of all farms in 1929 were classified as self-sufficing.[3]

Lake States Cut-Over Area.

This area consisted of 76 counties in Michigan, Minnesota, and Wisconsin, in which less than 50 percent of the approximate land area was in farms in 1930.

Hay and Dairy Area.

This area consisted of 187 counties in Wisconsin, Minnesota, Michigan, Ohio, Pennsylvania, New York, and Vermont. These were counties in which 25 percent or more of all farms were classified as dairy farms in the 1930 Census of Agriculture.[4]

Corn Belt.

This area consisted of 363 counties in the States of Ohio, Indiana, Illinois, Iowa, Minnesota, Missouri, South Dakota, Nebraska, and Kansas. These were counties in which 29 percent or more of the cropland and plowable pasture was planted to corn in 1929.

Spring Wheat Area.

This area consisted of 64 counties in North and South Dakota, and Montana, in which 30 percent or more of all cropland and plowable pasture was land from which wheat was harvested in 1929.

---

[2] *Cotton farm:* A farm from which 40 percent or more of the value of its products was derived from cotton (lint) or cottonseed.

[3] *Self-sufficing farm:* The value of farm products used by the farm family was 50 percent or more of the total value of all products of the farm.

[4] *Dairy farm:* A farm from which 40 percent or more of the value of its products was derived from milk, cream, butterfat, butter, and dairy cows and calves.

Winter Wheat Area.

This area consisted of 79 counties in Colorado, Kansas, Nebraska, and Texas, in which 30 percent or more of all cropland and plowable pasture was land from which wheat was harvested in 1929.

Ranching Area.

This area consisted of 64 counties in Colorado, Montana, Utah, and Oregon,[5] in which 40 percent or more of all farm acreage was in farms classified by the United States Census of Agriculture as stock ranches [6] in 1929. Only a small part of the total ranching area was sampled due to lack of adequate field staff for carrying on studies in the ranching States.

The delineation of areas of homogeneity with respect to type of agriculture constituted the first major step toward the selection of a controlled sample. Homogeneous farming areas are not necessarily homogeneous in many other respects. It was assumed, however, that type of agriculture and agricultural resources have a multiplicity of correlates, many of which are directly or indirectly associated with the rural relief situation.

The 9 areas delineated for sampling included 1,673 counties, somewhat more than half (54 percent) of all such political units in the country (see list A and figure A). While these areas do not cover the entire rural United States, they do comprise the largest number of aggregations of counties that are characterized simultaneously by a high degree of agricultural homogeneity and geographical contiguity.

The maximum sample was limited to about 140 counties, due to administrative limitations upon the amount of time allowed for getting the initial study under way and upon the amount of funds available for collecting data. It was not thought advisable to attempt to represent all rural areas of the country with so small a number of counties. Consequently, the counties lying outside the nine areas described above were not included. Moreover, in the States not touched by the nine areas there was no research organization or personnel for carrying on field work at the time.

The areas not sampled consisted of general and mixed farming areas which are often found between areas of dominant types of agriculture; that part of the Western Ranching Area lying in States with no administrative machinery for carrying on rural research; various localized farming regions, such as fruit and truck areas; and

---

[5] That part of the Ranching Area extending into other States was not included.

[6] *Stock ranch:* A farm where chief emphasis is on grazing rather than on production of crops and feeding of livestock, and on which 40 percent or more of the value of all farm products is derived from meat animals.

areas devoted to special crops, such as tobacco, beans, potatoes, rice, sugar beets, etc. Finally, certain very thinly populated nonagricultural regions, such as the Cascade Mountains in the far West, the Colorado-Mohave Desert, the Adirondacks and northern Maine, and the Florida Flatwoods and Everglades (see figure A), were also omitted.

SELECTION OF SAMPLE COUNTIES TO REPRESENT AREAS

The first major step toward the selection of a controlled sample of counties to represent the rural relief situation was a classification of the units into agricultural areas as described above. The second major step consisted of subgrouping the counties within each area on the basis of certain relevant factors.

It was contemplated that the items of information to be collected in the sample counties would be many and varied. Proposed field studies would be designed to provide information regarding nearly all aspects of the rural relief situation and would cover a considerable period of time. Hence, in stratifying the counties for the selection of the sample, indexes of fundamental and fairly permanent socio-economic conditions underlying the rural relief situation were used. They included the following: [7]

> Percent of all families in the county that were rural families.
> Percent of all rural families that were farm families.
> Percent of all farm operators that were tenants.
> Percent of all rural families whose heads were foreign born.
> Percent of all gainful workers in agriculture that were wage laborers.
> Land value per capita of the rural-farm population.

Each of these factors is, undoubtedly, correlated with other background variables which in turn are correlated with phases of rural relief. For example, a fairly close relationship was found in southern counties between the percent of Negroes in the rural population and the percent of farm tenancy. A fair degree of correlation between the proportion of Negroes in the general and in the relief population may be assumed. Hence, by controlling farm tenancy in selecting sample counties, it is probable that some control is exercised over both color and tenancy in the relief population. These intercorrelations among background factors underlying the rural relief situation eliminated the necessity of attempting to control any considerable number of variables in selecting the sample, for in selecting a county in which certain conditions are present, closely related conditions are *ipso facto* present.

The method of selecting counties from those grouped by agricultural areas may be shown by describing its application to the Corn

---

[7] The indexes were based on 1930 Census data.

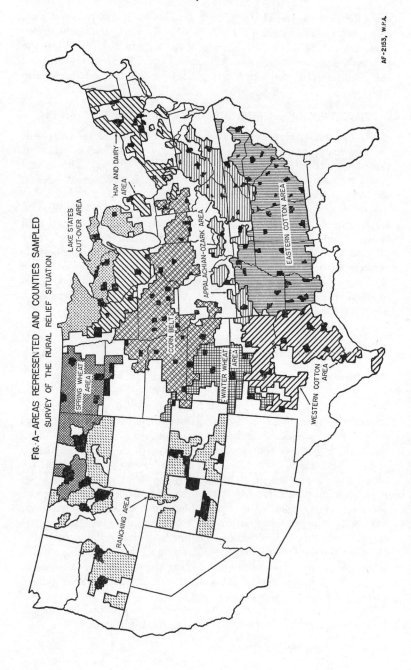

FIG. A—AREAS REPRESENTED AND COUNTIES SAMPLED
SURVEY OF THE RURAL RELIEF SITUATION

AF-2153, W.P.A.

Table A.—Scheme for Selecting Controlled
Sample of 27 out of 363 Corn Belt Counties

TABLE A.—SCHEME FOR SELECTING CONTROLLED SAMPLE OF 27 OUT OF 363 CORN BELT COUNTIES

[Counties selected in *italics*]

		X₁	X₂	X₃
Y₁	**Z₁**	Indiana: Carroll. Delaware. Grant. Hendricks. Miami. — Indiana: Parke. Ohio: Logan. Miami. *Putnam.* Illinois: Macoupin. — Kansas: Osage. Minnesota: Le Sueur. Missouri: Gentry.	Nebraska: Dixon. Franklin. Furnas. Harlan. Thayer. — Nebraska: Valley. Webster. Iowa: Butler. *Guthrie.* Keokuk. — Iowa: Taylor. Kansas: Nemaha. Pottawatomie.	Illinois: Bureau. Douglas. Kendall. Marshall. Menard. — Illinois: Piatt. Putnam. Sangamon. Tazewell. *Woodford.* — Indiana: Benton. Newton. Nebraska: Sarpy.
	Z₂	Indiana: *Fountain.* Henry. Madison. Montgomery. Pike. — Indiana: Union. Wayne. White. Ohio: Butler. Paulding. — Ohio: Warren. Wood. Kansas: Shawnee.	Illinois: Carroll. Hancock. McDonough. Ogle. Rock Island. — Iowa: Clinton. Iowa. Jones. Louisa. Missouri: Clinton. — Missouri: Holt. Kansas: Johnson. Nebraska: *Hitchcock.*	Iowa: Adair. *Calhoun.* Dallas. Dickinson. Humboldt. — Iowa: Sioux. Illinois: Ford. Grundy. Kankakee. Macon. — Illinois: Stark. Kansas: Chase. Nebraska: Clay.
	Z₃	Ohio: Champaign. Clark. *Clinton.* Greene. Madison. — Ohio: Marion. Montgomery. Illinois: Alexander. Gallatin. Greene. — Illinois: McHenry. Winnebago. Indiana: Johnson. Vermilion.	Illinois: Cass. Christian. De Kalb. Fulton. Kane. — Illinois: Mason. Mercer. Moultrie. Peoria. *Scott.* — Illinois: Vermilion. Will. Iowa: Muscatine. Nebraska: Burt.	Illinois: Henderson. Iroquois. La Salle. Lee. Livingston. — Illinois: McLean. Iowa: Cedar. *Ida.* Lyon. O'Brien. — Iowa: Tama. Nebraska: Butler. Fillmore. Merrick.
	Z₁	Kansas: Coffey. Linn. Phillips. *Smith.* Washington. — Iowa: Chickasaw. Fayette. Ringgold. Indiana: Randolph. Missouri: Henry. — Nebraska: Boone. Ohio: Darke. South Dakota: Gregory.	Nebraska: Antelope. Boyd. Greeley. Howard. Knox. — Nebraska: Pawnee. Kansas: Cloud. Decatur. Marshall. Republic. — Kansas: *Wabaunsee.* Minnesota: Cottonwood. South Dakota: Brule.	Iowa: Carroll. Fremont. Grundy. Sac. Story. — Nebraska: Cass. *Johnson.* Madison. Saline. Illinois: Knox. — Illinois: Logan. South Dakota: Bon Homme. Kingsbury.
		Indiana: Cass. Hamilton. … — Ohio: Henry. Preble — Iowa: Wapello. Kansas: …	Iowa: Adams. Buchanan. Des Moines. … — Iowa: Marion *Washington.* Worth. — Kansas: Geary. Nebraska.	Nebraska: Chase. Dodge. Kearney. — Iowa: Hancock. Hardin. Osceola. — South Dakota: Lincoln. Turner.

Z₃	Knox.	Illinois: Schuyler. Iowa: Winnebago.	Nebraska: Dawson. Ohio: Ross.	Iowa: Floyd.	Nebraska: Drundy. Thurston.	Warren. Minnesota: Faribault.	Pottawattamie	Cuming Pierce. Polk.	Minnehaha. Moody.
Z₁	Missouri: Benton. Cedar. De Kalb. *Hickory.* St. Clair.	Missouri: Worth. Kansas: Bourbon. Franklin. Graham. Jewell.	Kansas: Norton. Iowa: Monroe. Ohio: Fayette.	Minnesota: Jackson. Pipestone. Redwood. Watonwan. Iowa: *Black Hawk.*	Iowa: Delaware. Mitchell. Kansas: Cheyenne. Riley. South Dakota: Charles Mix.	South Dakota: Douglas. Missouri: Nodaway. Nebraska: Frontier.	Iowa: Boone. Cass. Crawford. *Marshall.* Monona.	Iowa: Palo Alto. Poweshiek. Wright. Nebraska: Colfax. Nuckolls.	Nebraska: Richardson. Illinois: Henry. Warren.
Y₃ Z₂	Kansas: Allen. Jackson. Lyon. Miami. Indiana: Boone.	Indiana: Fulton. Wabash. Iowa: Jefferson. Lee. Missouri: Bates.	Missouri: *Ray.* Colorado: Yuma. Nebraska: Sherman. Ohio: Van Wert.	Iowa: Cerro Gordo. Johnson. *Mahaska.* Union. Warren.	Minnesota: Blue Earth. Lyon. Martin. Murray. Nebraska: Dakota.	Nebraska. Lincoln. Redwillow. Missouri: Saline. South Dakota: Hanson.	Iowa: Benton. Cherokee. Emmet. Greene. Hamilton.	Iowa: Kossuth. *Page.* Nebraska: Jefferson. Lancaster. Nemaha.	Nebraska: Seward. Minnesota: Nobles. Nebraska: Stanton.
Y₃ Z₃	Indiana: Fayette. Jasper. Rush. *Shelby.* Tipton. Illinois: Boone.	Illinois: Jersey. Kansas: Atchison. Douglas. Missouri: Andrew. Pettis. Ohio: Hancock.	Ohio: Pickaway. Minnesota: Chippewa.	Nebraska: Adams. Custer. Gosper. Hayes. Platte. Kansas: Brown.	Kansas: Clay. Morris. Iowa: Clarke. Madison. South Dakota: *Brookings.* Davison.	South Dakota: Yankton. Minnesota: Brown.	Nebraska: Gage. *Hall.* Hamilton. Otoe. Phelps. York.	Iowa: Clay. Franklin. Shelby. South Dakota: Clay. Lake. Nebraska: Washington.	Illinois: De Witt. Minnesota: Rock

X = land value per capita of the rural farm population.
Y = percent of rural families that are farm families.
Z = percent of all gainful agricultural workers that are wage workers.

Subscript 1 indicates the lowest third of the 363 counties with respect to a given factor; subscript 2, the middle third; subscript 3, the highest third.

Belt. The 140 counties to which the sample was limited constituted about 8 percent of the 1,673 counties in all areas combined. There were 363 counties in the entire Corn Belt and the sampling ratio (8 percent) allowed for a selection of 29 counties. In order to facilitate the sampling technique this number was arbitrarily reduced to 27 counties.

Three background factors considered relevant by informed research scholars were used as the bases for classifying the 363 Corn Belt counties into 27 subgroups. These were (a) the percent of all rural families that were farm families in 1930, (b) the percent of all agricultural workers that were wage laborers in 1930, and (c) land value per capita of the rural farm population, 1930.

The 363 counties were first ranked from highest to lowest on the basis of per capita land value and broken into 3 equal groups of counties representing high, low, and intermediate values. Each of these three groups was then ranked on the basis of the rural-farm index, and was subdivided into equal groups of counties with high, low, and intermediate percentages of rural-farm population. These 2 steps gave 9 subgroups of about 40 counties each. These nine groups were in turn ranked on the basis of the farm labor index and divided into three equal groups.

The final result was a classification of the 363 counties into 27 subgroups, each having from 12 to 14 counties and each representing 1 of 27 phases of joint variation of 3 background factors (see table A).

The counties within each subgroup were considered homogeneous for practical purposes with respect to the three classificatory factors. In some other important respects, however, the counties in a particular subgroup differed widely among themselves. The subgroups did not, for example, form geographically contiguous subregions of the Corn Belt, but tended to scatter throughout a particular State or among several States. In making the final selection of the sample, one choice was made from each of the subgroups, the choice being governed by an endeavor to obtain a fairly even geographical distribution throughout the area and to select a county including approximately 8 percent of the total rural population of its subgroup. At the same time a State could be apportioned no larger number of counties than could be surveyed with the then existing research personnel. It was considered highly important that the sample include counties from each State overlapped by the areas sampled since many aspects of the relief problems to be investigated were related to administrative practices which varied from State to State. If upon initial contact by the field staff, the selected county was found unsuitable for survey purposes because of the lack of reliable sources of information or the lack of cooperation on the part of local relief officials, another county from the same subgroup was substituted in its place, the process of substitution being continued until a usable selection resulted.

In general, the sampling method applied to the Corn Belt counties was followed in the other eight areas. Some variation was necessary, however, due to differences in the total number of counties in the areas, and due to differences among areas with respect to the control factors used.

Considering the advice and judgment of experts in the field of rural sociology and economics, the background factors used in forming subgroups of counties making up the other eight areas were as follows:

Eastern Cotton Area:
1. Percent of all farm operators that were tenants.
2. Land value per capita of the rural-farm population.
3. Percent of all rural families that were farm families.

Western Cotton Area:
1. Land value per capita of the rural-farm population.
2. Percent of all rural families that were farm families.

Appalachian-Ozark Area:
1. Percent of all farm operators that were tenants.
2. Percent of all rural families that were farm families.

Lake States Cut-Over Area:
1. Land value per capita of the rural-farm population.
2. Percent of all rural families whose heads were foreign born.

Hay and Dairy Area:
1. Land value per capita of the rural-farm population.
2. Percent of all rural families that were farm families.

Spring Wheat Area:
1. Land value per capita of the rural-farm population.
2. Percent of all rural families that were farm families.

Winter Wheat Area:
1. Land value per capita of the rural-farm population.
2. Percent of all rural families that were farm families.

Ranching Area:
1. Land value per capita of the rural-farm population.
2. Percent of all rural families that were farm families.

The final list of sample units, including 138 counties, represented 9 major type of farming areas overlapping 33 States (see list B and figure A). These 138 counties, selected as representative of certain background factors considered relevant to the rural relief situation, were therefore assumed to be representative of the general aspects of the rural relief situation. The size of the samples varied from 7.4 percent of all counties in the Corn Belt to 18.8 percent of the counties in that part of the Ranching Area actually sampled (table B).

TABLE B.—PROPORTION OF ALL COUNTIES INCLUDED IN EACH AREA SAMPLE, AND PROPORTION OF ALL RURAL FAMILIES 1930, OF ALL RURAL RELIEF CASES OCTOBER 1933, AND OF ALL FARMS JANUARY 1935, FOUND IN SAMPLE COUNTIES IN NINE AREAS

Area	Counties			Families, 1930 [1]			Relief cases, October 1933 [2]			Farms, January 1935 [3]		
	Area total	Sample counties		Area total	Sample counties		Area total	Sample counties		Area total	Sample counties	
		Number	Percent		Number	Percent		Number	Percent		Number	Percent
All areas	1,673	138	8.2	6,830,298	554,870	8.1	643,103	49,989	7.8	4,208,625	342,610	8.1
Eastern Cotton	424	32	7.5	1,985,026	136,610	6.9	216,954	16,886	7.8	1,396,234	95,401	6.8
Western Cotton	151	12	7.9	715,803	66,252	9.3	53,450	4,031	7.5	482,291	45,053	9.3
Corn Belt	363	27	7.4	1,385,178	97,102	7.0	57,939	2,707	4.7	770,072	56,150	7.3
Hay and Dairy	187	16	8.6	1,211,253	113,985	9.4	75,152	5,843	7.8	590,696	57,997	9.8
Appalachian–Ozark	265	20	7.5	952,963	86,654	9.1	166,530	14,340	8.6	600,601	53,815	9.0
Winter Wheat	79	6	7.6	185,083	12,112	6.5	17,862	1,458	8.2	115,754	8,059	7.0
Spring Wheat	64	7	10.9	132,140	14,765	11.2	12,053	1,450	11.6	93,371	10,394	11.1
Lake States Cut-Over	76	6	7.9	179,980	12,044	6.7	36,846	2,238	6.1	118,514	7,912	6.7
Ranching	64	12	18.8	82,872	15,346	18.5	5,867	1,036	17.7	41,092	7,829	19.1

[1] Source: *Fifteenth Census of the United States: 1930*, Population.
[2] Source: *Unemployment Relief Census, October 1933*.
[3] Source: *United States Census of Agriculture: 1935*.

SELECTION OF SAMPLE COUNTIES TO REPRESENT STATES

Field studies were conducted in the 138 counties representing 9 agricultural areas from October 1934 to October 1935. During the spring of 1935 administrative need for information concerning the rural relief situation in particular States as well as in agricultural areas became pressing. In order to meet this need it was decided to devise a State sampling procedure and to select a list of counties for survey in each of a number of States. As an arbitrary standard, sample counties were to contain not less than 10 percent of the rural population of each State sampled.

The following procedure was used for selecting sample counties to represent separate States with respect to factors pertaining to the rural relief situation.

1. All counties within the State [8] were classified by principal type of farming. All counties falling within a particular type of farming area were indicated on a county outline map of the State.

2. The percent of all gainful workers, 10 years of age and over, engaged in nonagricultural enterprises was computed for each county.

---

[8] Counties largely urban in character, that is, counties containing very small rural populations in comparison with their urban populations, were excluded.

3. Where rural nonagricultural enterprise was of much importance (including 25 percent or more of the gainful workers, 10 years of age and over), the principal type of industry was determined and indicated along with the type of farming on the county outline map of the State.

4. On the basis of two background factors judged relevant to the purposes of the study, the counties of each State were classified into subgroups, the number of which was fairly close to 10 percent of all counties in the State concerned. Hence, for a State having 90 counties, the counties were classified into 9 subgroups of 10 counties each. The two factors used in classifying the counties into subgroups were: (1) percent of the rural population classified as rural-farm in 1930, and (2) percent of farm tenancy (or percent of farm labor in those States where this factor was of more importance than tenancy). In arriving at the subclasses the following steps were taken:

a. The counties of the State were ranked on the rural-farm index and divided into two or more equal groupings, each group having a different range of the index used for ranking the counties. The number of subgroupings depended upon the total number of counties in the array and therefore upon the total number of subgroups needed in the final classification.

b. Each of the initial groups of counties was ranked on the basis of the farm tenancy (or farm labor) index. The groups were then broken into equal numbers of secondary groups so that the total number of subgroups approached 10 percent of all counties being sampled.

(For illustration of procedure, see table C.)

5. One or more counties were selected from each subgroup. Selection was made of counties that contained approximately 10 percent of the total rural population [9] in the group of counties to which they belonged. These counties were selected from the subgroups so that counties previously selected as part of an area sample were included as part of the larger State sample wherever possible. In making the selection the following factors were included in their proper proportions as far as possible:

a. Type of farming as shown on county outline map.

b. Type of nonagricultural industry in counties where important, as shown on county outline maps.

c. Intensity of relief as shown on latest relief intensity maps.

---

[9] In actual practice it was not always possible to select counties to meet the requirement of a 10 percent sample. Hence, some disproportions exist in the final sample both within and among States.

TABLE C.—SCHEME FOR SELECTING CONTROLLED SAMPLE OF 10 OUT OF 86
OHIO COUNTIES

[Counties selected in *italics*]

Percent tenancy	Percent of all rural families that were rural-farm families in 1930		
	Lowest third of counties	Middle third of counties	Highest third of counties
Lowest third of counties	Carroll *Columbiana* Guernsey Harrison Lake Mahoning *Muskingum* Perry Trumbull Tuscarawas	Ashtabula *Geauga* Jackson Knox Medina Meigs Portage Vinton Washington	Coshocton. Delaware. Fairfield. Gallia. Mercer. *Monroe.* Morgan. Morrow. Noble. Pike.
Middle third of counties	*Athens* Belmont Erie Hocking Jefferson Lawrence Lorain Scioto Stark	Allen Ashland Holmes Huron Licking Marion *Putnam* Richland Sandusky Wayne	Auglaize. Crawford. Defiance. *Hardin.* Highland. Ross. Union. Williams. Wyandot.
Highest third of counties	*Brown* Butler Clermont Franklin Greene Lucas Montgomery *Ottawa* Summit Wood	Champaign Clark *Clinton* Fulton Logan Madison Miami Paulding Warren	Adams. Darke. Fayette. Hancock. Henry. Pickaway. Preble. *Seneca.* Shelby. Van Wert.

6. It was assumed that a sample drawn in the manner described would be properly weighted for all practical purposes so that no weighting of final results would be called for in order to correct for disproportions growing out of the selection of the county units.

Following the general procedure outlined above, a total of 304 sample counties were selected to represent 31 States [10] for purposes of the Survey of Current Changes in the Rural Relief Population. These counties included 117 of the 138 counties previously selected to represent 9 agricultural areas. In addition to the counties, 33 New Hampshire townships were selected,[11] largely on the bases of size of population and geographical distribution, to represent all townships in the State with less than 5,000 population. Forty Connecticut townships and forty-three Massachusetts townships selected by competent research students in those States were accepted

[10] Four sample counties in Arizona were included only in the Current Change Survey in October 1935.

[11] Included only in survey of June 1935.

as satisfactory for the Current Change Study. As in the case of New Hampshire, these sample townships were selected to represent all townships having less than 5,000 population [12] (see figure B and lists C and D).

The States sampled contained considerably more than three-fourths of the total rural population of the United States in 1930, while the total number of sample counties and townships contained about one-tenth of the total rural population of the United States. The remaining States were not sampled due to lack of a cooperative plan for rural research in those States and therefore to lack of a research staff for conducting field studies.

The size of the State samples averaged 12.2 percent of all counties. This ratio ranged from 9.0 percent in Alabama and Florida to 20.7 percent in Utah and 28.6 percent in Arizona. The relative size of the sample was necessarily large in the latter States due to the small number and heterogeneous character of the counties from which the samples were drawn (table D).

FIELD STUDIES CONDUCTED IN SAMPLE COUNTIES

Survey of the Rural Relief Situation, October 1934.

The first field study, "Survey of the Rural Relief Situation, October 1934," was made as of October 1934. Household schedule DRS–77A and county schedule DRS–77B were devised for this study (see schedules A and B). Approximately 29,800 household schedules were taken in the 138 counties selected to represent the 9 areas, and an additional 2,500 were filled in 6 locally selected Pacific Coast counties and in 40 Connecticut townships.[13]

Survey of Current Changes in the Rural Relief Population.

In February 1935 the "Survey of Current Changes in the Rural Relief Population" was inaugurated in the 138 sample counties. This study was designed to provide periodic information concerning the number and characteristics of rural relief and rehabilitation cases and to provide current information regarding the number and characteristics of opened, reopened, and closed cases.

---

[12] In these New England States, the primary divisions of the counties are known as towns or townships and include rural territory as well as compactly settled areas.

[13] For results of this study see Research Bulletins, Series F, Numbers 1–10, Division of Research, Statistics, and Finance, Federal Emergency Relief Administration.

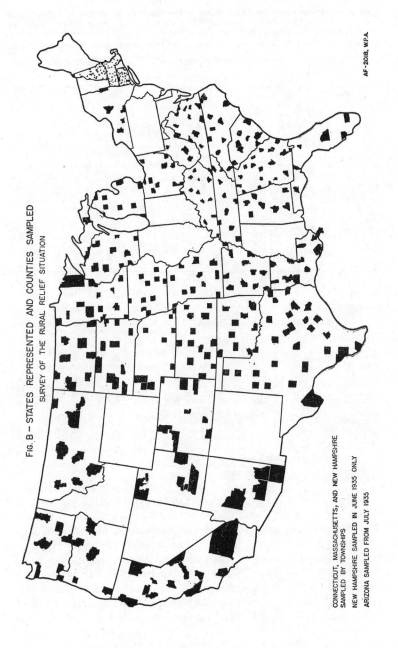

FIG. B — STATES REPRESENTED AND COUNTIES SAMPLED
SURVEY OF THE RURAL RELIEF SITUATION

AF-2018, W.P.A.

CONNECTICUT, MASSACHUSETTS, AND NEW HAMPSHIRE
SAMPLED BY TOWNSHIPS

NEW HAMPSHIRE SAMPLED IN JUNE 1935 ONLY

ARIZONA SAMPLED FROM JULY 1935

158 Farmers on Relief and Rehabilitation

TABLE D.—PROPORTION OF ALL COUNTIES INCLUDED IN EACH STATE SAMPLE, AND PROPORTION OF ALL RURAL FAMILIES 1930, OF ALL RURAL RELIEF CASES OCTOBER 1933, AND OF ALL FARMS JANUARY 1935, FOUND IN SAMPLE COUNTIES IN 31 STATES

State	Counties			Families, 1930 [1]			Relief Cases, October 1933 [2]			Farms, January 1935 [3]		
	State total	Sample counties		State total	Sample counties		State total	Sample counties		State total	Sample counties	
		Number	Percent		Number	Percent		Number	Percent		Number	Percent
All States sampled [4]	2,500	304	12.2	9,559,074	1,094,259	11.4	896,344	100,272	11.2	5,527,073	667,003	12.1
Alabama	67	7	9.0	408,990	40,064	9.8	69,178	7,030	10.2	273,455	28,653	10.5
Arizona	14	4	28.6	67,968	17,832	26.2	11,369	3,298	29.0	18,824	4,397	23.4
Arkansas	75	10	13.3	339,468	39,475	11.6	29,415	2,843	9.7	253,013	29,777	11.8
California	58	12	20.7	397,841	62,871	15.8	17,112	3,478	20.3	150,360	28,306	18.8
Colorado	63	8	12.7	125,986	12,601	10.0	5,772	503	8.7	63,644	6,341	10.0
Florida	67	6	9.0	174,251	19,961	11.5	46,958	5,533	11.7	72,857	9,728	13.4
Georgia	161	17	10.6	428,689	40,641	9.5	35,490	3,287	9.3	250,544	24,922	9.9
Iowa	99	10	10.1	373,350	37,671	10.1	10,683	1,142	10.7	221,986	22,123	10.0
Kansas	105	13	12.4	288,485	31,697	11.0	19,032	1,993	10.5	174,589	19,719	11.3
Kentucky	120	12	10.0	401,935	35,199	8.8	80,543	8,511	10.6	278,298	24,543	8.8
Louisiana	64	10	15.6	280,925	48,702	17.3	37,985	8,018	21.1	170,216	31,388	18.4
Michigan	83	11	13.3	380,313	41,258	10.8	48,479	4,044	8.3	196,517	25,268	12.9
Minnesota	87	13	14.9	298,762	50,804	17.0	9,514	2,297	24.1	203,302	36,526	18.0
Missouri	114	12	10.5	447,442	47,687	10.7	13,558	792	5.8	278,454	32,656	11.7
Montana	56	8	14.3	89,330	11,412	12.8	9,863	1,403	14.2	50,564	7,226	14.3
Nebraska	93	9	9.7	217,196	22,196	10.2	4,412	619	14.0	133,616	12,886	9.6
New York	62	5	8.1	529,357	41,718	7.9	34,498	1,529	4.4	177,025	16,084	9.1
North Carolina	100	12	12.0	463,589	46,717	10.1	34,950	2,177	6.2	300,967	30,290	10.1
North Dakota	53	8	15.1	119,076	21,149	17.8	8,351	2,159	25.9	84,606	15,590	18.4
Ohio	88	10	11.4	537,455	55,302	10.3	47,081	3,547	7.5	255,146	28,686	11.2
Oklahoma	77	9	11.7	351,539	38,312	10.9	74,803	8,434	11.3	213,325	24,291	11.4
Oregon	36	6	16.7	126,790	13,182	10.4	4,442	211	4.8	64,826	7,150	11.0
South Carolina	46	8	17.4	277,056	35,067	12.7	63,631	10,790	17.0	165,504	20,855	12.6
South Dakota	69	9	13.0	128,261	19,087	14.9	18,238	1,936	10.6	83,303	12,399	14.9
Tennessee	95	9	9.5	375,391	38,730	10.3	23,218	2,044	8.8	273,783	29,436	10.8
Texas	254	28	11.0	788,601	101,243	13.0	31,147	4,177	13.4	501,017	66,699	13.3
Utah	29	6	20.7	51,951	8,639	16.6	5,653	632	11.2	30,695	6,343	20.7
Virginia	100	13	13.0	341,848	40,577	11.9	5,356	778	14.5	197,632	25,038	12.7
Washington	39	6	15.4	178,853	19,979	11.2	11,910	266	2.2	84,381	9,985	11.8
West Virginia	55	4	7.3	257,165	18,647	7.3	65,287	5,029	7.7	104,747	7,830	7.5
Wisconsin	71	9	12.7	321,211	35,749	11.1	18,416	1,772	9.6	199,877	21,868	10.9

[1] Source: *Fifteenth Census of the United States: 1930,* Population.
[2] Source: *Unemployment Relief Census, October 1933.*
[3] Source: *United States Census of Agriculture: 1935.*
[4] New England States excluded.

Schedule DRS–109 was devised as the main instrument for collecting data for the Current Change Study (see schedules C and D). The schedule was used in its original form from February to June and in a considerably revised form after June. Samples representative of cross sections of the rural and town [14] relief population were taken in February, June, and October 1935. In addition to these cross-section studies, samples were taken of cases closed during the interval March to June inclusive, of cases opened, reopened, and closed each month July to October inclusive, and of cases

---

[14] *Town:* A center having from 2,500 to 4,999 inhabitants in 1930.

opened and reopened during November and December. These samples were taken as representative of the nine agricultural areas prior to June and as representative of both areas and States in June and succeeding months.

At the close of the year 1935 schedule DRS–409A (see schedule E) was devised for a study of rural families that had received relief in June 1935 but had been closed later. This schedule was taken in the sample counties of seven States only.[15] The study aimed to determine the sources of livelihood of the cases in December 1935 and the characteristics of families receiving their income from different sources, including special forms of public assistance.

Reporting of Public and Private Assistance in Rural and Town Areas.

The Survey of Current Changes in the Rural Relief Population was closed as of December 1935 when the F. E. R. A. ceased operation. At that time a new field study was inaugurated, namely, "Reporting of Public and Private Assistance in Rural and Town Sample Areas" (see schedule F).

This project was designed to obtain on a sampling basis current information concerning (a) the intensity, (b) the cost, (c) the types, and (d) the trend of public and private assistance in rural areas including towns up to 25,000 population.[16] The State sample was expanded for this survey to insure representation of towns up to 25,000 population.

SELECTION OF SAMPLE CASES WITHIN COUNTIES

In filling DRS–77A schedules as of October 1934 in 142 counties,[17] samples were taken from local agency files of case records. In order to keep the total number of cases within the limits of time and expense allowed for field work and tabulation, not more than 300 to 400 cases were selected from any 1 county regardless of the size of the case load in that county. The following sampling procedure was used in each county surveyed.

If there were—

> Fewer than 300 rural cases, all were enumerated.
> 300–399 rural cases, 2 out of every 3 cases were selected.
> 400–599 rural cases, every second case was selected.
> 600–899 rural cases, every third case was selected.

---

[15] Georgia, Iowa, Montana, North Carolina, South Dakota, West Virginia, and Wisconsin.

[16] For the results and methodology of this study, see monthly reports on "Current Statistics of Relief in Rural and Town Areas," Division of Social Research, Works Progress Administration.

[17] Including 138 counties in the 9 agricultural areas and 4 locally selected Pacific Coast counties.

900–1,199 rural cases, every fourth case was selected.
1,200–1,499 rural cases, every fifth case was selected.
1,500–1,799 rural cases, every sixth case was selected.
1,800–2,099 rural cases, every seventh case was selected.
2,100–2,699 rural cases, every ninth case was selected.
2,700 or more rural cases, every tenth case was selected.

In combining the results of the survey by areas, it was possible to apply proper county weights to correct for unequal sampling ratios.

In order to facilitate the selection of case samples, a complete card file of all cases was set up in each county in February 1935 with the inauguration of the Survey of Current Changes in the Rural Relief Population. For that file, control cards, form DRS–109B and revised form DRS–109D,[18] were used (see schedules G and H). One of these cards was filled for every rural and town relief or rehabilitation case in the county at the time that county began participating in the survey. The card file was kept up-to-date for each case. When a new case was extended assistance, a new card was filled. When a case left the rolls the card for that case was removed to a closed case file. If the case later returned to the relief rolls, the card was replaced in the active case file.

Samples were selected from the files of control cards. In drawing the February sample the cards were arranged alphabetically in three groups: (a) cases receiving unemployment relief only; (b) cases receiving rehabilitation loans only; and (c) cases receiving both relief and rehabilitation loans. The number of cards selected was determined according to the same procedure as that followed in October 1934.

In order to assure an adequate sample from each county and in order to avoid weighting results by counties, sampling from control cards for the DRS–109 schedule was done on a uniform 50 percent basis [19] after February 1935, selecting every second card from alphabetical groups. In October, certain exceptions were made, when in the interest of speed a few counties with very large relief case loads were sampled on a 25 percent basis, every fourth card being selected. The resulting disproportion was adjusted by applying proper weights to the final results of the survey.

In taking the DRS–409A schedules, the sampling ratio ranged from 5 percent to 50 percent, depending on the size of the population sampled. In the interest of economy of time and expense, no adjustments of these disproportions were made in the final tabulation of results.

---

[18] Revised July 1935.
[19] In Connecticut, schedules were filled for all cases in the sample townships.

COLLECTION OF DATA

Field Staff.

Field studies were conducted in the sample counties under a joint rural research plan by which the Division of Research, Statistics, and Finance of the Federal Emergency Relief Administration, the State Emergency Relief Administrations, and the State Colleges of Agriculture, or other institutions engaged in rural research in the States, agreed to cooperate in conducting investigations of rural relief. The rural sociologist or economist at the State College of Agriculture was appointed State Supervisor of Rural Research in each State where mutually satisfactory cooperative arrangements could be perfected among the agencies interested.

The State Supervisors of Rural Research were men exceptionally well qualified to supervise the field work necessary in connection with the rural studies.[20] As they were full-time workers on the staffs of their State colleges, they did not spend any considerable amount of time in the field in detailed supervision of field work but were responsible for its direction and for the prompt and accurate return of schedules to the national office.

In addition to the State Supervisor of Rural Research, the field personnel consisted of a full-time assistant supervisor and a survey staff, including clerical workers. The Assistant Supervisors of Rural Research were persons experienced in social and economic research who had graduate training equivalent at least to a master's degree. The clerical personnel was made up of local persons who were qualified for work under the provisions of the professional and technical works program carried on by the F. E. R. A. Most of these workers conformed to the "needs test" as applied by the State Emergency Relief Administration. However, no person was employed on the survey staff unless he was considered well qualified to perform the work required. Carefully written instructions were provided these workers by the Washington office and, in addition, personal instruction and training was given them by the State Supervisor or Assistant Supervisor of Rural Research.

Sources of Data.

In general, data entered on schedules taken in the sample counties were transcribed from family case record cards on file in local relief offices. Such records had previously been filled in connection with the investigation and social service activities of the agencies concerned. In some instances, information for specific items on the schedules was obtained by interviews with case workers and from local relief or rehabilitation officials. Some of the information given by the DRS–409 schedule was obtained through family interview.

---

[20] See attached list of State Supervisors.

Editing Schedules and Tabulating Results.

More than 270,000 DRS–109 and DRS–109A schedules were filled in the field during the months the survey was in progress. These schedules were edited in the field and were carefully re-edited in the Washington office. Each section on every schedule submitted was carefully examined to detect, wherever possible, erroneous, inconsistent, incomplete, or missing entries. In order to insure the greatest possible accuracy of the data, each schedule which needed revisions that could not be made by the editor from other entries was returned to the field for completion or revision. Coding, punching, and machine tabulation were done in Washington and New York.

REPRESENTATIVENESS OF SAMPLE

An accurate or representative sample is a miniature picture of a larger whole. The conclusions drawn from such a sample apply, within reasonable limits, to the entire field from which the sample was drawn. It is of greatest importance that a sample be selected in such a manner that its statistical values measure what they are supposed to measure; that is, so that they measure that larger whole predefined as constituting the population [21] to be studied. It is possible for a sample to be representative of a larger population of units, but due to bias in selection that population may not coincide with that which the sample was supposed to represent. Hence, the measure may not actually apply to the field presumably under investigation. In order for a sample to measure the large whole it is supposed to measure, it must include all the important phases of the whole and must include them in their proper proportions. Such a sample is said to be an unbiased or *valid* sample. If the sample is at the same time sufficiently large to reduce accidental errors and to produce stable measures the sample is said to be *reliable*.

Two major questions arise concerning the accuracy of the relief studies here described. The first question relates to the precision of the data themselves and the second question concerns the representativeness of the sample. The final results of the studies would be biased if there were constant errors in recording the original data. The accuracy of the data depends upon the correctness of the sources used. As has been pointed out, secondary sources were used almost exclusively in filling household schedules. Specific entries on agency case records as well as data supplied by such informants as case workers, case aides, or relief officials may often have been in error. Very few items were of such nature, however, that one would expect a constant error in reporting. Error in one direction would

---

[21] The term *population* is used in its technical sense to indicate the entire number of units represented by a sample.

probably be cancelled by errors in opposite directions. Hence, while inaccuracies may have been present in individual case schedules, averages were likely to be essentially correct. It may be pointed out that information was collected from E. R. A. agencies only, local poor relief being excluded. Relief standards maintained by these E. R. A. agencies were generally high, including the standards of maintaining complete and accurate records. Records were particularly good in the sample counties due to cooperation of local case workers and relief officials in the research aim to report accurate data.

One of the most pertinent questions that can be asked concerning any sample is whether it is representative of the whole which final generalizations are purported to encompass. In the discussion of this question in connection with the rural relief samples reviewed, it is necessary to exercise caution in the claims made for their accuracy. Samples selected from a totality for which no complete enumeration exists can never be directly tested statistically for their representativeness. The search for a solution must be directed largely to the application of logic and sound judgment rather than to the application of mathematical computations.

In undertaking the development of a procedure for selecting samples representative of the rural relief population, three major difficulties had to be recognized.

The relief situation in a particular locality as of a particular month may be largely a reflection of administrative policy.—Much of the variation in phases of rural relief is not a result of natural socioeconomic conditions about which *a priori* knowledge is available but is a result of unpredictable differences in programs and policies of relief administration. Such differences arise among counties within particular States as well as among the States themselves. Hence, temporary shortage of funds may result in curtailment of relief or in dropping certain classes of clients during a particular month. Special classes of relief clients may be shifted from the general relief rolls to special relief programs. Local relief administrators may order all employable members of a particular occupational group removed from relief because seasonal employment is considered available for them during a particular month. All cases may be closed pending reinvestigation of the eligibility of each client for relief. These and numerous other administrative differences and changes are unpredictable and beyond the reckoning of the investigator.

The relief situation in a locality as of a particular month may be largely a reflection of temporary factors that profoundly affect the relief program.—Temporary pick-up or shut-down of industrial plants may remove or add certain types of clients. Every year floods

occur in some localities, producing the necessity for temporary aid
to its victims. Loss of crops and livestock due to drought, insect
infestations, or other reasons occur in some localities yearly. In
years of widespread drought the extent of its devastation differs
widely among the localities affected.

*The major purpose of the relief surveys conducted made it neces-
sary that they cover many aspects of rural relief.*—The relief studies
under discussion were not made for the purpose of providing scien-
tific discoveries in the social field. Rather, these studies were made
for the purpose of providing information that would contribute to
the solution of pressing problems confronting the persons charged
with the task of administering relief. The questions which needed
answers were many, covering all phases of the rural relief situation.
Sampling for the answer to a single specific question would be relatively simple. It is known, however, that a sample representative
for one purpose will not necessarily be representative for other purposes. It was recognized from the beginning that the difficulties involved in the selection of a sample that would represent the rural-
relief population in its multitudinous aspects were enormous.

The natural reaction to the above discussion is that, due to lack
of statistical controls known to be relevant to the various aspects of
rural relief, a strictly random sample should have been taken. This
should have included a large number of counties, selected in such
manner as to allow each relevant factor an equal chance of inclusion.
On purely theoretical grounds this is probably true. Practical considerations, however, made the random sample impossible. The
optimum number of counties that the field staff of each State was
equipped to survey under existing limitations on time and expense
was known. In order to assure an approach to that optimum, it
was necessary to control the sample to the extent of predetermining
the number of counties in each State and in each area.

The question may still be raised, however, as to the advisability
of selecting counties at random within each State or area. Again,
practical considerations made the random sampling method impossible. In certain counties the relief case records were found to
be in such poor condition as to render the county useless as a sample.
In other counties local relief officials declined to cooperate with the
survey staff. Hence, in the final selection of the sample it was
necessary not only that the counties be as representative as possible
but that they be counties from which trustworthy information could
be had with as great ease as possible. This necessitated the selection
of a controlled sample.

In spite of the numerous pitfalls into which a sampling method
might lead when applied to the field of rural relief, it is believed
that the samples taken are accurate enough in their general aspects

for most practical purposes. This belief is based on the following considerations.

The way the sample was selected had an important bearing on its validity.—The factors used as controls in selecting sample counties for relief surveys were chosen on the basis of logic, reasoning, judgment, and common sense considerations on the part of those investigators who aided or advised in the development of the sampling procedure. The controls used were those readily available from the 1930 Census and which were judged relevant to the purposes of the studies contemplated.

The application of the sampling procedure resulted in the selection of a series of counties that were truly representative with respect to various background factors. They were representative not only of the factors directly controlled in selecting them, such as type of farming, farm tenancy, farm labor, farm and nonfarm distribution of the population, and per capita land value, but they proved to be representative also of other background variables. For example, data given by the 1935 Census of Agriculture were used for testing. That the sample counties were highly representative of most of the States with respect to part-time farming during 1934 and with respect to movement of population to farms during the depression is shown in accompanying tables [22] (tables E and F).

The fact that the counties were representative of numerous background factors does not, however, assure their representativeness with regard to the aspects of relief actually studied. Making a sample representative in some respects only increases the possibilities that it will be representative in other aspects. Representativeness with respect to other aspects is assured only to the extent that the background factors are relevant to the purposes of the study; i. e., relevant to those aspects in which one is interested.

Tests indicate that the sampling procedure followed actually gave a fair degree of control over aspects of the rural relief situation. They indicate that the factors judged relevant on *a priori* reasoning were actually pertinent to the purposes of the studies. In the tabulation of data, a few classifications of the relief population of each sample county were made. Hence, it was possible to determine the variation among sample counties with regard to certain aspects of rural relief, and to test this variation against the variation among the counties with respect to the control factors used in selecting the sample. The object of such tests was to determine whether the relationships among phases of relief and background factors expected on logical grounds were actually found in the results of the study.

---

[22] With respect to part-time farming and movement to farms, the results shown by States in the 1935 Census of Agriculture could have been obtained within reasonable limits of accuracy if the study had been limited to the sample counties.

TABLE E.—PROPORTION OF ALL FARM OPERATORS WHO WORKED 150 DAYS OR MORE OFF THEIR FARMS DURING 1934, FOR STATE AS A WHOLE AND FOR SAMPLE COUNTIES IN 31 STATES

State	State total			Sample counties		
	Total farmers	Part-time farmers		Total farmers	Part-time farmers	
		Number	Percent		Number	Percent
All States sampled [1]	5,527,073	448,013	8.1	667,455	52,100	7.8
Alabama	273,455	15,901	5.8	28,653	1,444	5.0
Arizona	18,824	3,318	17.6	4,397	768	17.5
Arkansas	253,013	11,375	4.5	29,779	1,378	4.6
California	150,360	26,121	17.4	28,305	5,690	20.1
Colorado	63,644	5,125	8.1	6,341	438	6.9
Florida	72,857	11,424	15.7	9,728	1,674	17.2
Georgia	250,544	16,631	6.6	25,379	1,464	5.8
Iowa	221,986	9,742	4.4	22,123	1,026	4.6
Kansas	174,589	11,752	6.7	19,719	1,250	6.3
Kentucky	278,298	20,227	7.3	24,543	1,638	6.7
Louisiana	170,216	8,820	5.2	31,388	1,575	5.0
Michigan	196,517	18,934	9.6	25,268	2,238	8.9
Minnesota	203,302	8,630	4.2	36,520	1,811	5.0
Missouri	278,454	19,100	6.9	32,658	2,072	6.3
Montana	50,564	4,197	8.3	7,226	501	6.9
Nebraska	133,616	4,497	3.4	12,886	486	3.8
New York	177,025	22,369	12.6	16,084	2,299	14.3
North Carolina	300,967	26,977	9.0	30,290	2,642	8.7
North Dakota	84,606	2,637	3.1	15,590	432	2.8
Ohio	255,146	29,353	11.5	28,686	2,336	8.1
Oklahoma	213,325	11,271	5.3	24,291	1,175	4.8
Oregon	64,826	10,009	15.4	7,150	1,082	15.1
South Carolina	165,504	14,947	9.0	20,855	2,038	9.8
South Dakota	83,303	3,056	3.7	12,399	493	4.0
Tennessee	273,783	22,462	8.2	29,436	2,303	7.8
Texas	501,017	34,209	6.8	66,699	3,442	5.2
Utah	30,695	4,289	14.0	6,343	777	12.2
Virginia	197,632	29,807	15.1	25,038	3,517	14.0
Washington	84,381	13,399	15.9	9,985	1,537	15.4
West Virginia	104,747	16,095	15.4	7,830	1,343	17.2
Wisconsin	199,877	11,339	5.7	21,868	1,231	5.6

[1] Data not available for townships in Connecticut and Massachusetts.

Source: *United States Census of Agriculture: 1935.*

TABLE F.—PROPORTION OF THE TOTAL FARM POPULATION JANUARY 1935 THAT REPORTED A NONFARM RESIDENCE 5 YEARS EARLIER, FOR STATE AS A WHOLE AND FOR SAMPLE COUNTIES IN 31 STATES

State	State total			Sample counties		
	Farm population, 1935	Moved from nonfarm residence		Farm population, 1935	Moved from nonfarm residence	
		Number	Percent		Number	Percent
All States sampled [1]	25, 997, 427	1, 566, 609	6. 0	3, 145, 315	183, 909	5. 8
Alabama	1, 386, 074	63, 665	4. 6	146, 955	6, 337	4. 3
Arizona	100, 083	10, 082	10. 1	21, 014	2, 585	12. 3
Arkansas	1, 180, 238	51, 763	4. 4	140, 138	6, 254	4. 5
California	608, 838	71, 078	11. 7	118, 922	12, 577	10. 6
Colorado	276, 198	26, 920	9. 7	25, 614	2, 325	9. 1
Florida	319, 658	22, 287	7. 0	36, 469	2, 156	5. 9
Georgia	1, 405, 944	57, 582	4. 1	141, 744	4, 359	3. 1
Iowa	967, 979	51, 168	5. 3	95, 657	5, 572	5. 8
Kansas	703, 743	48, 395	6. 9	78, 488	4, 956	6. 3
Kentucky	1, 307, 816	61, 326	4. 7	113, 368	6, 334	5. 6
Louisiana	859, 351	31, 186	3. 6	160, 439	5, 684	3. 5
Michigan	840, 514	110, 413	13. 1	108, 128	13, 317	12. 3
Minnesota	928, 487	49, 676	5. 4	164, 199	10, 207	6. 2
Missouri	1, 183, 499	81, 958	6. 9	147, 857	9, 796	6. 6
Montana	195, 262	15, 674	8. 0	26, 710	2, 296	8. 6
Nebraska	580, 694	23, 299	4. 0	55, 959	2, 290	4. 1
New York	784, 483	81, 514	10. 4	72, 683	8, 434	11. 6
North Carolina	1, 623, 481	50, 227	3. 1	163, 341	5, 402	3. 3
North Dakota	385, 614	11, 562	3. 0	71, 245	2, 365	3. 3
Ohio	1, 127, 405	105, 297	9. 3	124, 040	9, 993	8. 1
Oklahoma	1, 015, 562	71, 186	7. 0	114, 109	7, 466	6. 5
Oregon	248, 767	45, 141	18. 1	27, 544	5, 149	18. 7
South Carolina	948, 435	32, 510	3. 4	124, 344	3, 213	2. 6
South Dakota	358, 204	12, 950	3. 6	53, 855	2, 266	4. 2
Tennessee	1, 308, 420	59, 400	4. 5	146, 076	5, 621	3. 8
Texas	2, 332, 693	112, 774	4. 8	314, 465	11, 641	3. 7
Utah	138, 242	9, 198	6. 7	27, 625	1, 447	5. 2
Virginia	1, 053, 469	40, 053	3. 8	135, 545	4, 950	3. 7
Washington	335, 840	47, 818	14. 2	40, 575	6, 678	16. 5
West Virginia	561, 919	47, 150	8. 4	43, 011	4, 820	11. 2
Wisconsin	930, 515	63, 357	6. 8	105, 196	7, 419	7. 1

[1] Data not available for townships in Connecticut and Massachusetts.

Source: *United States Census of Agriculture: 1935.*

For example, one of the major purposes of the rural relief studies was to determine the distribution of the relief population between farm and nonfarm residence. As an index of this distribution, the percent of the rural relief cases located in the open country [23] was determined. This index is available for each of the sample counties. Significant and consistent relationships were found between this relief variable and the background factors used as controls. Figures C and D show this relationship in the Corn Belt, the area used for illustrative purposes.

In selecting the counties from the Corn Belt it was assumed that the residence distribution and other aspects of the rural relief

[23] Outside of centers having 50 or more inhabitants.

population would depend to some extent upon the fertility of the soil, upon the residence distribution of the general rural population, and upon the proportion of wage laborers among agricultural workers, and that a sample representative of these factors would also be representative of the relief variable. It appears that these assumptions were essentially correct. There was an unmistakable tendency for those counties having low per capita land value to have a large proportion of relief clients resident in the open country, and for those counties having high land values to have a small proportion of their relief clients in the open country. In other words, the relief variable is negatively correlated with the background factor.[24] This negative relationship is not disturbed by the subgrouping of the counties on the basis of the other two background factors. Regardless of the subgroupings, counties with high land values had low proportions of open country relief cases. Counties with low land values had high proportions of open country relief cases, and counties with intermediate land values had intermediate values of the relief index (figure C).

As was to be expected on logical grounds, a positive relationship was found between the residence distribution of the general rural population and the residence distribution of the rural relief population. Some relationship between the farm labor index and the relief index was also found. The data do not show sufficient consistency, however, to indicate clearly the nature or significance of this relationship (figure C and table G).

The relationship between the background factors and the proportion of the relief population resident in the open country is not entirely consistent but is disturbed in several instances by administrative factors and by the operation of temporary emergencies. Hence, three counties (Hall and Johnson, Nebraska, and Hutchinson, South Dakota) with very high land values show large proportions of agricultural families on relief due to the very great impoverishment of the rural-farm population by drought in 1934 and by adverse weather conditions during the spring of 1935. An unduly high proportion of open country residents were on relief in Hickory County, Missouri, because of drought in 1934 and floods in 1935. An unexpectedly low percent of the agricultural population was on relief in Brookings, South Dakota, due to the administrative shift of farmers from general relief to a special program of rural rehabilitation (table G).

---

[24] The rank-difference coefficient of correlation was found to be —.53.

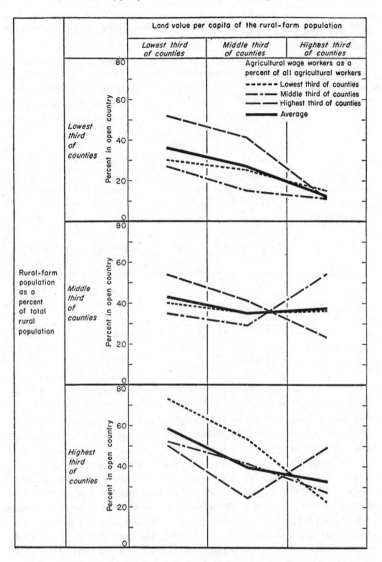

Fᵢ𝘨. C – RELATIONSHIP BETWEEN BACKGROUND FACTORS AND THE
PERCENT OF THE RURAL RELIEF POPULATION
LOCATED IN OPEN COUNTRY IN 27 SAMPLE
CORN BELT COUNTIES
June 1935

AF-2015, W.P.A.

TABLE G.—RELATIONSHIP BETWEEN BACKGROUND FACTORS AND THE PERCENT OF THE RURAL RELIEF POPULATION LOCATED IN OPEN COUNTRY IN 27 SAMPLE CORN BELT COUNTIES, JUNE 1935

Rural-farm population as percent of total rural population	Agricultural wage workers as a percent of all agricultural workers	Land value per capita of the rural-farm population		
		Lowest third of counties	Middle third of counties	Highest third of counties
		Percent in open country	Percent in open country	Percent in open country
Lowest third of counties	Lowest third of counties	30 Putnam	25 Guthrie	15 Woodford
	Middle third of counties	27 Fountain	15 Hitchcock	11 Calhoun
	Highest third of counties	52 Clinton	41 Scott	11 Ida
Middle third of counties	Lowest third of counties	40 Smith	35 Wabaunsee	36 Johnson
	Middle third of counties	35 Hancock	29 Washington	54 Hutchinson
	Highest third of counties	54 Morgan	41 Whiteside	23 Pierce
Highest third of counties	Lowest third of counties	73 Hickory	53 Black Hawk	22 Marshall
	Middle third of counties	52 Ray	41 Mahaska	27 Page
	Highest third of counties	50 Shelby	24 Brookings	49 Hall

It seems clear that the factors used in selecting a controlled sample for relief purposes were relevant. This does not mean that the sampling procedure followed was a perfect one, for administrative factors, as well as such emergency conditions as drought, flood, hail, insect infestation, strikes, etc., were not taken into account in selecting it. However, the sampling procedure followed gave sufficient control of the variation in the general aspects of rural relief to assure a fairly representative sample and thereby to render the main conclusions of the studies conducted reliable for most practical purposes.

Statistical tests indicated that the sample counties were, in general, representative with respect to certain aspects of the rural relief population of October 1933.—As shown above, it was found *a posteriori* that the background factors used in stratifying counties for the selection of samples were relevant in that they controlled a certain amount of the variation in aspects of rural relief. Possibility of bias due to local administrative policy and other local conditions was, however, implicit in the sampling method used. The only complete check on the extent of such bias would be a comparison of relief aspects found in the sample counties with those in all counties from which the sample was drawn. Unfortunately no such check was possible since no complete enumeration was made during the period when studies were being conducted in the sample counties.

Only one complete census of the rural relief population was ever taken.[25] That enumeration was made as of October 1933, only 6 months after the organization of the Federal Emergency Relief Administration. Considerable information was collected by that census. However, the published information is not satisfactory as a means of checking relief samples taken more than a year later. In the interim between the time the Relief Census was taken and the time the sample studies were made, important changes took place in the rural relief field. These changes are reflected in such factors as the great drought of 1934, the extension of Federal relief to include all counties of the country, the development of a special program of rural rehabilitation, the development of a works program, and the development of higher standards of relief administration. In view of these changes it is not to be expected that the various aspects of rural relief in 1935 would be entirely similar to those of October 1933.

While the rural relief samples of 1935 cannot legitimately be checked against the rural relief universe of October 1933, it is possible to check the extent to which the selected counties constituted a sample representative of some phases of the rural relief population of that month. From county data in the Unemployment Relief Census, the representativeness of the sample counties was tested in two respects, (a) with respect to aggregate numbers of rural relief cases and (b) with respect to average number of persons per rural relief case.

A close estimate of the aggregate number of rural cases receiving relief in the 9 agricultural areas in October 1933 could have been made from a count of the cases in the 138 sample counties. For example, the 138 counties contained 8.1 percent of all rural families in the 9 areas in 1930. They contained 7.8 percent of all rural relief cases in the same areas as reported by the Unemployment Relief Census, a fairly close agreement. Such close agreement between these ratios was not found in each of the nine separate areas though in most areas a fairly satisfactory comparison was obtained (table B). Likewise, a reasonably close estimate of the number of rural cases receiving relief in 31 States in October 1933 could have been made from a count of cases in the 304 sample counties selected to represent these States. The 304 sample counties selected from 31

---

[25] *Unemployment Relief Census, October 1933*, Federal Emergency Relief Administration.

States contained 11.4 percent of all rural families in those States in 1930. They contained 11.2 percent of all rural relief cases reported by the Unemployment Relief Census. The relief ratio showed considerable departures in some individual States (table D). Such discrepancies were to be expected, however, due to local administrative factors contingent upon the developmental stage of rural relief in October 1933.

The State samples were representative with respect to the average size of rural cases in October 1933. In 283 counties selected to represent 29 States [26] the ratio of rural relief persons to cases was the same as in all counties from which the samples were selected, the ratio being 4.5 persons per case. In nine of the separate States the average number of persons per case was the same for the sample as for the State. In each of 13 States the sample average departed from the State average by only one-tenth person per case. In no State was the discrepancy greater than two-tenths person per case.

The fact that the sample counties were representative in these respects increases the confidence that they were representative in other respects, and the fact that they were representative of aspects of rural relief in October 1933 increases confidence although it does not prove that they were also representative in the months in which interest centers.

Close comparison between the averages given by the area and State samples indicated that the two samples were actually representative of the same relief population.—This in itself was not so much an argument for the validity as for the reliability of the sampling procedure; that is, the procedure produced consistent results. In other words, it may be said that regardless of whether the samples provided unbiased pictures of the populations they were supposed to represent, they did provide consistent pictures of *a* relief population.

Beginning with June 1935, tabulations of the data given by the Survey of Current Changes in the Rural Relief Population were made by States for all States sampled. In order to preserve the continuity of the previous surveys, however, tabulations were also made by areas, combining the information collected in 138 counties selected from 9 agricultural areas. Hence, in June and October the results of two cross-section studies of the rural relief population were available for comparison. Results of the one study were derived from a sample of about 29,000 schedules taken in 138 counties selected from 9 agricultural areas. Results of the other study were derived from a larger sample of nearly 61,000 schedules taken in 300 counties and 83 New England townships. The larger sample in-

---

[26] Colorado and Virginia excluded due to lack of, or small number of, cases in sample counties. New England States excluded due to lack of information by townships.

cluded 117 of the counties and about 23,000 of the schedules of the smaller sample. The one sample was, however, in all respects at least twice as large as the other (table H). Moreover, the larger sample included all types of agricultural, and of most rural non-agricultural, enterprises in the United States.

TABLE H.—COMPARISON OF LARGER AND SMALLER SAMPLE WITH RESPECT TO SIZE AND WITH RESPECT TO SPECIFIED RELIEF ITEMS, JUNE 1935

Item	Smaller sample [1]	Larger sample [2]
SIZE OF SAMPLE		
Percent of all counties sampled	8. 2	12. 1
Percent of all counties in United States	4. 5	9. 8
Percent of all rural families (1930) in areas or States sampled	8. 1	12. 1
Percent of all rural families (1930) in United States	4. 4	8. 8
Percent of all farm operators (1935) in areas or States sampled	8. 1	12. 1
Percent of all farm operators (1935) in United States	5. 0	10. 0
Total number of case schedules taken	29, 258	60, 674
Total number of cases in sample counties and townships	58, 516	120, 471
RELIEF ITEMS		
Percent of rural relief cases among all rural families, 1930	10. 5	10. 8
Percent of relief farmers among all farmers, 1935	5. 5	5. 7
Percent of unemployable cases among all rural cases	12. 6	12. 0
Percent of village cases among all rural cases	38. 8	39. 1
Percent of farm operator heads among all heads	31. 0	31. 6
Percent of farm laborer heads among all heads	11. 7	13. 1
Percent of nonagricultural heads among all heads	39. 5	38. 0
Percent of normal families among all cases	73. 0	72. 4
Percent of broken families among all cases	10. 9	10. 6
Percent change in number of rural cases, June to October 1935	−24. 9	−24. 7
Average number of persons per rural case	4. 3	4. 3
Percent of persons under 16 years of age among all relief persons	43. 3	42. 9
Percent of persons 16 to 24 years of age among all relief persons	16. 3	16. 0
Percent of persons 25 to 64 years of age among all relief persons	35. 1	35. 8
Percent of persons 65 years and over among all relief persons	5. 2	5. 2
Average number of workers per employable case	1. 5	1. 5
Percent of 1-person households among all rural cases	9. 5	9. 9

[1] 138 counties.
[2] 300 counties and 83 New England townships.

Notwithstanding the great difference in size and geographical coverage of the two June samples, when the results were compared it was found that nearly all of the general conclusions drawn from the one were substantiated by the other. For example, the relationship between the relief population and the general population was not widely different in the two samples (10.5 and 10.8 percent). The distribution of the relief population with respect to residence, employability, occupational characteristics, age, and household composition was not significantly different in the two samples. The percent decrease of the case load from June to October 1935 was almost identical in the two samples (24.9 and 24.7 percent) (table H).

What significance is to be attached to the close correspondence between the results of the area and State samples? Two probabilities are indicated. It is probable that the rural relief population in the nine areas originally sampled was, as a whole, not essentially different in many respects from that in the combined areas not sampled (see discussion of areas not sampled, page 148). It is further probable that the counties and townships selected as State samples or as parts of State samples but lying outside the original 9 areas (there were 117 such counties and 83 New England townships) represent fairly well that portion (or most of that portion) of rural United States outside the 9 areas. It appears that provisional generalizations concerning the general aspects of rural relief and embracing the entire rural United States may be made from either sample. Such generalizations would in all probability be sufficiently accurate for practical purposes.

LIST A.—COUNTIES IN NINE AGRICULTURAL AREAS

Eastern Cotton Area

Alabama:
Autauga.
Barbour.
Bibb.
Blount.
Bullock.
Butler.
Calhoun.
Chambers.
Cherokee.
Chilton.
Choctaw.
Clarke.
Clay.
Cleburne.
Coffee.
Colbert.
Conecuh.
Coosa.
Covington.
Crenshaw.
Cullman.
Dale.
Dallas.
De Kalb.
Elmore.
Escambia.
Etowah.
Fayette.
Franklin.
Geneva.
Greene.
Hale.
Henry.
Houston.
Jackson.
Lamar.
Lauderdale.
Lawrence.
Lee.
Limestone.
Lowndes.
Macon.
Madison.
Marengo.
Marion.

Alabama—Continued.
Marshall.
Monroe.
Montgomery.
Morgan.
Perry.
Pickens.
Pike.
Randolph.
Russell.
St. Clair.
Shelby.
Sumter.
Talladega.
Tallapoosa.
Tuscaloosa.
Walker.
Washington.
Wilcox.
Winston.
Arkansas:
Ashley.
Bradley.
Calhoun.
Chicot.
Clark.
Clay.
Cleburne.
Cleveland.
Columbia.
Conway.
Craighead.
Crittenden.
Cross.
Dallas.
Desha.
Drew.
Faulkner.
Garland.
Grant.
Greene.
Hempstead.
Hot Spring.
Howard.
Independence.
Izard.

Arkansas—Continued.
Jackson.
Jefferson.
Lafayette.
Lawrence.
Lee.
Lincoln.
Little River.
Logan.
Lonoke.
Miller.
Mississippi.
Monroe.
Montgomery.
Nevada.
Ouachita.
Perry.
Phillips.
Pike.
Poinsett.
Pope.
Pulaski.
Randolph.
St. Francis.
Saline.
Scott.
Sharp.
Union.
Van Buren.
White.
Woodruff.
Yell.
Georgia:
Baker.
Baldwin.
Banks.
Barrow.
Bartow.
Ben Hill.
Bleckley.
Bulloch.
Burke.
Butts.
Calhoun.
Campbell.
Candler.

Eastern Cotton Area—Continued.

Georgia—Continued.
Carroll.
Catoosa.
Chattahoochee.
Chattooga.
Cherokee.
Clarke.
Clay.
Clayton.
Cobb.
Colquitt.
Columbia.
Coweta.
Crawford.
Crisp.
Dawson.
De Kalb.
Dodge.
Dooly.
Douglas.
Early.
Elbert.
Emanuel.
Evans.
Fayette.
Floyd.
Forsyth.
Franklin.
Glascock.
Gordon.
Greene.
Gwinnett.
Hall.
Hancock.
Haralson.
Harris.
Hart.
Heard.
Henry.
Houston.
Irwin.
Jackson.
Jasper.
Jefferson.
Jenkins.
Johnson.
Lamar.
Laurens.
Lee.
Lincoln.
McDuffie.
Macon.
Madison.
Marion.
Meriwether.
Miller.
Mitchell.
Monroe.
Montgomery.
Morgan.
Murray.
Newton.
Oconee.
Oglethorpe.
Paulding.
Peach.

Georgia—Continued.
Pickens.
Pike.
Polk.
Pulaski.
Putnam.
Quitman.
Randolph.
Richmond.
Rockdale.
Schley.
Screven.
Spalding.
Stephens.
Stewart.
Sumter.
Talbot.
Taliaferro.
Taylor.
Telfair.
Terrell.
Tift.
Toombs.
Treutlen.
Troup.
Turner.
Twiggs.
Upson.
Walker.
Walton.
Warren.
Washington.
Webster.
Wheeler.
Whitfield.
Wilcox.
Wilkes.
Wilkinson.
Worth.
Louisiana :
Avoyelles.
Bienville.
Bossier.
Caddo.
Caldwell.
Catahoula.
Claiborne.
Concordia.
De Soto.
East Carroll.
Evangeline.
Franklin.
Grant.
Jackson.
Lincoln.
Madison.
Morehouse.
Natchitoches.
Ouachita.
Pointe Coupee.
Rapides.
Red River.
Richland.
Sabine.
St. Landry.
Tensas.

Louisiana—Continued.
Union.
Vernon.
Washington.
Webster.
West Carroll.
Winn.
Mississippi :
Adams.
Alcorn.
Amite.
Attala.
Benton.
Bolivar.
Calhoun.
Carroll.
Chickasaw.
Choctaw.
Claiborne.
Clarke.
Clay.
Coahoma.
Covington.
De Soto.
Franklin.
George.
Grenada.
Hinds.
Holmes.
Humphreys.
Issaquena.
Itawamba.
Jasper.
Jefferson.
Jefferson Davis.
Jones.
Kemper.
Lafayette.
Lamar.
Lauderdale.
Lawrence.
Leake.
Lee.
Leflore.
Lincoln.
Lowndes.
Madison.
Marion.
Marshall.
Monroe.
Montgomery.
Neshoba.
Newton.
Noxubee.
Oktibbeha.
Panola.
Pike.
Pontotoc.
Prentiss.
Quitman.
Rankin.
Scott.
Sharkey.
Simpson.
Smith.
Sunflower.

Eastern Cotton Area—Continued.

Mississippi—Continued.
Tallahatchie.
Tate.
Tippah.
Tishomingo.
Tunica.
Union.
Walthall.
Warren.
Washington.
Wayne.
Webster.
Wilkinson.
Winston.
Yalobusha.
Yazoo.
Missouri:
Dunklin.
New Madrid.
Pemiscot.
North Carolina:
Anson.
Cabarrus.
Catawba.
Cleveland.
Cumberland.
Franklin.
Gaston.
Halifax.
Harnett.
Hoke.
Iredell.
Johnston.
Lee.
Lincoln.

North Carolina—Contd.
Mecklenburg.
Montgomery.
Northampton.
Polk.
Richmond.
Robeson.
Rowan.
Rutherford.
Sampson.
Scotland.
Stanly.
Union.
Warren.
South Carolina:
Abbeville.
Aiken.
Allendale.
Anderson.
Bamberg.
Barnwell.
Calhoun.
Cherokee.
Chesterfield.
Clarendon.
Colleton.
Darlington.
Dillon.
Dorchester.
Edgefield.
Fairfield.
Greenville.
Greenwood.
Hampton.
Kershaw.

South Carolina—Contd.
Lancaster.
Laurens.
Lee.
Lexington.
McCormick.
Marlboro.
Newberry.
Oconee.
Orangeburg.
Pickens.
Richland.
Saluda.
Spartanburg.
Sumter.
Union.
York.
Tennessee:
Carroll.
Chester.
Crockett.
Dyer.
Fayette.
Gibson.
Hardeman.
Hardin.
Haywood.
Henderson.
Lake.
Lauderdale.
Lawrence.
McNairy.
Madison.
Shelby.
Tipton.

Western Cotton Area

Oklahoma:
Beckham.
Bryan.
Caddo.
Choctaw.
Comanche.
Cotton.
Creek.
Garvin.
Grady.
Greer.
Harmon.
Haskell.
Hughes.
Jackson.
Jefferson.
Kiowa.
Le Flore.
Lincoln.
Love.
McClain
McCurtain.
McIntosh.
Marshall.
Muskogee.
Okfuskee.
Okmulgee.

Oklahoma—Continued.
Pottawatomie.
Roger Mills.
Seminole.
Sequoyah.
Stephens.
Tillman.
Wagoner.
Washita.
Texas:
Anderson.
Angelina.
Austin.
Bastrop.
Bee.
Bell.
Bosque.
Bowie.
Brazos.
Burleson.
Caldwell.
Cameron.
Camp.
Cass.
Cherokee.
Childress.
Coleman.

Texas—Continued.
Collin.
Collingsworth.
Colorado.
Coryell.
Cottle.
Crosby.
Dallas.
Dawson.
Delta.
Denton.
De Witt.
Ellis.
Erath.
Falls.
Fannin.
Fayette.
Fisher.
Foard.
Fort Bend.
Franklin.
Freestone.
Gonzales.
Grayson.
Gregg.
Grimes.
Guadalupe.

Western Cotton Area—Continued.

Texas—Continued.
  Hall.
  Hamilton.
  Hardeman.
  Harrison.
  Haskell.
  Henderson.
  Hidalgo.
  Hill.
  Hockley.
  Hopkins.
  Houston.
  Howard.
  Hunt.
  Johnson.
  Jones.
  Karnes.
  Kaufman.
  Knox.
  Lamar.
  Lamb.
  Lavaca.
  Lee.
  Leon.
  Limestone.
  Live Oak.

Texas—Continued.
  Lubbock.
  Lynn.
  McLennan.
  Madison.
  Marion.
  Martin.
  Milam.
  Mitchell.
  Montgomery.
  Morris.
  Nacogdoches.
  Navarro.
  Nolan.
  Nueces.
  Panola.
  Polk.
  Rains.
  Red River.
  Robertson.
  Rockwall.
  Runnels.
  Rusk.
  Sabine.
  San Augustine.
  San Jacinto.

Texas—Continued.
  San Patricio.
  Scurry.
  Shelby.
  Smith.
  Somervell.
  Starr.
  Stonewall.
  Taylor.
  Terry.
  Titus.
  Travis.
  Trinity.
  Upshur.
  Van Zandt.
  Walker.
  Waller.
  Washington.
  Wharton.
  Wheeler.
  Wichita.
  Wilbarger.
  Williamson.
  Wilson.
  Wood.

Appalachian-Ozark Area

Arkansas:
  Boone.
  Carroll.
  Crawford.
  Franklin.
  Johnson.
  Madison.
  Marion.
  Newton.
  Searcy.
  Stone.
  Washington.
Georgia:
  Dade.
  Fannin.
  Gilmer.
  Habersham.
  Lumpkin.
  Rabun.
  Towns.
  Union.
  White.
Illinois:
  Franklin.
  Hamilton.
  Hardin.
  Johnson.
  Pope.
  Saline.
  Williamson.
Kentucky:
  Adair.
  Allen.
  Bell.
  Breathitt.

Kentucky—Continued.
  Butler.
  Caldwell.
  Carter.
  Casey.
  Clay.
  Clinton.
  Crittenden.
  Cumberland.
  Edmonson.
  Elliott.
  Estill.
  Floyd.
  Grayson.
  Greenup.
  Harlan.
  Hopkins.
  Jackson.
  Johnson.
  Knott.
  Knox.
  Larue.
  Laurel.
  Lawrence.
  Lee.
  Leslie.
  Letcher.
  Lincoln.
  Livingston.
  McCreary.
  Magoffin.
  Martin.
  Meade.
  Menifee.
  Metcalfe.

Kentucky—Continued.
  Monroe.
  Morgan.
  Muhlenberg.
  Ohio.
  Owsley.
  Perry.
  Pike.
  Powell.
  Pulaski.
  Rockcastle.
  Rowan.
  Russell.
  Wayne.
  Whitley.
  Wolfe.
Missouri:
  Bollinger.
  Camden.
  Carter.
  Crawford.
  Dent.
  Douglas.
  Iron.
  Madison.
  Oregon.
  Reynolds.
  St. Francois.
  Ste. Genevieve.
  Shannon.
  Taney.
  Washington.
  Wayne.

Appalachian-Ozark Area—Continued.

North Carolina:
Alexander.
Alleghany.
Ashe.
Avery.
Buncombe.
Burke.
Caldwell.
Chatham.
Cherokee.
Clay.
Graham.
Haywood.
Henderson.
Jackson.
McDowell.
Macon.
Madison.
Mitchell.
Moore.
Randolph.
Swain.
Transylvania.
Watauga.
Wilkes.
Yancey.
Oklahoma:
Adair.
Cherokee.
Delaware.
Latimer.
Pushmataha.
Tennessee:
Anderson.
Benton.
Bledsoe.
Blount.
Bradley.
Campbell.
Cannon.
Carter.
Claiborne.
Clay.
Cocke.
Coffee.
Cumberland.
Decatur.
De Kalb.
Fentress.
Franklin.
Grainger.
Grundy.
Hamblen.
Hancock.
Hawkins.
Hickman.
Houston.
Humphreys.
Jackson.

Tennessee—Continued.
Jefferson.
Johnson.
Lewis.
McMinn.
Macon.
Marion.
Marshall.
Maury.
Monroe.
Morgan.
Overton.
Perry.
Pickett.
Polk.
Putnam.
Rhea.
Roane.
Scott.
Sequatchie.
Sevier.
Smith.
Stewart.
Sullivan.
Unicoi.
Union.
Van Buren.
Warren.
Washington.
Wayne.
White.
Williamson.
Virginia:
Albemarle.
Alleghany.
Amherst.
Appomattox.
Bedford.
Botetourt.
Buchanan.
Campbell.
Carroll.
Craig.
Culpeper.
Floyd.
Franklin.
Giles.
Grayson.
Greene.
Henry.
Lee.
Madison.
Montgomery.
Nelson.
Orange.
Page.
Patrick.
Rappahannock.
Rockbridge.

Virginia—Continued.
Russell.
Scott.
Smyth.
Spotsylvania.
Stafford.
Tazewell.
Wise.
West Virginia:
Barbour.
Boone.
Braxton.
Calhoun.
Clay.
Doddridge.
Fayette.
Gilmer.
Grant.
Greenbrier.
Hampshire.
Hancock.
Hardy.
Harrison.
Jackson.
Kanawha.
Lewis.
Lincoln.
Logan.
McDowell.
Marion.
Mason.
Mercer.
Mineral.
Mingo.
Monongalia.
Monroe.
Morgan.
Nicholas.
Pendleton.
Pleasants.
Pocahontas.
Preston.
Putnam.
Raleigh.
Randolph.
Ritchie.
Roane.
Summers.
Taylor.
Tucker.
Tyler.
Upshur.
Wayne.
Webster.
Wetzel.
Wirt.
Wood.
Wyoming.

Lake States Cut-Over Area

Michigan:
Alcona.
Alger.
Alpena.

Michigan—Continued.
Antrim.
Baraga.
Benzie.

Michigan—Continued.
Charlevoix.
Cheboygan.
Chippewa.

Lake States Cut-Over Area—Continued.

Michigan—Continued.
Clare.
Crawford.
Delta.
Dickinson.
Emmet.
Gladwin.
Gogebic.
Grand Traverse.
Houghton.
Iosco.
Iron.
Kalkaska.
Keweenaw.
Lake.
Leelanau.
Luce.
Mackinac.
Manistee.
Marquette.
Mason.
Menominee.
Midland.
Missaukee.

Michigan—Continued.
Montmorency.
Newaygo.
Ogemaw.
Ontonagon.
Oscoda.
Otsego.
Presque Isle.
Roscommon.
Schoolcraft.
Wexford.
Minnesota :
Aitkin.
Beltrami.
Carlton.
Cass.
Clearwater.
Cook.
Crow Wing.
Hubbard.
Itasca.
Koochiching.
Lake.
Lake of the Woods.

Minnesota—Continued.
Pine.
Roseau.
St. Louis.
Wisconsin :
Ashland.
Bayfield.
Burnett.
Douglas.
Florence.
Forest.
Iron.
Langlade.
Lincoln.
Marinette.
Oconto.
Oneida.
Price.
Rusk.
Sawyer.
Taylor.
Vilas.
Washburn.

Hay and Dairy Area

Michigan :
Arenac.
Bay.
Genesee.
Ingham.
Jackson.
Kent.
Lapeer.
Livingston.
Macomb.
Mecosta.
Muskegon.
Oakland.
Osceola.
Ottawa.
St. Clair.
Sanilac.
Washtenaw.
Minnesota :
Anoka.
Becker.
Benton.
Carver.
Chisago.
Dakota.
Dodge.
Douglas.
Freeborn.
Goodhue.
Houston.
Isanti.
Kanabec.
Kandiyohi.
McLeod.
Meeker.
Mille Lacs.
Morrison.

Minnesota—Continued.
Mower.
Olmsted.
Otter Tail.
Pennington.
Pope.
Red Lake.
Rice.
Scott.
Sherburne.
Sibley.
Stearns.
Steele.
Todd.
Wabasha.
Wadena.
Waseca.
Washington.
Winona.
Wright.
New York :
Albany.
Allegany.
Broome.
Cattaraugus.
Cayuga.
Chautauqua.
Chemung.
Chenango.
Clinton.
Columbia.
Cortland.
Delaware.
Dutchess.
Genesee.
Greene.
Jefferson.

New York—Continued.
Lewis.
Livingston.
Madison.
Montgomery.
Oneida.
Onondaga.
Orange.
Oswego.
Otsego.
Rensselaer.
St. Lawrence.
Saratoga.
Schoharie.
Steuben.
Sullivan.
Tioga.
Tompkins.
Washington.
Wyoming.
Ohio :
Ashtabula.
Belmont.
Columbiana.
Delaware.
Geauga.
Jefferson.
Licking.
Lorain.
Medina.
Portage.
Stark.
Trumbull.
Tuscarawas.
Union.
Wayne.

Hay and Dairy Area—Continued.

Pennsylvania:
Beaver.
Bedford.
Bradford.
Bucks.
Chester.
Crawford.
Cumberland.
Erie.
Franklin.
Juniata.
Lawrence.
Lebanon.
Mercer.
Montgomery.
Montour.
Susquehanna.
Tioga.
Washington.
Wayne.
Wyoming.
Vermont:
Addison.
Caledonia.
Chittenden.
Franklin.
Lamoille.
Orange.
Orleans.
Rutland.

Vermont—Continued.
Washington.
Windham.
Windsor.
Wisconsin:
Adams.
Barron.
Brown.
Buffalo.
Calumet.
Chippewa.
Clark.
Columbia.
Crawford.
Dane.
Dodge.
Door.
Dunn.
Eau Claire.
Fond du Lac.
Grant.
Green.
Green Lake.
Iowa.
Jackson.
Jefferson.
Juneau.
Kenosha.
Kewaunee.
La Crosse.

Wisconsin—Continued.
Lafayette.
Manitowoc.
Marathon.
Marquette.
Monroe.
Outagamie.
Ozaukee.
Pepin.
Pierce.
Polk.
Portage.
Racine.
Richland.
Rock.
St. Croix.
Sauk.
Shawano.
Sheboygan.
Trempealeau.
Vernon.
Walworth.
Washington.
Waukesha.
Waupaca.
Waushara.
Winnebago.
Wood.

Corn Belt

Colorado:
Yuma.
Illinois:
Alexander.
Boone.
Brown.
Bureau.
Carroll.
Cass.
Champaign.
Christian.
Coles.
De Kalb.
De Witt.
Douglas.
Edgar.
Ford.
Fulton.
Gallatin.
Greene.
Grundy.
Hancock.
Henderson.
Henry.
Iroquois.
Jersey.
Kane.
Kankakee.
Kendall.
Knox.
La Salle.
Lee.

Illinois—Continued.
Livingston.
Logan.
McDonough.
McHenry.
McLean.
Macon.
Macoupin.
Marshall.
Mason.
Menard.
Mercer.
Morgan.
Moultrie.
Ogle.
Peoria.
Piatt.
Putnam.
Rock Island.
Sangamon.
Schuyler.
Scott.
Shelby.
Stark.
Tazewell.
Vermilion.
Warren.
Whiteside.
Will.
Winnebago.
Woodford.

Indiana:
Benton.
Boone.
Carroll.
Cass.
Clinton.
Decatur.
Delaware.
Fayette.
Fountain.
Fulton.
Gibson.
Grant.
Hamilton.
Hancock.
Hendricks.
Henry.
Howard.
Jasper.
Johnson.
Knox.
Madison.
Miami.
Montgomery.
Morgan.
Newton.
Parke.
Pike.
Pulaski.
Putnam.
Randolph.
Rush.

Corn Belt—Continued.

Indiana—Continued.
Shelby.
Tippecanoe.
Tipton.
Union.
Vermilion.
Wabash.
Warren.
Wayne.
White.
Iowa :
Adair.
Adams.
Audubon.
Benton.
Black Hawk.
Boone.
Bremer.
Buchanan.
Buena Vista.
Butler.
Calhoun.
Carroll.
Cass.
Cedar.
Cerro Gordo.
Cherokee.
Chickasaw.
Clarke.
Clay.
Clinton.
Crawford.
Dallas.
Delaware.
Des Moines.
Dickinson.
Emmet.
Fayette.
Floyd.
Franklin.
Fremont.
Greene.
Grundy.
Guthrie.
Hamilton.
Hancock.
Hardin.
Harrison.
Henry.
Humboldt.
Ida.
Iowa.
Jasper.
Jefferson.
Johnson.
Jones.
Keokuk.
Kossuth.
Lee.
Linn.
Louisa.
Lyon.
Madison.
Mahaska.
Marion.

Iowa—Continued.
Marshall.
Mills.
Mitchell.
Monona.
Monroe.
Montgomery.
Muscatine.
O'Brien.
Osceola.
Page.
Palo Alto.
Pocahontas.
Pottawattamie.
Poweshiek.
Ringgold.
Sac.
Scott.
Shelby.
Sioux.
Story.
Tama.
Taylor.
Union.
Wapello.
Warren.
Washington.
Webster.
Winnebago.
Woodbury.
Worth.
Wright.
Kansas :
Allen.
Atchison.
Bourbon.
Brown.
Chase.
Cheyenne.
Clay.
Cloud.
Coffey.
Decatur.
Doniphan.
Douglas.
Franklin.
Geary.
Graham.
Jackson.
Jefferson.
Jewell.
Johnson.
Linn.
Lyon.
Marshall.
Miami.
Morris.
Nemaha.
Norton.
Osage.
Phillips.
Pottawatomie.
Republic.
Riley.
Shawnee.

Kansas—Continued.
Smith.
Wabaunsee.
Washington.
Minnesota :
Blue Earth.
Brown.
Chippewa.
Cottonwood.
Faribault.
Jackson.
Lac qui Parle.
Le Sueur.
Lyon.
Martin.
Murray.
Nobles.
Pipestone.
Redwood.
Renville.
Rock.
Watonwan.
Yellow Medicine.
Missouri :
Andrew.
Atchison.
Bates.
Benton.
Cedar.
Clinton.
De Kalb.
Gentry.
Henry.
Hickory.
Holt.
Nodaway.
Pettis.
Ray.
St. Clair.
Saline.
Worth.
Nebraska :
Adams.
Antelope.
Boone.
Boyd.
Buffalo.
Burt.
Butler.
Cass.
Cedar.
Chase.
Clay.
Colfax.
Cuming.
Custer.
Dakota.
Dawson.
Dixon.
Dodge.
Dundy.
Fillmore.
Franklin.
Frontier.
Furnas.

Corn Belt—Continued.

Nebraska—Continued.
  Gage.
  Gosper.
  Greeley.
  Hall.
  Hamilton.
  Harlan.
  Hayes.
  Hitchcock.
  Howard.
  Jefferson.
  Johnson.
  Kearney.
  Knox.
  Lancaster.
  Lincoln.
  Madison.
  Merrick.
  Nance.
  Nemaha.
  Nuckolls.
  Otoe.
  Pawnee.
  Phelps.
  Pierce.
  Platte.
  Polk.
  Redwillow.
  Richardson.
  Saline.

Nebraska—Continued.
  Sarpy.
  Saunders.
  Seward.
  Sherman.
  Stanton.
  Thayer.
  Thurston.
  Valley.
  Washington.
  Wayne.
  Webster.
  York.
Ohio:
  Auglaize.
  Butler.
  Champaign.
  Clark.
  Clinton.
  Darke.
  Fayette.
  Greene.
  Hancock.
  Henry.
  Logan.
  Madison.
  Marion.
  Miami.
  Montgomery.
  Paulding.

Ohio—Continued.
  Pickaway.
  Preble.
  Putnam.
  Ross.
  Van Wert.
  Warren.
  Wood.
South Dakota:
  Bon Homme.
  Brookings.
  Brule.
  Charles Mix.
  Clay.
  Davison.
  Douglas.
  Gregory.
  Hanson.
  Hutchinson.
  Kingsbury.
  Lake.
  Lincoln.
  McCook.
  Miner.
  Minnehaha.
  Moody.
  Sanborn.
  Turner.
  Union.
  Yankton.

Spring Wheat Area

Montana:
  Cascade.
  Chouteau.
  Daniels.
  Dawson.
  Fallon.
  Fergus.
  Hill.
  Judith Basin.
  Pondera.
  Prairie.
  Richland.
  Roosevelt.
  Sheridan.
  Stillwater.
  Teton.
  Valley.
  Wibaux.
North Dakota:
  Adams.
  Barnes.
  Benson.
  Billings.

North Dakota—Contd.
  Bottineau.
  Burke.
  Burleigh.
  Cavalier.
  Divide.
  Dunn.
  Eddy.
  Emmons.
  Foster.
  Golden Valley.
  Grant.
  Hettinger.
  Logan.
  McHenry.
  McIntosh.
  McKenzie.
  McLean.
  Mercer.
  Morton.
  Mountrail.
  Nelson.
  Oliver.

North Dakota—Contd.
  Pierce.
  Ramsey.
  Renville.
  Rolette.
  Sheridan.
  Sioux.
  Slope.
  Stark.
  Stutsman.
  Towner.
  Walsh.
  Ward.
  Wells.
  Williams.
South Dakota:
  Brown.
  Campbell.
  Corson.
  Edmunds.
  McPherson.
  Spink.
  Walworth.

Winter Wheat Area

Colorado:
  Sedgwick.
Kansas:
  Barber.
  Barton.
  Clark.
  Comanche.

Kansas—Continued.
  Dickinson.
  Edwards.
  Ellis.
  Ellsworth.
  Ford.
  Gove.

Kansas—Continued.
  Grant.
  Gray.
  Harper.
  Harvey.
  Haskell.
  Hodgeman.

Winter Wheat Area—Continued.

Kansas—Continued.
Kingman.
Kiowa.
Lane.
Lincoln.
McPherson.
Marion.
Meade.
Mitchell.
Ness.
Osborne.
Ottawa.
Pawnee.
Pratt.
Rawlins.
Reno.
Rice.
Rooks.
Rush.
Russell.
Saline.
Sedgwick.
Seward.

Kansas—Continued.
Sheridan.
Stafford.
Stanton.
Stevens.
Sumner.
Thomas.
Trego.
Nebraska :
Banner.
Cheyenne.
Deuel.
Kimball.
Perkins.
Oklahoma :
Alfalfa.
Beaver.
Blaine.
Canadian.
Cimarron.
Custer.
Dewey.
Ellis.

Oklahoma—Continued.
Garfield.
Grant.
Harper.
Kay.
Kingfisher.
Major.
Noble.
Texas.
Woods.
Woodward.
Texas :
Armstrong.
Carson.
Castro.
Floyd.
Gray.
Hale.
Hansford.
Lipscomb.
Ochiltree.
Swisher.

Ranching Area

Colorado :
Archuleta.
Costilla.
Custer.
Dolores.
Eagle.
Garfield.
Grand.
Gunnison.
Hinsdale.
Huerfano.
Jackson.
Larimer.
Las Animas.
Moffat.
Montezuma.
Ouray.
Park.
Rio Blanco.
Routt.
Saguache.
San Miguel.

Montana :
Beaverhead.
Big Horn.
Broadwater.
Carter.
Custer.
Garfield.
Glacier.
Golden Valley.
Granite.
Jefferson.
Lewis and Clark.
Madison.
Meagher.
Musselshell.
Park.
Powder River.
Powell.
Rosebud.
Sanders.
Sweet Grass.
Wheatland.

Oregon :
Baker.
Crook.
Grant.
Harney.
Jefferson.
Klamath.
Lake.
Malheur.
Wallowa.
Wheeler.
Utah :
Daggett.
Garfield.
Grand.
Iron.
Kane.
Morgan.
Piute.
Rich.
Summit.
Tooele.
Wasatch.
Washington.

LIST B.—SAMPLE COUNTIES REPRESENTING NINE AGRICULTURAL AREAS

Eastern Cotton Area

Alabama:
  Bullock.
  Calhoun.
  Conecuh.
  Winston.
Arkansas:
  Calhoun.
  Craighead.
  Pike.
Georgia:
  Chattooga.
  Dodge.
  Heard.
  Jenkins.
  McDuffie.

Georgia—Continued.
  Madison.
  Mitchell.
  Pike.
  Webster.
Louisiana:
  Concordia.
  Morehouse.
  Natchitoches.
  Webster.
Mississippi:
  Lawrence.
  Tippah.
  Washington.
  Winston.

Missouri:
  Pemiscot.
North Carolina:
  Cabarrus.
  Sampson.
South Carolina:
  Allendale.
  Calhoun.
  Fairfield.
  Pickens.
Tennessee:
  Henderson.

Western Cotton Area

Oklahoma:
  Jackson.
  Lincoln.
Texas:
  Bastrop.
  Cass.

Texas—Continued.
  Collin.
  Houston.
  Karnes.
  McLennan.
  Montgomery.

Texas—Continued.
  Shelby.
  Terry.
  Wilbarger.

Appalachian-Ozark Area

Arkansas:
  Madison.
Georgia:
  Lumpkin.
Illinois:
  Franklin.
Kentucky:
  Johnson.
  Knox.
  Lee.
  Muhlenberg.

Missouri:
  Shannon.
North Carolina:
  Jackson.
  Wilkes.
Tennessee:
  Cocke.
  White.
  Williamson.

Virginia:
  Bedford.
  Lee.
  Page.
West Virginia:
  Boone.
  Marion.
  Nicholas.
  Pendleton.

Lake States Cut-Over Area

Michigan:
  Gogebic.
  Oscoda.
  Schoolcraft.

Minnesota:
  Pine.

Wisconsin:
  Forest.
  Sawyer.

Hay and Dairy Area

Michigan:
  Sanilac.
Minnesota:
  Benton.
  Olmsted.
  Otter Tail.
New York:
  Broome.
  Livingston.

New York—Continued.
  Oneida.
  Washington.
Ohio:
  Geauga.
  Stark.

Pennsylvania:
  Bradford.
  Wayne.
  Wyoming.
Wisconsin:
  Chippewa.
  Sauk.
  Walworth.

Methodology of Rural Current Change Studies 185

Corn Belt

Illinois:
  Scott.
  Whiteside.
  Woodford.
Indiana:
  Fountain.
  Hancock.
  Morgan.
  Shelby.
Iowa:
  Black Hawk.
  Calhoun.
  Guthrie.

Iowa—Continued.
  Ida.
  Mahaska.
  Marshall.
  Page.
  Washington.
Kansas:
  Smith.
  Wabaunsee.
Missouri:
  Hickory.
  Ray.

Nebraska:
  Hall.
  Hitchcock.
  Johnson.
  Pierce.
Ohio:
  Clinton.
  Putnam.
South Dakota:
  Brookings
  Hutchinson.

Spring Wheat Area

Montana:
  Chouteau.
North Dakota:
  Burke.

North Dakota—Contd.
  Emmons.
  Hettinger.
  Ramsey.

South Dakota:
  Corson.
  Edmunds.

Winter Wheat Area

Colorado:
  Sedgwick.
Kansas:
  Pawnee.

Kansas—Continued.
  Saline.
Oklahoma:
  Harper.

Oklahoma—Continued.
  Kingfisher.
Texas:
  Carson.

Ranching Area

Colorado:
  Archuleta.
  Garfield.
  Routt.
Montana:
  Garfield.

Montana—Continued.
  Granite.
  Madison.
  Meagher.
Oregon:
  Baker.

Oregon—Continued.
  Crook.
Utah:
  Garfield.
  Grand.
  Piute.

LIST C.—SAMPLE COUNTIES AND TOWNSHIPS REPRESENTING 34 STATES

Alabama:
  Calhoun.
  Conecuh.
  Dale.
  Dallas.
  Marshall.
  Shelby.
  Winston.
Arizona:[1]
  Cochise.
  Graham.
  Pinal.
  Yavapai.
Arkansas:
  Calhoun.
  Craighead.
  Grant.
  Madison.
  Marion.
  Miller.
  Phillips.
  Pike.
  Prairie.
  Yell.

California:
  Glenn.
  Humboldt.
  Kings.
  Lake.
  Lassen.
  Madera.
  Mono.
  Monterey.
  San Bernardino.
  San Joaquin.
  Ventura.
  Yuba.
Colorado:
  Alamosa.
  Archuleta.
  Garfield.
  Kiowa.
  Kit Carson.
  Routt.
  Sedgwick.
  Teller.

Connecticut:
  Fairfield County:
    Easton.
    Monroe.
    New Fairfield.
    Wilton.
  Hartford County:
    Burlington.
    Granby.
    Rocky Hill.
    Simsbury.
    South Windsor.
    Suffield.
  Litchfield County.
    Barkhamsted.
    Bethlehem.
    Canaan.
    Goshen.
    Harwinton.
    Kent.
  Middlesex County:
    Durham.
    East Haddam.

[1] In survey during October, November, and December 1935 only.

Connecticut—Continued.
Middlesex Cty.—Contd.
Essex.
Middlefield.
New Haven County:
Beacon Falls.
Cheshire.
Madison.
Orange.
Oxford.
Prospect.
Southbury.
New London County:
East Lyme.
Lebanon.
Montville.
Preston.
Voluntown.
Tolland County:
Coventry.
Hebron.
Somers.
Tolland.
Windham County:
Ashford.
Canterbury.
Pomfret.
Woodstock.
Florida:
Bradford.
Broward.
Jefferson.
Lee.
Polk.
Washington.
Georgia:
Chattooga.
Dodge.
Greene.
Heard.
Jenkins.
Jones.
Lumpkin.
McDuffie.
McIntosh.
Madison.
Mitchell.
Murray.
Muscogee.
Pike.
Tattnall.
Ware.
Webster.
Iowa:
Appanoose.
Black Hawk.
Calhoun.
Emmet.
Guthrie.
Ida.
Mahaska.
Marshall.
Monona.
Washington.
Kansas:
Barber.
Ford.

Kansas—Continued.
Gove.
Greenwood.
Hamilton.
Jefferson.
Neosho.
Pawnee.
Russell.
Saline.
Seward.
Smith.
Wabaunsee.
Kentucky:
Boone.
Hickman.
Johnson.
Knox.
Larue.
Lee.
Mercer.
Metcalfe.
Rowan.
Scott.
Todd.
Webster.
Louisiana:
Acadia.
Concordia.
Morehouse.
Natchitoches.
Plaquemines.
Pointe Coupee.
Tangipahoa.
Terrebonne.
Vernon.
Webster.
Massachusetts:
Barnstable County:
Dennis.
Eastham.
Mashpee.
Berkshire County:
Alford.
Cheshire.
Florida.
Richmond.
Sheffield.
Bristol County:
Freetown.
Rehoboth.
Westport.
Dukes County:
Gay Head.
Oak Bluffs.
Essex County:
Essex.
Georgetown.
Middleton.
Salisbury.
Franklin County:
Buckland.
Colrain.
Shutesbury.
Warwick.
Whately.

Massachusetts—Contd.
Hampden County:
Chester.
Monson.
Tolland.
Hampshire County:
Belchertown.
Cummington.
Southampton.
Middlesex County:
Ashland.
Carlisle.
Littleton.
Stow.
Townsend.
Norfolk County:
Avon.
Wrentham.
Plymouth County:
Duxbury.
Plympton.
Scituate.
Worcester County:
Boylston.
Charlton.
Hubbardston.
Millville.
New Braintree.
Michigan:
Barry.
Berrien.
Gogebic.
Kalkaska.
Leelanau.
Mecosta.
Monroe.
Oscoda.
Presque Isle.
Sanilac.
Schoolcraft.
Minnesota:
Benton.
Big Stone.
Hubbard.
Kittson.
Olmsted.
Otter Tail.
Pennington
Pine.
Pope.
Redwood.
Rock.
St. Louis.
Scott.
Missouri:
Adair.
Douglas.
Franklin.
Hickory.
Holt.
Johnson.
Miller.
Newton.
Pemiscot.
Ralls.

Counties and Townships Representing 34 States—Continued.

Missouri—Continued.
  Ray.
  Shannon.
Montana :
  Chouteau.
  Daniels.
  Garfield.
  Granite.
  Lake.
  Madison.
  Meagher.
  Prairie.
Nebraska :
  Box Butte.
  Hall.
  Hitchcock.
  Johnson.
  Morrill.
  Pierce.
  Richardson.
  Sheridan.
  Thayer.
New Hampshire : [2]
  Belknap County :
    Gilmanton.
  Carroll County :
    Eaton.
    Tamworth.
  Cheshire County :
    Alstead.
    Chesterfield.
    Troy.
  Coos County :
    Dummer.
    Northumberland.
    Pittsburg.
  Grafton County :
    Dorchester.
    Enfield.
    Franconia.
    Haverhill.
    Hebron.
    Holderness.
    Thornton.
  Hillsborough County :
    Deering.
    Greenville.
    Hudson.
    Milford.
    Peterborough.
  Merrimack County :
    Bow.
    Canterbury.
    Warner.
  Rockingham County :
    Fremont.
    Newington.
    Newton.
    North Hampton.
    Nottingham.
  Strafford County :
    Milton.
    Strafford.

New Hampshire—Contd.
  Sullivan County :
    Charlestown.
    Springfield.
New York :
  Broome.
  Livingston.
  Oneida.
  Schuyler.
  Washington.
North Carolina :
  Alamance.
  Cabarrus.
  Caldwell.
  Chowan.
  Franklin.
  Gates.
  Harnett.
  Jackson.
  Onslow.
  Pasquotank.
  Perquimans.
  Stokes.
North Dakota :
  Burke.
  Emmons.
  Hettinger.
  McHenry.
  McKenzie.
  Ramsey.
  Richland.
  Stutsman.
Ohio :
  Athens.
  Brown.
  Clinton.
  Geauga.
  Hardin.
  Monroe.
  Muskingum.
  Ottawa.
  Putnam.
  Seneca.
Oklahoma :
  Carter.
  Custer.
  Harper.
  Hughes.
  Jackson.
  Kingfisher.
  Lincoln.
  Pushmataha.
  Rogers.
Oregon :
  Baker.
  Clatsop.
  Crook.
  Josephine.
  Morrow.
  Polk.
South Carolina :
  Allendale.
  Calhoun.

South Carolina—Contd.
  Colleton.
  Fairfield.
  Georgetown.
  Lee.
  Newberry.
  Pickens.
South Dakota :
  Brookings.
  Corson.
  Custer.
  Edmunds.
  Grant.
  Hand.
  Hutchinson.
  Jackson.
  Meade.
Tennessee :
  Anderson.
  Cocke.
  Fayette.
  Franklin.
  Hawkins.
  Henderson.
  Stewart.
  White.
  Williamson.
Texas :
  Bastrop.
  Bosque.
  Brewster.
  Burleson.
  Carson.
  Cass.
  Collin.
  Colorado.
  Fisher.
  Floyd.
  Freestone.
  Frio.
  Hansford.
  Houston.
  Karnes.
  Lamb.
  McLennan.
  Montgomery
  Palo Pinto.
  San Saba.
  Shelby.
  Starr.
  Sutton.
  Terry.
  Upshur.
  Upton.
  Webb.
  Wilbarger.
Utah :
  Box Elder.
  Garfield.
  Grand.
  Piute.
  Sevier.
  Weber.

[2] In survey during June 1935 only.

Counties and Townships Representing 34 States—Continued.

Virginia:
  Alleghany.
  Bedford.
  Charles City.
  King William.
  Lee.
  Mathews.
  Mecklenburg.
  Page.
  Powhatan.
  Pulaski.
  Southampton.

Virginia—Continued.
  Stafford.
  Westmoreland.
Washington:
  Adams.
  Benton.
  Chelan.
  Cowlitz.
  Jefferson.
  Stevens.
West Virginia:
  Boone.
  Marion.

West Virginia—Contd.
  Nicholas.
  Pendleton.
Wisconsin:
  Calumet.
  Chippewa.
  Crawford.
  Forest.
  La Crosse.
  Portage.
  Sauk.
  Sawyer.
  Walworth.

LIST D.—STATES SAMPLED, BY REGIONS

Northern States:
  Iowa.
  Kansas.
  Michigan.
  Minnesota.
  Missouri.
  Nebraska.
  New York.
  North Dakota.
  Ohio.
  South Dakota.
  Wisconsin.

Southern States:
  Alabama.
  Arkansas.
  Florida.
  Georgia.
  Kentucky.
  Louisiana.
  North Carolina.
  Oklahoma.
  South Carolina.
  Tennessee.
  Texas.
  Virginia.
  West Virginia.

Western States:
  Arizona (October 1935
    only).
  California.
  Colorado.
  Montana.
  Oregon.
  Utah.
  Washington.
New England States:
  Connecticut.
  Massachusetts.
  New Hampshire (June
    1935 only).

SCHEDULE A

SURVEY OF THE RURAL RELIEF SITUATION—RURAL HOUSEHOLDS RECEIVING RELIEF OR REHABILITATION ADVANCES IN OCTOBER 1934

F. E. R. A. FORM DRS-77A
SCHEDULE NO. _____
NAME OF AGENCY: _____

COUNTY _____ STATE _____

DATE _____
FILLED BY _____
RESIDENCE _____

LINE NUMBER	CASE NUMBER	NAME OF HEAD OF CASE	SEX OF HEAD OF RELIEF CASE		NUMBER OF PERSONS IN RELIEF CASE		PERSONS 16-64 YEARS OF AGE				USUAL OCCUPATION OF HEAD					KIND OF RELIEF RECEIVED IN OCTOBER			VALUE OF RELIEF RECEIVED IN OCTOBER (Exclusive of rehabilitation advances)	VALUE OF REHABILITATION ADVANCES RECEIVED IN OCTOBER	RECEIVED RELIEF DURING					EXPECTED TO BE ON RELIEF IN FEBRUARY 1935		WAS RELIEF CASE ON RURAL REHABILITATION IN OCTOBER		OTHER PERSONS IN FAMILY
			MALE	FEMALE	TOTAL	UNDER 16 YEARS OF AGE	NONE	NO PERSON EMPLOYED OR SEEKING WORK	ONE OR MORE MALES	NO MALES; ONE OR MORE FEMALES	OWNER	TENANT OR CROPPER	UNSKILLED LABORER	NO USUAL OCCUPATION	ALL OTHERS	WORK RELIEF ONLY	DIRECT RELIEF ONLY	DIRECT AND WORK			MAY	JUNE	JULY	AUGUST	SEPTEMBER	YES	NO	YES	NO	
		2	3	4	5	6	7	8	9	10	11	12	13	14	15	16	17	18	19	20	21	22	23	24	25	26	27	28	29	30
1																														
2																														
3																														
20																														

TOTAL _____ { A ___
                { B ___

137296°—37——14

SCHEDULE B

F. E. R. A. FORM DRS–77B   COUNTY_____
DATE_____   STATE_____
FILLED BY_____

SURVEY OF THE RURAL RELIEF SITUATION

Rural Rehabilitation Schedule

I. CASES RECEIVING ADVANCES UNDER THE RURAL REHABILITATION PROGRAM.
  1. MONTH AND YEAR FIRST CASE WAS PLACED ON ROLLS_____
  2. NUMBER OF NEW CASES ENROLLED:

a. BEFORE JULY 1, 1934_____	_____
b. DURING JULY_____	_____
c. DURING AUGUST_____	_____
d. DURING SEPTEMBER_____	_____
e. DURING OCTOBER_____	_____
f. TOTAL NEW CASES_____	_____

  3. TOTAL CASES REMAINING ON ROLLS OCTOBER 31, 1934_____
  4. TOTAL CASES DROPPED FROM ROLLS_____(2f) MINUS (3)
    a. BECAUSE NO FURTHER AID NECESSARY_____
    b. FOR NONFULFILLMENT OF CONTRACT_____
    c. FOR OTHER REASONS (SPECIFY UNDER REMARKS)_____
  5. NUMBER OF CASES RETURNED FROM REHABILITATION TO RELIEF THROUGH
    OCTOBER 31, 1934_____
II. NUMBER OF CASES EXPECTED TO BE ON RURAL REHABILITATION ROLLS IN
  FEBRUARY 1935_____
  1. CASES TO BE CARRIED OVER FROM OCTOBER_____
  2. NEW CASES TO BE ADDED AFTER OCTOBER 31_____

F. E. R. A. FORM DRS-109

SCHEDULE C

FEDERAL EMERGENCY RELIEF ADMINISTRATION

HARRY L. HOPKINS, ADMINISTRATOR

DIVISION OF RESEARCH, STATISTICS AND FINANCE

CORRINGTON GILL, DIRECTOR

SURVEY OF CURRENT CHANGES IN THE RURAL RELIEF POPULATION

AGENCY.............. COUNTY.......... STATE........

NAME OF CLIENT............................

ADDRESS............................ CASE NO....

A. FOR NEW CASES

DATE OF FIRST RELIEF ORDER

B. FOR CLOSED CASES

DATE OF LAST RELIEF ORDER

C. FOR REOPENED RELIEF CASES

DATE OF FIRST RELIEF ORDER IN PRESENT RELIEF PERIOD	DATE OF LAST RELIEF ORDER IN PREVIOUS RELIEF PERIOD

D. FOR REHABILITATION CASES

DATE OF TRANSFER FROM RELIEF	DATE OF OPENING	DATE OF CLOSING

E. COLOR OF HEAD OF HOUSEHOLD— CHECK ONE (X)

WHITE	NEGRO	OTHER
( )	( )	( )

IF "OTHER" SPECIFY.

F. ACRES IN FARM OR HOMESTEAD

	AT TIME OF OPENING	AT TIME OF CLOSING
USUAL		

G. RESIDENCE—CHECK ONE (X)

OPEN COUNTRY	VILLAGE 50–2499	TOWN 2500–4999
( )	( )	( )

H. YEAR LAST MOVED TO THIS COUNTY

I. IF 1930 OR AFTER: COUNTY OR STATE FROM WHICH MOVED

(COUNTY)   (STATE)

J. RECEIVED RELIEF DURING—CHECK (X)

1932	1933	1934
( )	( )	( )

SCHEDULE C—Continued.

K. PERSONAL AND OCCUPATIONAL DATA

ALL PERSONS IN RELIEF CASE

PERSONS 16-64 YEARS OF AGE WORKING OR SEEKING WORK

LINE NO.	RELATIONSHIP TO HEAD OF HOUSEHOLD	SEX	YEAR OF BIRTH	CODE (LEAVE BLANK)	WORKING OR SEEKING WORK: YES/NO	CURRENT EMPLOYMENT STATUS — OCCUPATION	INDUSTRY	CODE (LEAVE BLANK)	WEEKLY EARNINGS	CODE (LEAVE BLANK)	DATE LAST NONRELIEF JOB ENDED	CODE (LEAVE BLANK)	LAST EMPLOYMENT AT USUAL OCCUPATION — OCCUPATION	INDUSTRY	CODE (LEAVE BLANK)	MONTH AND YEAR ENDED	CODE (LEAVE BLANK)	ALTERNATE OCCUPATION — OCCUPATION	INDUSTRY
1	2	3	4	A	5	6	7	B	8	C	9	D	10	11	E	12	F	13	14
1	HEAD																		
2																			
3																			
4																			
5																			
6																			
7																			
8																			
9																			
10																			
11																			
12																			
13																			
14																			

L. REASON FOR OPENING OR REOPENING—CHECK ONE (X)

1 ( ).
2 ( ) LOSS OF JOB IN ORDINARY EMPLOYMENT.
3 ( ) LOSS OR DEPLETION OF ASSETS.
4 ( ) CROP FAILURE OR LOSS OF LIVESTOCK.
5 ( ) OTHER—SPECIFY.

M. REASON FOR CLOSING—CHECK ONE (X) CHECK FOR CLOSED OR REOPENED CASES

1 ( ).
2 ( ) SECURED ORDINARY EMPLOYMENT.
3 ( ) CROP MARKETED OR INCREASED CROP PRICES.
4 ( ) TRANSFER TO OTHER AGENCY.
5 ( ) OTHER—SPECIFY.

N. IF THE CASE WAS CLOSED FOR REASONS 1 OR 2 GIVE THE FOLLOWING INFORMATION FOR THE MEMBER OF THE HOUSEHOLD INVOLVED

LINE NUMBER SHOWN IN K 1	OCCUPATION	INDUSTRY	WEEKLY EARNINGS

O. IF HEAD WAS ENGAGED IN AGRICULTURE SINCE AGE 16

YEARS ENGAGED IN AGRICULTURE				LAST TENURE STATUS								
1-3	4-6	7-9	10 OR MORE	OWNER OR MANAGER	CROPPER	RENTER	LABORER	N.A.	ACRES OPERATED	PRINCIPAL PRODUCT	DATE ENDED	REASON FOR ENDING

P. IF CASE IS ON REHABILITATION ROLLS

MONTH AND YEAR	DATE ENROLLED	TOTAL COMMITMENT	YEAR OF LAST REPAYMENT	ADVANCES TO DATE			REPAYMENTS TO DATE	BALANCE DUE	METHOD OF REPAYMENT—CHECK (X) EMPLOYMENT ON—		
				TOTAL	REHABILITATION GOODS	SUBSISTENCE GOODS			SELF-LIQUIDATING PROJECT	WORK DIVISION PROJECT	OTHER
FEB. 1935				$	$	$	$	$			
				$	$	$	$	$			
				$	$	$	$	$			
				$	$	$	$	$			

Q. IF CASE RECEIVED RELIEF

AMOUNT OF RELIEF RECEIVED				PROPOSED FOR REHABILITATION YES/NO
MONTH AND YEAR	WORK RELIEF	DIRECT RELIEF	BOTH WORK AND DIRECT RELIEF	
FEB. 1935				

DATE............ FILLED BY................

DATE............ FILLED BY................

SCHEDULE D

FEDERAL EMERGENCY RELIEF ADMINISTRATION

HARRY L. HOPKINS, ADMINISTRATOR

DIVISION OF RESEARCH, STATISTICS AND FINANCE

CORRINGTON GILL, DIRECTOR

SURVEY OF CURRENT CHANGES IN THE RURAL RELIEF POPULATION

AGENCY _____ COUNTY _____ STATE _____

NAME OF CLIENT _____ CASE NO. _____

ADDRESS _____

F. E. R. A. FORM DRS-109A

A. MONTH OF SURVEY

B. REASON FOR OPENING OR REOPENING: CHECK ONE (X).

1. LOSS OF EMPLOYMENT (WITHIN FOUR MONTHS).
   A. ( ) WORKS PROGRAM.
   B. ( ) PRIVATE OR REGULAR GOVERNMENT.
   C. ( ) OWN ACCOUNT.
   D. ( ) OTHER (SPECIFY BELOW).
2. ( ) LOSS OR DEPLETION OF ASSETS.
3. ( ) DECREASED EARNINGS FROM CURRENT EMPLOYMENT.
4. ( ) LOSS OF RESETTLEMENT STATUS.
5. ( ) CROP FAILURE OR LOSS OF LIVESTOCK.
6. ( ) INCREASED NEEDS (SPECIFY BELOW).
7. ( ) OTHER (SPECIFY BELOW).

IF 1D, 5, OR 7 IS CHECKED SPECIFY.

C. EMERGENCY RELIEF AND EMERGENCY EMPLOYMENT HISTORY

PERIOD	DATE OF FIRST ASSISTANCE	PRO-GRAM	DATE OF LAST ASSISTANCE
FIRST			
SECOND			
THIRD			
FOURTH			
FIFTH			

D. RESIDENCE—CHECK ONE (X)

TIME	OPEN COUNTRY	VIL-LAGE 50-2499	TOWN 2500-4999
JUNE 1935	( )	( )	( )
MONTH OF SURVEY	( )	( )	( )

E. YEAR LAST MOVED TO THIS COUNTY _____

IF 1930 OR AFTER: COUNTY AND STATE FROM WHICH MOVED

COUNTY	STATE

F. COLOR OF HEAD OF HOUSEHOLD—CHECK ONE (X)

WHITE	NEGRO	OTHER (SPECIFY)
( )	( )	( )

G. IF CASE RECEIVED RELIEF

AMOUNT OF RELIEF RECEIVED

WORK RELIEF	DIRECT RELIEF	BOTH WORK AND DIRECT RELIEF
$	$	$

REFERRED TO RESETTLEMENT ADMINISTRATION

YES	NO

H. KIND OF CASE—CHECK ONE (X).
NEW ( ) REOPENED ( ) CLOSED ( )

J. REASON FOR CLOSING: CHECK ONE (X).

1. EMPLOYMENT SECURED.
   A. ( ) WORKS PROGRAM.
   B. ( ) PRIVATE OR REGULAR GOVERNMENT.
   C. ( ) OWN ACCOUNT.
   D. ( ) OTHER (SPECIFY BELOW).
2. ( ) INCREASED EARNINGS FROM CURRENT EMPLOYMENT.
3. ( ) CROPS MARKETED OR INCREASED CROP PRICES.
4. ( ) LOANS (SPECIFY SOURCE BELOW).
5. ( ) GOVERNMENT BENEFIT (SPECIFY BELOW).
6. ASSISTANCE PROVIDED BY:
   A. ( ) RESETTLEMENT ADMINISTRATION.
   B. ( ) LOCAL AGENCY (SPECIFY BELOW).
   C. ( ) LANDLORD.
   D. ( ) RELATIVES OR FRIENDS.
   E. ( ) OTHER (SPECIFY BELOW).
7. ( ) ADMINISTRATIVE POLICY.
8. ( ) CLIENT MOVED OR FAILED TO REPORT.
9. ( ) OTHER (SPECIFY BELOW).

IF 1D, 4, 5, 6B, 6E, OR 9 IS CHECKED SPECIFY

K. IF THE CASE WAS CLOSED FOR REASON 1, A TO D, SECTION J, GIVE THE FOLLOWING INFORMATION FOR THE MEMBER OF THE HOUSEHOLD INVOLVED

LINE NUMBER SHOWN IN SECTION L, COLUMN 1	OCCUPATION	INDUSTRY	WEEKLY EARNINGS	HOURS WORKED
			$	

L. PERSONAL DATA — ALL PERSONS IN RELIEF CASE

OCCUPATIONAL DATA — ALL PERSONS 16–64 YEARS OF AGE WORKING OR SEEKING WORK

LINE NO. (1)	RELATIONSHIP TO HEAD OF HOUSEHOLD 2	SEX 3	YEAR OF BIRTH 4	CODE (LEAVE BLANK) 4A	MARITAL STATUS 5	IN SCHOOL (CHECK) YES 6	NO 7	LAST GRADE COMPLETED: GRADE AND HIGH SCHOOL 8	COLLEGE 9	PRESENT STATUS: ENTER YES, NO, N. A. — WORKING 10	SEEKING WORK 11	CURRENT EMPLOYMENT: IF UNEMPLOYED LAST EMPLOYMENT — OCCUPATION 12	INDUSTRY 13	IF CURRENTLY EMPLOYED — WEEKLY EARNINGS 14	HOURS WORKED 15	IF UNEMPLOYED DATE LAST NONRELIEF JOB ENDED 16	USUAL OCCUPATION AND INDUSTRY — OCCUPATION 17	INDUSTRY 18
1	HEAD																	
2																		
3																		
4																		
5																		
6																		
7																		
8																		
9																		
10																		
11																		
12																		
13																		
14																		
15																		

M. IF HEAD WAS ENGAGED IN AGRICULTURE DURING LAST 10 YEARS

YEARS ENGAGED 1–3	4–6	7–10	LAST STATUS — OWNER OR MANAGER	CROPPER	TENANT	LABORER	N. A.	ACRES OPERATED	DATE ENDED

FILLED BY .... DATE ......

EDITED BY .... DATE ......

W. P. A.   FORM DRS–409A

A. REASON FOR CLOSING: RELIEF PERIOD WHICH INCLUDED JUNE 1935: CHECK (X)

1. EMPLOYMENT SECURED.
   A. ( ) WORKS PROGRAM.
   B. ( ) PRIVATE OR REGULAR GOVERNMENT.
   C. ( ) OWN ACCOUNT.
   D. ( ) OTHER (SPECIFY BELOW).
2. ( ) INCREASED EARNINGS FROM CURRENT EMPLOYMENT.
3. ( ) CROP MARKETED OR INCREASED CROP PRICES.
4. ( ) LOANS (SPECIFY SOURCE BELOW).
5. ( ) GOVERNMENT BENEFIT (SPECIFY BELOW).
6. ASSISTANCE PROVIDED BY:
   A. ( ) RESETTLEMENT ADMINISTRATION.
   B. ( ) LOCAL AGENCY (SPECIFY BELOW).
   C. ( ) LANDLORD.
   D. ( ) RELATIVES OR FRIENDS.
   E. ( ) OTHER (SPECIFY BELOW).
7. ( ) ADMINISTRATIVE POLICY (SPECIFY BELOW).
8. ( ) CLIENT MOVED OR FAILED TO REPORT.
9. ( ) OTHER (SPECIFY BELOW).

IF 1D, 4, 5, 6B, 6E, 7, OR 9 IS CHECKED—SPECIFY

B. DATE OF THIS CLOSING

SCHEDULE E

WORKS PROGRESS ADMINISTRATION

HARRY L. HOPKINS, ADMINISTRATOR

CORRINGTON GILL   HOWARD B. MYERS, DIRECTOR
ASSISTANT ADMINISTRATOR   DIVISION OF SOCIAL RESEARCH

SURVEY OF RURAL HOUSEHOLDS THAT RECEIVED RELIEF IN JUNE AND WERE CLOSED PRIOR TO DEC. 1, 1935

E.   IDENTIFICATION OF HOUSEHOLD

NAME OF CLIENT............   CASE NO............

RESIDENCE: STATE............

COUNTY............   IN JUNE SAMPLE
VILLAGE OR TOWN............   YES ( )   NO ( )
                                           DATE OF
NAME OF FIELD AGENT............   INTERVIEW............
NAME OF SCHEDULE CLERK............ SCHEDULE NO............

F. COLOR OF HEAD OF HOUSEHOLD CHECK ONE (X)

WHITE	NEGRO	OTHER (SPECIFY)
( )	( )	

H. RESIDENCE—CHECK TWO (X)

TIME	OPEN COUNTRY	VILLAGE (50–2499)	TOWN (2500–4999)
JUNE 1935	( )	( )	( )
DEC. 1935	( )	( )	( )

L.

1. REASON FOR REOPENING PRESENT RELIEF PERIOD: CHECK ONE (X)

1. LOSS OF EMPLOYMENT.
   A. ( ) WORKS PROGRAM.
   B. ( ) PRIVATE OR REGULAR GOVERNMENT.
   C. ( ) OWN ACCOUNT.
   D. ( ) OTHER (SPECIFY BELOW).
2. ( ) LOSS OR DEPLETION OF ASSETS.
3. ( ) DECREASED EARNINGS FROM CURRENT EMPLOYMENT.
4. ( ) LOSS OF RESETTLEMENT STATUS.
5. ( ) CROP FAILURE OR LOSS OF LIVESTOCK.
6. ( ) INCREASED NEEDS (SPECIFY BELOW).
7. ( ) OTHER (SPECIFY BELOW).

IF 1D, 6, OR 7 IS CHECKED—SPECIFY

FOR CASES REOPENED SINCE JUNE 1935 AND RECEIVING EMERGENCY UNEMPLOYMENT RELIEF DURING DECEMBER 1935

2. DATE OF FIRST ORDER IN THIS RELIEF PERIOD

DATE OF LAST ORDER IN PREVIOUS RELIEF PERIOD

3. TYPE AND AMOUNT OF RELIEF RECEIVED IN DECEMBER

DIRECT RELIEF	WORK RELIEF	DIRECT AND WORK RELIEF

C. IF CASE WAS CLOSED MORE THAN ONCE SINCE JUNE 1935

MONTH OF CLOSING	REASON FOR CLOSING

D. HOUSEHOLD RECEIVED STATE OR LOCAL RELIEF OR AID DURING DECEMBER 1935: YES ( ) NO ( )

IF YES IS CHECKED

| TYPE OF RELIEF | RELIEF AGENCY | | VALUE |
	PUBLIC OR PRIVATE	NAME OF AGENCY	
(1)	(2)	(3)	(4)
			$

G. FAMILY UNDER CARE RESETTLEMENT ADMINISTRATION: YES ( ) NO ( ) IF YES IS CHECKED

DATE ACCEPTED	ADVANCES TO DATE	
MO.	TOTAL	$
DAY	CAPITAL GOODS	
YR.	SUBSISTENCE GOODS	
	AMOUNT REPAID	

I. YEAR LAST MOVED TO THIS COUNTY

IF 1930 OR LATER

MOVED FROM ANOTHER COUNTY OF THIS STATE	MOVED FROM ANOTHER STATE
(NAME COUNTY)	(NAME STATE)

J. YEARS PRIOR TO 1935 AND MONTHS DURING 1935 IN WHICH HOUSEHOLD RECEIVED EMERGENCY UNEMPLOYMENT RELIEF: CHECK (X)

1933	1934	1935									
		JAN.	FEB.	MAR.	APR.	MAY	JUNE	JULY	AUG.	SEPT.	OCT.	NOV.
( )	( )	( )	( )	( )	( )	( )	( )	( )	( )	( )	( )	( )

K. IF HEAD WAS ENGAGED IN AGRICULTURE DURING PAST 10 YEARS

LAST FARM OCCUPATION

LINE NO.	YEARS ENGAGED CHECK ONE (X)	DATE ENDED ____ OR IF CURRENT ( )	STATUS: CHECK ONE (X)	NUMBER OF ACRES OPERATED
(1)	(2)	(3)		(4)
1	1–3 ( )		OWNER OR MANAGER ( )	CROP ACRES
2	4–6 ( )		TENANT ( )	CASH CROP ACRES
3	7–10 ( )		CROPPER ( )	OTHER ACRES
4			LABORER ( )	TOTAL ACRES
5			N. A. ( )	TYPE OF CASH CROP

M. IF CASE WAS REOPENED SINCE JUNE 1935

MONTH OF REOPENING	REASON FOR REOPENING

N. OTHER SOURCES OF INCOME DECEMBER 1935

SOURCE	AMOUNT
1. RELATIVES AND FRIENDS	$
2. BANK ACCOUNTS, SAVINGS	
3. SALE OF PERSONAL BELONGINGS	
4. CREDIT ESTABLISHED	
5. SALE OF FARM PRODUCE	
A. CROPS	
B. LIVESTOCK	
C. LIVESTOCK PRODUCTS	
6. A. A. A. PAYMENTS	
7. VETERANS COMPENSATION AND PENSIONS	
8. OTHER SOURCES (SPECIFY)	

SCHEDULE E—Continued.

P. REASON FOR INELIGIBILITY FOR W. P. EMPLOYMENT

CODE
1. PHYSICALLY OR MENTALLY UNFIT
2. NEEDED AT HOME
3. NO LONGER ELIGIBLE FOR RELIEF
4. OTHER (SPECIFY)

Q. REASON FOR NOT WORKING OR SEEKING WORK

CODE
1. HOUSEWIFE
2. UNPAID HOME WORKER
3. STUDENT
4. CHRONIC ILLNESS OR PHYSICAL DISABILITY
5. FEEBLE-MINDEDNESS OR INSANITY
6. OTHER (SPECIFY)

R. REASON FOR ENDING GOVERNMENT EMERGENCY EMPLOYMENT

CODE
1. SECURED ORDINARY EMPLOYMENT
2. LAID OFF OR PROJECT ENDED
3. INJURED OR ILLNESS
4. DISCHARGED
5. OTHER (SPECIFY)

O. PERSONAL AND OCCUPATIONAL DATA

ALL PERSONS IN HOUSEHOLD — ALL PERSONS 16–64 YEARS OF AGE — ALL PERSONS 16–64 YEARS OF AGE WORKING OR SEEKING WORK

LINE NO. (1)	RELATIONSHIP TO HEAD OF HOUSEHOLD (2)	IN HOUSEHOLD JUNE 1935 (CHECK) YES (3)	NO (4)	SEX (M. OR F.) (5)	YEAR OF BIRTH (6)	MARITAL STATUS (M., S., WID., SEP., DIV.) (7)	IN SCHOOL (CHECK) YES (8)	NO (9)	EDUCATION LAST GRADE COMPLETED — GRADE AND HIGH SCHOOL (10)	COLLEGE (11)	PRESENT STATUS WORKING (12)	SEEKING WORK (13)	CERTIFIED FOR W.P. EMPLOYMENT (IF "NO", ENTER NUMBER SHOWN IN "P") (14)	IF NOT WORKING OR SEEKING WORK, REASON (ENTER NUMBER SHOWN IN "Q") (15)	IF UNEMPLOYED DATE LAST NONRELIEF JOB ENDED (16)	USUAL EMPLOYMENT OCCUPATION (17)	INDUSTRY (18)
1	HEAD																
2																	
3																	
4																	
5																	
6																	
7																	
8																	
9																	
10																	
11																	
12																	
13																	
14																	
15																	

REMARKS:

7. EMPLOYMENT DURING THE MONTH OF DECEMBER 1935

(1) LINE NO. SHOWN IN "O"	(2) DATE BEGAN	TYPE OF EMPLOYMENT		(5) OCCUPATION	(6) INDUSTRY	(7) DATE ENDED	(8) IF GOV'T EMERGENCY REASON FOR ENDING (ENTER NO. SHOWN IN "R")	(9) TOTAL EARNINGS	(10) HOURS WORKED
		(3) GOVERNMENT EMERGENCY (NAME AGENCY)	(4) ORD. EMPL. (CHECK)					$	

8. EMPLOYMENT ON GOVERNMENT EMERGENCY PROJECTS (EXCEPT E. R. A. PROJECTS) JULY 1, 1935 TO NOV. 30, 1935

(1) LINE NO. SHOWN IN "O"	(2) DATE BEGAN	(3) AGENCY	(4) OCCUPATION	(5) INDUSTRY	(6) DATE ENDED	(7) REASON FOR ENDING (ENTER NO. SHOWN IN "R")	(8) MONTHLY RATE OF EARNINGS
							$

DRS-162

SCHEDULE F

SOCIAL RESEARCH DIVISION, W. P. A.

NUMBER OF CASES AIDED AND AMOUNT OF OBLIGATIONS INCURRED FOR PUBLIC AND PRIVATE ASSISTANCE IN RURAL AND TOWN SAMPLE AREAS

AGENCY_____

STATE_____ COUNTY_____

SIGNATURE OF PERSON REPORTING_____

DATE_____ REPORT FOR MONTH OF_____ 19____

LINE NO.	TYPE OF ASSISTANCE (1)	NUMBER OF CASES AIDED (2)	AMOUNT (3)	LINE NO.
1	PUBLIC ASSISTANCE (ENTRIES FOR PUBLIC AGENCIES):			1
2	CATEGORICAL OR SPECIAL ASSISTANCE:			2
3	STATUTORY AID TO DEPENDENT CHILDREN_____		$_____	3
4	STATUTORY OLD AGE ASSISTANCE_____			4
5	STATUTORY AID TO THE BLIND_____			5
6	STATUTORY VETERAN'S AID_____			6
7	GENERAL ASSISTANCE [1]_____			7
8	OTHER (SPECIFY):			8
	A. _____			
	B. _____			
9	NET UNDUPLICATED TOTAL OF CASES RECEIVING PUBLIC ASSISTANCE_____			9
10	PRIVATE ASSISTANCE (ENTRIES FOR PRIVATE AGENCIES)_____			10
11	OTHER ASSISTANCE (ENTRIES FOR COMBINATION PUBLIC AND PRIVATE AGENCIES)_____			11

[1] Additional information concerning general public assistance:

[LINE 7, CONTINUED]

LINE NO.	RESIDENT FAMILIES			UNATTACHED RESIDENT PERSONS		TOTAL NUMBER OF PERSONS IN CASES RECEIVING GENERAL PUBLIC ASSISTANCE	LINE NO.
	NUMBER OF FAMILIES (4)	NUMBER OF PERSONS REPRESENTED (5)	AMOUNT (6)	NUMBER OF PERSONS (7)	AMOUNT (8)	(9)	
7	_____	_____	$_____	_____	$_____	_____	7

REMARKS:

SCHEDULE G

SURVEY OF CURRENT CHANGES IN THE RURAL RELIEF POPULATION

( ) REHABILITATION   CONTROL CARD DRS 109-B
( ) RELIEF

NAME.. CASE NO. ....

USUAL   F. O. ( )   TEN. ( )   CROP. ( )   O. C. ( )   TOWN ( )
OCCUPATION   LAB. ( )   OTH. ( )   NONE ( )   RESIDENCE VILL. ( )   CITY ( )

STATE....................... COUNTY .... NO. OF PERSONS IN HOUSEHOLD........

	J	F	M	A	M	J	J	A	S	O	N	D
OPENED OR REOPENED...........................												
CLOSED..												
CARRIED OVER................................												
TRANSFERRED TO REHABILITATION................												
TO BE INCLUDED IN SAMPLE.....................												
SCHEDULE FILLED FROM RECORDS.................												
FINANCIAL INFORMATION ENTERED...............												
SCHEDULE SENT TO SUPERVISOR.................												
SCHEDULE RETURNED BY SUPERVISOR............												

SCHEDULE H

SURVEY OF CURRENT CHANGES IN THE RURAL RELIEF POPULATION CONTROL CARD DRS 109-D

NAME .... CASE NO. ....

STATE .... COUNTY .... NUMBER IN HOUSEHOLD ....

USUAL   F. O. ( )   TEN. ( )   CROP. ( )   TOWN ( )   VILL. ( )
OCCUPATION   LAB. ( )   OTH. ( )   NONE ( )   RESIDENCE

	J	F	M	A	M	J	J	A	S	O	N	D
OPENED OR REOPENED...........................												
CARRIED OVER................................												
CLOSED..												
CLOSED BECAUSE OF:												
WORKS PROGRAM...........................												
RESETTLEMENT ADMINISTRATION.............												
OTHER REASONS..........................												
CASE INCLUDED IN 50 PERCENT SAMPLE........												
SCHEDULE FILLED FROM RECORDS.................												

STATE SUPERVISORS OF RURAL RESEARCH

[Personnel record as of Nov. 10, 1936]

Name	State	Period of cooperation
Allred, C. E	Tennessee	Jan. 16, 1935, to date.
Anderson, W. A	New York	Sept. 16, 1934, to July 1, 1935.
Beers, Howard W	Washington	May 16, 1935, to Sept. 15, 1935.
	Wisconsin	Sept. 16, 1935, to Feb. 1, 1936.
	New Jersey	Feb. 4, 1936, to date.
Boyer, Philips B	Tennessee	Nov. 1, 1934, to Jan. 15, 1935.
Brannen, C. O	Arkansas	Oct. 1, 1934, to date.
Breithaupt, L. R	Oregon	Jan. 2, 1936, to date.
Burgess, P. S	Arizona	Oct. 1, 1935, to date.
Coen, B. F	Colorado	Oct. 1, 1934, to Dec. 31, 1935.
Coffey, W. C	Minnesota	May 16, 1935, to date.
Dennis, W. V	Pennsylvania	Oct. 16, 1934, to date.
Duncan, O. D	Oklahoma	Sept. 16, 1934, to date.
Eastman, M. Gale	New Hampshire	June 1, 1935, to Jan. 31, 1936.
Gabbard, L. P	Texas	Oct. 1, 1934, to date.
Geddes, Joseph A	Utah	June 1, 1935, to date.
Gillette, John M	North Dakota	Nov. 1, 1934, to date.
Hamilton, C. H	North Carolina	Sept. 16, 1934, to June 30, 1936.
Hill, George W	Wisconsin	Feb. 1, 1936, to date.
Hill, Randall C	Kansas	Sept. 16, 1934, to date.
Hoffsommer, H. C	Alabama	Oct. 1, 1934, to Aug. 31, 1935.
Hummel, B. L	Virginia	Nov. 1, 1934, to date.
Kirkpatrick, E. L	Wisconsin	Oct. 1, 1934, to Sept. 15, 1935.
Kraenzel, Carl F	Montana	July 16, 1935, to date.
Kumlien, W. F	South Dakota	Oct. 1, 1934, to date.
Landis, Paul H	Washington	Oct. 1, 1935, to date.
Larson, Olaf F	Colorado	Jan. 2, 1936, to date.
Lively, Charles E	Ohio	Jan. 1, 1935, to date.
Moore, E. H	Oregon	Nov. 23, 1934, to Sept. 30, 1935.
Morgan, E. L	Missouri	June 25, 1935, to date.
Mumford, Eben	Michigan	Oct. 1, 1934, to date.
Nelson, Lowry	Utah	Sept. 24, 1934, to Dec. 26, 1934.
Nicholls, W. D	Kentucky	Sept. 16, 1934, to date.
Peterson, George M	California	Nov. 1, 1934, to June 15, 1935.
Smith, T. Lynn	Louisiana	Oct. 1, 1934, to date.
Wakeley, Ray E	Iowa	Sept. 16, 1934, to date.
Whetten, Nathan L	Connecticut	Oct. 16, 1934, to date.
Williams, B. O	South Carolina	Mar. 1, 1935, to date.
Zimmerman, Carle C	Massachusetts	May 16, 1935, to date.

Temporary State Supervisors of Rural Research

Name	State	Name	State
Anderson, T. W	Georgia.	Johansen, Sigurd	New Mexico.
	Florida.	Lindstrom, D. E	Illinois.
	Alabama.	Link, Irene L	West Virginia.
Broderick, Katherine	Indiana.	Lounsbury, Thomas	New York.
Callin, A. E	Nebraska.	McClure, John H	Alabama.
Creek, Charles R	Indiana.	Matthews, M. Taylor	North Carolina.
DeFord, John F	Nebraska.	Minear, Kenneth	West Virginia.
Durham, W. E	Mississippi.	Rapp, Robert E	California.
Facinoli, John	West Virginia.	Wilson, Edwin E	Do.
Galbraith, Charles S	Florida.		

Appendix C
GLOSSARY

GLOSSARY

(The definitions given herewith are those used in the Survey of Current Changes in the Rural Relief Population.)

Accessions.—New or reopened relief cases as of a given period.

Acres Operated.—Total acres in farm, regardless of whether under cultivation or not. May be owned, rented, part owned, or part rented.

Aged.—Persons 65 years of age and over.

Assets. (See *Loss or Depletion of Assets.*)

Broken Family.—Mother and children or father and children.

Capital Goods (as type of rehabilitation advance).—The purchase, rental, construction, or repairs of land, buildings, home equipment, livestock, work animals, feed, seed, fertilizer, equipment, farm tools, or machinery, and any other capital outlays required to carry out the rural rehabilitation program (F. E. R. A. Form RD–22a).

Carry-Over.—Cases receiving relief in a given month that were brought forward from an earlier month.

Case. (See *Relief Case.*)

Cash Crop Acres.—Crop acres cultivated for the purpose of selling more than 50 percent of the produce grown on them.

Children.—Persons under 16 years of age.

Client. (See *Rehabilitation Client.*)

Closed Relief Case.—A case to which an agency has ceased giving relief from F. E. R. A. funds, whether or not the household continues to receive aid from some other Government agency. Thus a household transferred from general relief to the Resettlement Administration after July 1, 1935, is a closed relief case; a household in which a worker formerly on E. R. A. work relief was transferred to the Federal Works Program after July 1, 1935, is a closed relief case, provided the household no longer receives general relief.

Crop Acres.—Acres actually cultivated by a farmer during one crop season. The number of crop acres reported for farmers in this survey was the number operated during the year of the survey or the most recent year in which the farmer engaged in farming.

Cropper. (See *Farm Cropper.*)

Current Employment.—The current employment of a worker whose household was on relief continuously from February through

205

June was the nonrelief employment lasting 1 week or more during February.

The current employment of a worker whose household came on relief from March through June was any nonrelief employment during the week in which the first relief order was received.

Current Occupation.—The occupation engaged in by a person currently employed.

Depletion of Assets. (See *Loss or Depletion of Assets.*)

Direct Relief.—Material relief in the form of cash or orders for food, clothing, fuel, household necessities, rent, transportation, moving, and medical care, in return for which the client is not required to work.

Drought Relief.—Assistance extended to families in the drought areas, often in the form of feed and seed loans with the requirement that they be repaid by work on E. R. A. projects.

Employable Person. (See *Worker.*)

Employed.—Working for wages, salary, commission, profit, or other contribution to the family income, or enrolled on a pay roll, or occupying a farm with the intention of resuming active work when conditions permit. Thus, a farm operator residing on a farm, who has suspended operations, as in the drought area, but who intends to resume active farming, is considered employed; a person operating a farm or working on his own account, even though losing money, is considered employed; a person who works regularly on the home farm, or in shop or store, and by this work contributes to the family income is considered employed even though he receives no wages or salary; a worker on strike, on vacation, or temporarily laid off due to illness or disability is considered employed, as long as he is still on a pay roll; a person working as an apprentice is considered employed. A full-time day school student or a housewife occupied full time in doing her own housework is not considered employed.

Farm.—A tract of land of at least 3 acres or producing agricultural products of at least $250 value per year, which is directly farmed by a farm operator, either by his labor alone or with the assistance of members of his household or hired employees, or operated by a partnership of farm operators.

A farm may consist of a single tract of land or of a number of separate tracts, and these several tracts may be held under different tenures, as when one tract is owned by the farmer and another is rented by him. When a landowner has one or more tenants or managers, the land operated by each is considered a farm.

Farm Cropper.—A farm operator who operates hired land only and to whom the landlord furnishes all the work animals; i. e., a farm operator who contributes only his labor and receives in return a share of the crop. In this study, croppers were reported separately from other tenants only in the cotton areas.

Farm Experience.—Number of years a person was engaged in agriculture since 16 years of age.

Farm Laborer.—A worker whose usual or current occupation is work on a farm, with or without wages, under the supervision of the farm operator. This definition includes the wife, children 16 years of age or over, or other members of the farm operator's household who work regularly and most of the time on the household farm (*home farm laborers*), whether they receive money wages, a share of the crop, or board and room. It does not include household members who perform only incidental chores on the farm. Unless otherwise stated, a farm laborer in this study is one whose *usual occupation* is that of farm laborer.

Farm Operator.—A worker whose usual or current occupation is the management of a farm, whether as owner or tenant. (See *Farm, Farm Owner, Farm Tenant, Farm Cropper.*) Unless otherwise stated, a farm operator in this study is one whose *usual occupation* is that of farm operator.

Farm Owner.—A farm operator who owns all or part of the land which he operates. Salaried farm managers and squatters or homesteaders who are operating farms are classified in this study as farm owners. (See *Farm.*)

Farm Tenant.—A farm operator who operates hired land only, furnishing all or part of the working equipment and stock, whether he pays cash or a share of the crop, or both, as rent.

Farmer. (See *Farm Operator.*)

General Relief.—Cash, orders, and/or rental payments, provided wholly or in part by Federal, State, county, or municipal funds designated for the purpose of aiding the unemployed. Not regarded as general relief are services, such as medical care, without material aid; Federal surplus commodities; mothers' pensions, or other forms of special allowances not reported to the State E. R. A.; earnings or allotments from the Civilian Conservation Corps; transient relief; Works Program wages. (See *Direct Relief, Drought Relief,* and *Work Relief.*)

Government Benefit (as reason for closing relief case).—A payment from the Agricultural Adjustment Administration.

Grade Attainment.—The last year successfully completed in grade school, high school, or college.

Head of Household.—If the household consists of only one family, the head of that family is the head of the household. If the household consists of two or more families, the oldest family head is head of the household, unless he or she is 65 years of age or over.

In such a case the oldest family head who is less than 65 years of age is head of the household.

In cases of households consisting only of two or more single, widowed, divorced, or separated persons, without children, the person with the largest earnings or property rights is head of the household.

In cases of married couples, with or without children, the husband-father is head, except when he is over 64 years of age and is living with a son or daughter 21–64 years of age who is working or seeking work. In such a case that son or daughter is considered the head.

In the case of a widowed, divorced, separated, or single person with children, the parent is head except when he or she is over 64 years of age and is living with a son or daughter 21–64 years of age who is working or seeking work. In such a case that son or daughter is head.

In cases in which a male and a female are equally eligible on all other grounds to be considered the head, the male is the head. If two or more persons of the same sex are equally eligible on all other grounds to be considered head of a household, the oldest is the head.

Home Farm Laborer.   (See *Farm Laborer.*)

Inexperienced Worker.—A worker 16 to 64 years of age inclusive who has never had employment which lasted for 4 consecutive weeks.   (See **Worker.**)

Loss or Depletion of Assets (as reason for opening relief case).—Loss or depletion of cash reserves, bank deposits, or income-providing investments; cessation of payments on annuities or insurance settlements; loss by fire, etc. Withdrawal of support by relatives or friends is not considered loss or depletion of assets.

New Case.—A case accepted on relief rolls during the month of the survey which had never before received relief from the agency accepting it.

Nonfamily Man.—A man not living with wife or with children.

Nonfamily Woman.—A woman not living with husband or with children.

Normal Family.—Husband and wife, or husband, wife, and children.

Open Country.—Territory outside centers of 50 or more population.

Private Relief Agency.—A relief agency supported principally by private funds. Example: Red Cross.

Public Relief Agency.—A relief agency supported by public funds raised by Federal, State, or local taxation.

Regular Government Employment.—Nonrelief, nonemergency employment under Federal, State, county, or municipal governments, as contrasted with work relief, or with emergency government employment.

Rehabilitation Advances.—Money, materials, real estate, or chattels. (See *Capital Goods* and *Subsistence Goods.*)

Rehabilitation Client.—A person who has at some time received material and/or advisory aid under the rural rehabilitation program and who has not been removed from the active rehabilitation rolls.

Relief. (See *General Relief.*)

Relief Agency. (See *Public Relief Agency* and *Private Relief Agency.*)

Relief Case.—One or more related or unrelated persons who live together, receive assistance as one unit, and are considered as one case by the agency giving the assistance. If two or more families or nonfamily persons or a combination of families and nonfamily persons live together but are treated by the relief agency as separate cases, each is considered a separate case in this survey. Members of the immediate family away from home temporarily, on vacation, in hospital, in jail, etc., are included in a relief case, provided they are expected to return within 6 months of the time of enumeration. (See *General Relief.*)

Relief Household. (See *Relief Case.*)

Relief Period.—The period of time between opening or reopening and closing of a relief case.

Renter. (See *Farm Tenant.*)

Reopened Case.—A case which had been given relief at some time previously, and which was again accepted for relief by the same agency after having received no relief for at least 1 full calendar month or after having lost Works Progress Administration employment or Resettlement status.

Rural.—Open country and village.

Rural Rehabilitation.—A program designed to aid needy agricultural households through loans or grants of capital or subsistence goods and through advice in farm and home management. This program was administered by Rural Rehabilitation Divisions of State and local E. R. A.'s, prior to July 1, 1935, and after that date by the Resettlement Administration.

Seeking Work.—Unemployed and actively looking for a job; or, if temporarily ill or disabled, expecting to look for work as soon as possible; or apparently wanting employment, although not actually looking for work.

Students looking for temporary work during vacation periods, or looking for part-time work after full-time school hours, are not regarded as seeking work.

Semiskilled Worker.—Manual worker whose occupation calls for only a short period or no period of preliminary training and for which only a moderate degree of judgment or manual dexterity is necessary. Examples: factory operative, truck driver.

Separations.—Closed relief cases as of a given period.

Sharecropper. (See *Farm Cropper.*)

Skilled Worker.—Manual worker whose occupation usually calls for a long period of training or apprenticeship, and for a degree of judgment and/or manual dexterity above that required of semiskilled workers. Examples: foreman, blacksmith, carpenter, machinist.

Subsistence Goods (as type of rehabilitation advance).—Cash and/or such commodities or services as food, clothes, fuel, medical care, or any other necessities of life which the rural rehabilitation cases might need, pending their complete rehabilitation (F. E. R. A. Form RD–22a).

Tenant. (See *Farm Tenant.*)

Tenure.—The occupational status of a farm operator; i. e., owner, tenant, cropper.

Town.—Center of 2,500 to 5,000 population.

Turn-Over.—The total volume of movement of cases onto and off the relief rolls during a given period of time. (See *Accessions* and *Separations.*)

Unemployable Person.—A person under 16 or over 64 years of age, or a person 16 to 64 years of age who is neither working nor seeking work. (See *Employed, Worker,* and *Seeking Work.*)

Unskilled Worker.—Manual worker whose occupation calls for no special training, judgment, or manual dexterity. Examples: domestic servant, common laborer.

Usual Occupation.—The occupation in nonrelief employment, of at least 4 consecutive weeks' duration at which a worker has been employed the greatest length of time during the last 10 years. If the worker has spent approximately the same length of time at two or more occupations, the one at which he worked last is his usual occupation.

Village.—Center of 50 to 2,500 population.

Worker.—A person 16 to 64 years of age inclusive, working or seeking work. (See *Employed* and *Seeking Work.*)

Work Relief.—Relief given under the requirement that some work be done on temporary emergency employment projects undertaken by municipal, county, State, or Federal Government (or several of these in cooperation). Wage payments to workers employed on the Federal Works Program under the Emergency Relief Appropriation Act of 1935 are not considered work relief. In this study drought relief was classified separately from work relief, although some of it was extended in the form of loans to be repaid by work on E. R. A. projects.

Working. (See *Employed.*)

Youth.—Persons 16 to 24 years of age inclusive.

INDEX

211

INDEX

○